Deadline

CHICAGO STUDIES IN PRACTICES OF MEANING

A SERIES EDITED BY ANDREAS GLAESER, WILLIAM MAZZARELLA,

WILLIAM H. SEWELL JR., KAUSHIK SUNDER RAJAN, AND LISA WEDEEN

Published in collaboration with the Chicago Center for Contemporary Theory

http://ccct.uchicago.edu

Recent books in the series

GUERRILLA MARKETING: COUNTERINSURGENCY AND
CAPITALISM IN COLOMBIA *by Alexander L. Fattal*

WHAT NOSTALGIA WAS: WAR, EMPIRE, AND THE TIME
OF A DEADLY EMOTION *by Thomas Dodman*

THE MANA OF MASS SOCIETY *by William Mazzarella*

THE SINS OF THE FATHERS: GERMANY, MEMORY,
METHOD *by Jeffrey K. Olick*

THE POLITICS OF DIALOGIC IMAGINATION: POWER
AND POPULAR CULTURE IN EARLY MODERN
JAPAN *by Katsuya Hirano*

AMERICAN VALUE: MIGRANTS, MONEY, AND MEANING IN
EL SALVADOR AND THE UNITED STATES *by David Pedersen*

QUESTIONING SECULARISM: ISLAM, SOVEREIGNTY, AND THE
RULE OF LAW IN MODERN EGYPT *by Hussein Ali Agrama*

THE MAKING OF ROMANTIC LOVE: LONGING AND SEXUALITY IN EUROPE,
SOUTH ASIA, AND JAPAN, 900–1200 CE *by William M. Reddy*

THE MORAL NEOLIBERAL: WELFARE AND CITIZENSHIP
IN ITALY *by Andrea Muehlebach*

THE GENEALOGICAL SCIENCE: THE SEARCH FOR JEWISH ORIGINS
AND THE POLITICS OF EPISTEMOLOGY *by Nadia Abu El-Haj*

Deadline

Populism and the Press in Venezuela

ROBERT SAMET

The University of Chicago Press
Chicago and London

The University of Chicago Press, Chicago 60637

The University of Chicago Press, Ltd., London

Published 2019

Printed in the United States of America

28 27 26 25 24 23 22 21 20 19   1 2 3 4 5

ISBN-13: 978-0-226-63356-5 (cloth)

ISBN-13: 978-0-226-63373-2 (paper)

ISBN-13: 978-0-226-63387-9 (e-book)

DOI: https://doi.org/10.7208/chicago/9780226633879.001.0001

Library of Congress Cataloging-in-Publication Data

Names: Samet, Robert, author.

Title: Deadline : populism and the press in Venezuela / Robert Samet.

Other titles: Chicago studies in practices of meaning.

Description: Chicago : The University of Chicago Press, 2019. |
    Series: Chicago studies in practices of meaning

Identifiers: LCCN 2019000624 | ISBN 9780226633565 (cloth : alk. paper) |
    ISBN 9780226633732 (pbk. : alk. paper) | ISBN 9780226633879 (e-book)

Subjects: LCSH: Crime and the press—Venezuela—Caracas. | Crime—Political
    aspects—Venezuela—Caracas. | Populism—Venezuela. | Denunciation
    (Criminal law)—Venezuela.

Classification: LCC PN5102 .S26 2019 | DDC 323.44/5—dc23

LC record available at https://lccn.loc.gov/2019000624

♾ This paper meets the requirements of ANSI/NISO Z39.48-1992
(Permanence of Paper).

CONTENTS

ACKNOWLEDGMENTS

It seems fitting that a note of gratitude should preface a book about grievances. This project was more than a decade in the making. Many people contributed generously of themselves in the process of research, writing, and rewriting. My list of debts begins with the Venezuelan journalists who had no reason to trust me, a perfect stranger, and yet nonetheless chose to do so. I have tried to be worthy of their confidence and to emulate their spirit of openness. Special thanks to Altagracia Anzola, Felicita Blanco, Laura Dávila Truelo, Alex Delgado, Oliver Fernández, Gustavo Frisneda, David González, Felipe González Roa, Sandra Guerrero, Santiago Gutiérrez, María Isoliett Iglesias, Mayela León, Sabrina Machado, Ricardo Mateus, Javier Mayorca, Thabata Molina, María Alejandra Monagas, Jenny Oropeza, Efrén Pérez Hernández, Jose Pernalete, Wilmer Poleo, Deivis Ramírez Miranda, Gustavo Rodríguez, Eligio Rojas, Fernando Sánchez, and Luis Vallenilla. Thank you also to the editors of *Últimas Noticias* and *El Nacional* who welcomed me into their newsrooms, an experience that taught me much about what it means to uphold lofty ideals under adverse conditions.

The decision to conduct fieldwork in Venezuela was made at Stanford University. Sylvia Yanagisako shaped the project from its inception, often in ways that I did not immediately recognize. Paulla Ebron served as a model of intellectual curiosity and kept me well supplied with reading material. James Ferguson encouraged my interest in populism and helped me link what I observed in Venezuela to larger social and economic patterns. Thomas Blom Hansen arrived near the end of the writing process and offered a number of suggestions that turned out to be decisive in framing my argument. Ted Glasser, Terry Karl, and Fred Turner generously adopted me from outside their respective disciplines and encouraged my interdisciplinary inclinations. Kathleen Coll, Claudia Engel, Miyako Inoue, and Liisa

Malkki were wonderful interlocutors and mentors who offered crucial advice along the way.

At Stanford, I was fortunate to be surrounded by an exceptional cohort of peers. Nikhil Anand, Hannah Appel, Elif Babül, Maura Finkelstein, Rania Sweis, and Austin Zeiderman shaped my development as an anthropologist and continue to be some of my closest interlocutors. Peter Samuels pushed me intellectually, and I was all too happy to follow his example through many a late-night writing session. Natalia Roudakova played the role of informal mentor even after she left Stanford for the University of California, San Diego. I also owe a hearty thanks to Tania Ahmad, Mike Ananny, Isabel Awad, Mun Young Cho, Aisha Ghani, Rachael Joo, Dolly Kikon, Daniel Kreiss, Yoon-Jung Lee, Serena Love, Lise Marken, Tomas Matza, Ramah McKay, Curtis Murungi, Zhanara Nauruzbayeva, Bruce O'Neill, Kevin O'Neill, Seeta Peña Gangadharan, Angel Roque, Joshua Samuels, Erica Williams, and Thet Win, who were wonderful companions.

Research for this book was made possible by the Wenner-Gren Foundation; National Science Foundation grant no. 0719667; Stanford University's Department of Anthropology, Vice Provost for Graduate Education, and Center for Latin American and Caribbean Studies; the Union College Faculty Research Fund; and the Latin American Security, Drugs, and Democracy fellowship administered by the Social Science Research Council (SSRC) and the Universidad de los Andes with funds provided by the Open Society Foundation.

During my time in Venezuela, a number of friends kept me sane and safe. When I arrived, Alejandro Damián took me under his wing and taught me everything that I needed to know about surviving Caracas. Not only was Ale the person whom family knew that they could call in an emergency, he introduced me to the Ávila, María Lionza, and El Coyuco. Charlie Devereux and Tiffany Fairey brought me into their home and showed me more kindness than I could ever have expected. Watching Finn and Mia grow up was truly a blessing. The list goes on. It includes Lurdes Basolí, Elodie Bernardeau, Quinlan Bowman, Rory Carroll, Amy Cooper, Graham Dick, Rachel Jones, Carlos Lagorio, Blandine Lievois, Clara Long, Simon May, Damian Oropeza, Jose Orozco, Ligimat Pérez, the crew at Casa Azul (especially Mike Fox, Carlos Martinez, and Jojo Farrell), and my neighbors, Luisa, Suki, and Pepi.

These acknowledgments would be incomplete without giving credit to the research assistants who worked on this project, especially Carmelo Velásquez, who straddled the divide between friend and colleague. Carmelo came to understand this project from the inside out. His easygoing charm opened doors across Caracas, and he made the solitary business of research a real joy. I was also lucky to have the help of Carlos Carrero, Åsa Odin Ekman, Sylvia Gomez, Luis Leonardo (Leo) Lameda, and Lila Vanoria at various points in my research.

Experiencing the highs and lows of the Chávez era is something that I shared with a number of colleagues. When I arrived in Venezuela, Naomi Schiller was in the process of wrapping up her research on Catia TVe and grassroots media producers in Caracas. Where other anthropologists may have felt encroached upon, she welcomed me as a fellow traveler, for which I am truly grateful. Alejandro Velasco and Julie Skurski have been two of my most generous interlocutors. Alejandro read the manuscript in its entirety and helped me better hone the substance of my argument. Julie generously worked through an early draft of the introduction. David Smilde provided helpful suggestions on the book's conclusion, as did Yanilda González. Rebecca Jarman and Cory Fischer-Hoffman supplied me with a wealth of insights that I have only barely managed to incorporate; likewise Aaron Kappeler, with whom I recently had the pleasure of sharing an office and many fruitful conversations. Thanks are also due to Andrés Antillano, Andrés Cañizález, George Ciccariello-Maher, Amy Cooper, Fernando Coronil, Luis Duno-Gottberg, Victor Hugo Febres, Lorena Freitez, Rebecca Hanson, Mariya Ivancheva, Dorothy Kronick, Boris Muñoz, Elsie Rosales, Yana Stainova, Matt Wilde, and Verónica Zubillaga.

This book was shaped by several ongoing conversations on Latin American politics. I had the good fortune to participate in the inaugural cohort of the Drugs, Security, and Democracy fellowship program sponsored by the SSRC and Open Society Foundation. Thanks to Desmond Arias, Adam Baird, Damion Blake, Diana Bocarejo, Guadalupe Correa-Cabrera, José Miguel Cruz, Graham Denyer Willis, Angelica Duran Martinez, Alex Fattal, Anthony Fontes, Yanilda González, Paul Hathazy, David Holiday, Jessica Mack, Juan Felipe Moreno, Cleia Noia, Ellen Sharp, Winifred Tate, Kimberly Theidon, Ana Villarreal, and Michael Wolff. At the University of Massachusetts Amherst, I participated in the "On Protest" working group, spearheaded by Sonia Alvarez, Angélica Bernal, Barbara Cruikshank, and Jillian Schwedler. My thanks to them and to the other participants, especially Roberto Alejandro, Martha Balaguera, Ivelisse Cuevas-Molina, Charles Hale, Kevin Henderson, Jeff Juris, Elva Orozco, Ana María Ospina, Tyler Schuenemann, and Millie Thayer.

At Union College, I have been surrounded by a phenomenal group of scholars who have pushed my thinking on populism, politics, and the role of ethnography in knowledge production. Karen Brison, Aaron Kappeler,

Arsalan Khan, Steve Leavitt, Michelle Osborn, and Jeff Witsoe convened a workshop on the book's opening chapter. The final version is vastly improved thanks to their exacting standards. I thank them for this and for their friendship. I have also benefited from ongoing conversations with Cigdem Cidam, Joseph García, George Gmelch, Janet Grigsby, Jennifer Matsue, Teresa Meade, Daniel Mosquera, Hans Mueller, Leahanna Pelish, Stacie Raucci, Guillermina Seri, and Leo Zaibert.

In addition to my colleagues at Union College, a number of others read and commented on chapter drafts at various stages. Thank you to Graham Denyer Willis, John French, Daniel Hallin, Roopa Krithivasan, Kevin O'Neill, Natalia Roudakova, Naomi Schiller, and Winifred Tate. A special mention goes to Daniel Goldstein, who read multiple drafts of the book and helped me move it toward publication. Austin Zeiderman has been a generous reader and an indefatigable source of advice even while living on another continent. Maura Finkelstein provided intellectual and moral support when it was needed most, as did Ali Aslam. Thank you also to Thea Riofrancos, to Ieva Jusionyte, and to the brilliant group of scholars who participated in the workshop "Populism in the Americas" at Harvard University: Ali Aslam, Gianpaolo Baiocchi, Angélica Bernal, Nusrat Chowdhury, Jason Frank, Laura Grattan, Jeff Juris, and Ritchie Savage. Last, but certainly not least, a tremendous note of appreciation to William Mazzarella, who recommended submitting the manuscript to the University of Chicago Press. He has been a source of inspiration since even before this project got under way and is someone whose example I try to emulate.

Working with the University of Chicago Press has been an enriching experience. I am grateful to the two anonymous reviewers who read the manuscript and for the helpful workshop with the Practices in Meaning series editors: Andreas Glaeser, William Mazzarella, William Sewell, Kaushik Sunder Rajan, and Lisa Wedeen. I could not have asked for a more engaged, thoughtful editor than Priya Nelson. My thanks to her and to Dylan Montanari, who shepherded me through the publishing process. Credit also goes to Lori Meek Schuldt for her careful copyediting and her attention to prose. I would also like to take this opportunity to thank the editors of the publications in which earlier versions of my work have appeared, particularly, for chapter 5, "The Photographer's Body: Populism, Polarization and the Uses of Victimhood in Venezuela," *American Ethnologist* 40, no. 3 (2013): 525–39; and, for chapter 6, "The Denouncers: Populism and the Press in Venezuela," *Journal of Latin American Studies* 49, no. 1 (2017): 1–27.

My family has been the foundation for everything that I have done. There is no one who makes me prouder than my sister and role model, Lauren.

Since we were kids, she has always been a trouper and a *luchadora*. At the same time, she has always been incredibly generous and giving of herself. My father, Jan Samet, has been my greatest advocate. His love of knowledge is what gave me the courage to pursue a PhD and to write this book. He has never told me what to do with my life, but he has stood by my decisions as if they were his own. My mother, Sylvia Samet, has been both copyeditor and voice of practical reason. She has put so much time into this book and has always been available for help at all hours of the day or night. Whenever she approved of a paragraph or a chapter, I knew that it had passed an important hurdle.

Finally, I thank my spouse, Elif Babül, who has suffered this book as if it were her own. I read nearly every sentence of this book aloud to her. She would then insist on reading it for herself and proceed to make it better. Our friendship was the best thing that happened to me in graduate school. It is with tremendous gratitude that I dedicate this book to her and to our son, Elan. I anticipate more joy and laughter as we move forward together. Especially now that the book is done.

Media and the Logic of Populism

Gabriel's son went out one Wednesday afternoon to buy new motorcycle tires in Caracas, Venezuela.[1] He never returned. The sixteen-year-old boy was shot in broad daylight just blocks from his home. I met Gabriel two days later as he was speaking to a pack of crime journalists outside the Caracas city morgue. What made the story newsworthy was not the boy's death—scores of young men are murdered in Caracas every month—but rather his father's willingness to make a series of public accusations, or *denuncias*. He named the gang that murdered his son, he accused the police of complicity, and he denounced the government of President Hugo Chávez for failing to intervene. Eventually, one of the reporters pushed a microphone under his chin. "As a parent, how do you feel? No doubt you've seen other cases like this one, but this time it touches you personally." Excerpts of Gabriel's grief-filled response were repeated on the afternoon news and in the papers the next morning.

> You see in the news that in Iraq they killed twenty people with a bomb, but here they kill a hundred every week. How is a country supposed to function like this? If the police and the government know who the gangs are, why don't they confront them? They know that [this gang] has been operating in our neighborhood for ten years. The whole world knows it, but they keep killing without fear. If they had killed the son of some high official, the police would have overrun the place by now. But those of us without connections have to be content with divine justice. Who am I going to run to? Who am I going to tell? Nobody!

There was nobody for him to tell, that is, except the press.

Denunciations like this one were a regular occurrence on the Caracas crime beat. In 2015, the central morgue handled almost as many homicides per month as New York City witnessed in the course of the entire year.[2] This was not a sudden outbreak of violence. Since the late 1980s, Venezuela's capital—which has a population one-third the size of New York—has experienced alarming levels of crime owing to the boom and bust of the country's petroeconomy. Venezuela is one of the world's leading oil producers. When global oil prices collapsed in the mid-1980s, Venezuela's already profound social and economic crisis deepened. The origins of Caracas's crime problem are to be found in this crisis and subsequent changes to the fabric of the city, which were implemented under threat of economic austerity.[3]

President Chávez came to power on promises to roll back austerity, but the crime problem became even more pronounced under his leadership (1999–2013). Since 2006, Venezuela has had the highest homicide rate in South America (greater than 50 per 100,000 inhabitants), and Caracas has consistently ranked among the deadliest cities in the world (greater than 100 homicides per 100,000 inhabitants).[4] Failure to curb violent crime made "insecurity" one of the most hotly contested issues of the Chávez era.[5] For many Venezuelans, crime symbolized everything wrong with their country, and no institution played a more prominent role in publicizing the problem than the private press.

It was the press and not crime that drew me to Caracas. When I began this project in 2007, Caracas boasted the most diverse, politically dynamic media ecology of any city in the Western Hemisphere. It had a powerful private press, an expanding state press, and a vigorous community media movement, all of which spanned the print, broadcast, and (later) digital spectrums. Journalism in Venezuela was booming. It was also embattled. Media wars over crime were a microcosm of a polarized political landscape that pitted *chavismo* (the movement headed by President Chávez, aka the Bolivarian Revolution) against "the opposition."[6] My research was initiated at a moment in which the private press was considered to be the opposition's most powerful representative. Television channels such as Globovisión and RCTV and newspapers such as *El Nacional* and *El Universal* took on the functions of political parties, and they hammered home a litany of problems, among them crime and insecurity.

This book is based on nearly three years of ethnographic research on crime journalism in Caracas, the bulk of it carried out between 2007 and 2014.[7] I became interested in crime news because it reflected ongoing political struggles in Venezuela. For President Chávez and his supporters, the steady barrage of crime stories threatened to overshadow the progressive gains of the Bolivarian Revolution. For the opposition, these stories were proof of institutional failure, and they served as a platform for antigovernment mobilization. Crime journalists were at the heart of these battles over the politics of security. Rather than proclaiming neutrality and retreating from the fray, they fashioned a role for themselves as the voice of crime victims and avatars of the popular will.

Polarized battles over crime journalism in Caracas foreshadowed what has become the new normal in democracies around the world. Long before the so-called post-truth moment arrived on the doorsteps of North America and Western Europe, Venezuela was consumed with talk of truth and lies, facts and fictions, accurate reporting and libelous speech. During the Chávez era, these battles reached a fever pitch. President Chávez and his supporters accused the private press of distorting facts in the service of a transnational conspiracy. Prominent figures in the media shot back that the Chávez administration was promoting systematic falsehoods and eroding press freedom. The situation was so extreme that even the most basic facts were hard to ascertain. Truth, it seemed, was in the eyes of the beholder.

Scarcely two decades into the twenty-first century, scholars, activists, and policy makers confront a puzzle. Press freedom coupled with new media technology was supposed to spread liberal democracy around the world. Instead, it became an engine for the global rise of populism and illiberal politics more broadly. What happened? Pundits have offered up a chorus of explanations. Most of them amount to normative dismissals of populism or liberal hand-wringing about partisanship in the media. This book offers a more rigorous explanation of the relationship between populism and the press that I hope will serve as a road map going forward. It does so ethnographically, by following the practices of crime journalists in Caracas. One practice in particular—the use of denuncias like the one described earlier—holds the key to unlocking a much larger puzzle. Close attention to the journalistic art of denunciation allows us to observe how media create the conditions of possibility for populist mobilization.

The crux of my argument centers on how denuncias construct an image of "the people" or "the popular will." Appeals to the people or to popular sovereignty (rule by the people) are the common denominator of every populist movement. That much is known. What contemporary scholars have so far neglected is the crucial role that media play in articulating this collective fiction. The task at hand is to revisit "the people" not as an actually existing entity, but as a particular kind of imagined community that is constructed through a nexus of media practices.

Focusing on media practices circumvents a pair of common misnomers about the relationship between populism and the press. The first assumes that the press is little more than a tool of charismatic leaders and demagogues. Much of the attention on populism in Venezuela has concentrated on the figure of Hugo Chávez and his use of the media. This obsession with populist leaders like Chávez and their telegenic powers tends to obscure the conditions of possibility that give rise to these leaders in the first place. The second misnomer attributes the success of populist movements to the ease with which ordinary people are manipulated by "the media." There is no doubt that the press represents powerful economic interests and that these interests work to direct popular opinion. However, such accounts grant far too little agency to people who identify with populist movements and far too much to instruments of mass persuasion.

My objective is not to dismiss charismatic leaders or economic elites but to ground analysis of the media's role in populism in something even more fundamental—grievances or demands. Populism's raw material is a proliferation of grievances, injuries, and wrongdoings that are directed against the state or other powerful institutions. To understand the role of media in the origin and trajectory of populist movements, we are best served focusing on such grievances and the communicative practices through which they are relayed.

Working alongside crime journalists allowed me to observe how a particular subset of grievances was amplified and broadcast by news outlets in Caracas. Few experiences are more traumatizing than a homicide, a kidnapping, or a sexual assault. The collective impact of thousands of such assaults propelled a reactionary backlash that transformed the politics of security in Venezuela from the inside out. When I arrived in Caracas, the Chávez government emphasized economic justice and social rehabilitation as the solution to the crime problem. Chávez explicitly rejected tough-on-crime rhetoric as an attack on the poor and a tool of neoliberalism. A decade later, his successor, President Nicolás Maduro, did just the opposite and embraced what criminologists call "punitive populism." This shift in the presidential discourse on security was driven in part by media depictions of violent crime. Going inside the world of crime journalists sheds light on the gradual transformation of the Bolivarian Revolution and the ever-evolving crisis of Venezuelan democracy.[8]

The Chávez Era

Caracas in the Chávez era was, for many, a beacon of hope. It was a laboratory for experiments with progressive politics across the global south and the epicenter of the celebrated "left turn" in Latin American politics. Venezuela's capital city became synonymous with a rejection of neoliberal economic policies and a search for alternatives to the so-called Washington Consensus. The Chávez government was responsible for a progressive constitution that enshrined a multitude of political, social, and economic rights. It was also the first government in the hemisphere to openly oppose the George W. Bush administration and the US-led war on terror in the wake of 9/11. Not since the early years of Venezuelan democracy in the late 1950s had so many eyes turned toward Caracas. Political battles that played out during this period felt significant, not just for Venezuela or Latin America but on a global scale.[9]

Caracas in the Chávez era also had the distinction of being the world's most polarized city not at war. The Bolivarian Revolution had popular appeal, but it also created a powerful backlash, especially among elites and the political classes that it displaced. An imaginary divide cut across the city. The political antagonism between supporters and opponents of the late Hugo Chávez was the most salient feature of everyday life in Caracas. Jobs were won and lost, friendships made and broken, institutions funded and dismantled based on where a person was judged to stand vis-à-vis the divide between "*chavistas*" (supporters of President Chávez) and "the opposition." Residents of Caracas (*caraqueños*) were experts at interpreting the signs of political allegiance. Sometimes these signs were obvious—for example, the bright red colors worn by many of the president's supporters. Other times, they had to be divined by way of speculation, rumor, and innuendo.[10]

This is the kind of schism that uncareful observers describe as ontological. It was certainly true that these two political movements shared fundamentally different worldviews on everything from economic programs to international relations to urban aesthetics. The Bolivarian Revolution drew inspiration from anticolonial struggles in Latin America during the Cold War, whereas the opposition was most often associated with the free market revolutions under way in North America and Western Europe. However, chavismo and the opposition were more closely related than is sometimes acknowledged. For starters, there were deep historical ties. Both movements were part of a political alliance that emerged during the 1980s in reaction to the economic collapse of the petrostate and the perceived failures of Venezuelan democracy. Because of these historical ties there were also biographical ties. More than a few leaders within the opposition were former chavistas, and there were considerably more personal interactions between the two camps than usually recognized. Most important, there were strong resemblances at the level of political practice.

If we bracket, for a moment, the disparate political outlooks and focus on political practice, some interesting affinities snap into view. For example, we might observe that both chavismo and the opposition were majoritarian movements that styled themselves as the only true representative of the Venezuelan people. We might also note that both of these movements defined themselves not in terms of what they stood for but what they stood against. For chavismo that meant neoliberalism, imperialism, and above all else, the opposition and its mouthpiece, the media; for the opposition that meant socialism, insecurity, the influence of Cuba, and above all else, Hugo Chávez. There was also the fact that, for both camps, the denunciation of their adversaries served as a platform for mobilizing a seemingly endless stream of rallies, protests, and demonstrations. The list could go on. What I am driving at, however, is that both chavismo and the opposition were case studies in populism.

The shared populism of chavismo and the opposition is essential for understanding the politics of security during the Chávez era. Conventional accounts of Venezuela usually emphasize the populism of the former and imply the liberal-democratic credentials of the latter. Nothing could be further from the truth. Although it can run the risk of painting two highly contrasting political projects with the same brush, I have chosen to emphasize the populist affinities between chavismo and the opposition because it shows how the politics of security in Venezuela was tied to a much larger pattern of mobilization and countermobilization. The logic of populism provides a framework for understanding the peregrinations of both chavismo and the opposition. It helps explain why these two projects emerged in tandem, how they transformed over time, and the ways in which certain objects (crime, corruption, the economy) became the focus of political contestation.

"Víctor Javier, We Love You"

In this polarized setting, accusations ricocheted back and forth between media outlets on either side of the chavista/opposition divide. Everyone in Caracas knew what it meant to "make a denunciation" (*hacer una denuncia*) to the press because the press was inundated with them. Accusatory practices such as denunciation are usually associated with investigative reporting, but in Venezuela they had taken over the entire journalistic field. Denuncias dominated call-in radio and television talk shows. They featured in opinion columns, letters to the editor, and online comment sections. They informed the content of such traditional news beats as national politics, international politics, city and regional news, health care, education, and entertainment. Even advertising was a vehicle for denuncias. Everyone was denouncing everyone.

Crime journalists routinely published denuncias that linked soaring crime rates to the failures of the Chávez administration, but attacking the government was not the only or even the primary reason that most people took their accusations to the press. The media were seen as a vehicle through which injustices large and small could be rectified. People went to crime reporters with cases that had stalled in the courts or that were being ignored by the police; they denounced low-level corruption, extrajudicial killings, police brutality, and the wrongful incarceration of loved ones; they worked to publicize patterns of crime in their neighborhoods and to call attention to specific perpetrators; and they used the press to clear the names of people unjustly accused of crimes.

Denuncias provided the impetus for an entire style of reporting. Crime journalists took specific grievances—for example, a police killing or a neighborhood terrorized by gang violence—and transformed them into larger demands. Understanding the significance of denuncias means understanding the process whereby particular grievances came to stand for an entire chain of political and institutional failures.

Take the case of Víctor Javier, a young bus driver who disappeared in the dead of night. The story began with a search for the missing man. On the morning of June 13, 2008, his relatives showed up at the city morgue looking for the crime reporters. Like everyone in Caracas, they knew that the morgue in Bello Monte was the best place to find the reporters. In a brief interview, Víctor Javier's mother told us that she believed her son had been kidnapped, murdered, or both. Despite taking the case to the authorities, the police did nothing to locate the young man. For that reason the family had organized a search party and began scouring the city.[11]

The next morning they found Víctor Javier's body in a wooded ravine off the side of the highway thanks, in part, to a tip from a spirit medium. Under normal circumstances, this case would have barely registered in the press except for one small detail. Víctor Javier was a driver for one of the many private bus lines that crisscrossed the city. Robberies on buses were common, but in April 2008 the situation worsened. In response to a growing number of attacks, the city's bus drivers and transportation workers blocked the highways to denounce insecurity. Around this same time, crime reporters started keeping a tally of how many transportation workers had been murdered in the city that year. Víctor Javier was number thirty-six.

Counting victims was a common practice among reporters because it allowed them to connect individual cases to wider patterns of violence. Most news outlets published a weekend homicide count, a number that functioned as a general barometer of insecurity. Similarly, the number of drivers killed told a story about a highly vulnerable system of transportation that millions of people used every day. As the count of murdered bus drivers and taxi drivers mounted, so did the pressure on the government to secure the daily commute.

A few hours after Víctor Javier's body was discovered, the new minister of interior and justice was scheduled to hold a televised press conference. During the question-and-answer session, a reporter inquired about Víctor Javier and "thirty-five other transport workers murdered in Caracas." The minister's response was both clumsy and insensitive. He told the journalist that Víctor Javier did not deserve to be counted among the ranks of murdered transportation workers because he was not killed in the course of his duties and because he was a probable delinquent.[12]

On Sunday morning a line of buses descended on the morgue. Across the windows of each vehicle were hand-painted messages: "Víctor Javier we love you," "Víctor Javier was my friend," and "Enough of all this death." In a matter of minutes, several hundred people filled the narrow street and the small carport in front of the morgue.[13]

For Víctor Javier's family and friends, the protest was about clearing the young man's good name and their own. I overheard a short, round woman lecturing one of the reporters. "In the barrios we are workers. We are not *malandros* [delinquents], we are professionals." Beside her, a young woman lamented. "The insecurity is everywhere in Caracas, but most of all it is in the barrios."[14] Then there was Juan Rosal, complaining furiously about the treatment of his son and his family: "If it is the child of [poor] 'Pablo Pueblo' that dies, then they say that he was a delinquent. But if a murder takes place in a wealthy neighborhood like this one, you can be sure that they are going to investigate the case."[15] Not only was Rosal trying to clear his son's name, he was also publicly denouncing the police, the minister, and the whole system of justice: "The police did nothing to find him and now this minister comes along and says that my son was not a bus driver. He died with his uniform on! Not one of my four children is a delinquent. I would like to tell [the minister] to leave his bodyguards behind and come visit my neighborhood at night."[16]

The case of Víctor Javier made an effective denunciation because it allowed reporters to connect his death to a larger pattern of insecurity through numbers, through protests, and through direct accusations against a high-ranking authority. It merged with other murders, other protests, and other condemnations to give the impression of a growing crisis in the city's transportation system. All of this had an impact. The same day that Víctor Javier's family and friends descended on the morgue en masse, President Chávez announced plans for a new security initiative titled Plan Ruta Segura (Plan Secure Route) that would place one police officer and two National Guards on every bus. This hastily assembled program was a direct response to growing pressure from transport workers, pressure that crime journalists were effectively channeling.

Denuncias

Over the course of my fieldwork, I came to see the use of denuncias as the defining characteristic of journalism in Chávez era. The term *denuncia* is a juridical expression that is usually translated as "denunciation," "accusation," or "complaint." In Venezuela and most of Latin America it has two closely related usages, with which everyone is familiar. A denuncia can refer to the official report that plaintiffs file with the police or the courts to initiate an investigation or a trial. In a strictly legal sense, denuncias are written documents tied to bureaucratic institutions. However, the term denuncia also refers to accusations made outside the formal legal realm. When crime reporters and their sources talk about "making a denuncia," they are usually referring to a public accusation that circumvents the police or the judiciary and goes straight to the court of popular opinion. Such denuncias are acts of bearing witness to injustice or wrongdoing. More than a form or even a genre, they are recognized as a testimonial practice, one that links journalists, their sources, and their audiences.[17]

As a technique of truth telling, denunciation is fundamental to the legal and political tradition of Latin America.[18] My research traces denuncias all the way back to the *denunciatio* of canon law in medieval Europe, itself an adaptation of Roman law.[19] Early versions of the denuncia likely arrived in the Americas as a part of the Spanish Inquisition's legal apparatus. A similar practice was evident in letters of complaint addressed to the Spanish crown by colonial subjects.[20] That said, the denuncias that proliferated across Latin America during the twentieth century more closely resembled the style of denunciation practiced in revolutionary France, which tied the defense of the nation to mass publicity.[21] Matters of jurisprudence went from being the province of kings and their courts to being an extension of the sovereign people. If elite rule remains a material reality in Latin America, it is a reality that must nevertheless address itself to "the people" vis-à-vis technologies of mass communication.[22]

Venezuelan journalists viewed the judicious use of denuncias as a fundamentally democratic practice, an act of consciousness raising, and an exercise of free speech. By speaking truth to power, such press-fueled revelations could provide the impetus for democratic reforms or even spark revolution. If the use of denuncias was tied to journalists' vision of democracy, these were not instruments of rational-critical debate, nor were they the outgrowth of a Habermasian public sphere. Denuncias were not, in other words, linked to a vision of liberal democracy. Rather, they were tools of popular mobilization. Under the right circumstances, the right denuncia had the power to mobilize the will of *el pueblo* (the people) toward revolutionary ends. A well-timed denuncia could even help topple governments. During the early 1990s, press-fueled denunciations of corruption in Venezuela did just that. These denuncias were tied to the downfall of the two political parties that had governed Venezuela since the late 1950s, the return of populist mobilization, and the rise of Hugo Chávez.

Theories of populism go a long way toward explaining the political significance of denuncias. *Populism* is an admittedly slippery term and one that spurs ongoing debate. In this book, *populism* refers to a political logic that reduces the political space to a Manichean struggle between the will of "the people"—the rightful source of sovereign authority—and its enemy, "the power bloc."[23] Populist movements are movements that claim to represent the righteous majority against the illegitimate usurpation of power. This definition builds on the work of Ernesto Laclau and an earlier generation of Latin American scholars.[24] Denuncias resemble what Laclau calls an "articulating practice," and they function as discursive building blocks of populist movements.[25] That is because mass mediated denuncias have the capacity to link or "articulate" a whole series of otherwise disparate demands in a way that creates the basis for a shared political identity. This was precisely how journalists on the Caracas crime beat understood their work. They were not simply exposing the sordid details of crime. They were voicing the grievances of the Venezuelan people.

The Logic of Populism

No region is more closely associated with populism than Latin America. Among area scholars there are, broadly speaking, two approaches to the topic.[26] The first comes at populism from the bottom up, concentrating on the conditions that give rise to populist movements. Pioneered during the 1960s and 1970s by social scientists including Gino Germani, Torcuato di Tella, Francisco Weffort, and Ernesto Laclau, this approach explains how and why people come to identify with mass movements.[27] The second approach to populism in Latin America can be traced to the early twenty-first century and such scholars as Kurt Weyland, who redefined populism as charismatic leadership.[28] Although it can be useful for comparative purposes—in Venezuela the work of Kirk Hawkins comes to mind—this approach defines populism narrowly in a way that tends to mystify the phenomenon and obscure the roots of political discontent.[29]

This book approaches populism from the ground up, concentrating on the practices that form the popular will. I define *populism* as a particular logic or pattern of political mobilization that is rooted in democracy's founding fiction, the principle of popular sovereignty. This logic is polarizing. It is also, as I will explain, militantly democratic. Approaching populism as a political logic that is internal to democracy means setting aside the outcomes of populist movements and focusing instead on the populist imagination. Such an approach avoids many of the normative (usually negative) assumptions about populism—for example, that it appeals to base emotions, promotes unreason, or paves the way for authoritarianism. It also provides analytical purchase on a notoriously slippery concept.

The capriciousness of populism is well known.[30] We find populist movements in nearly every corner of the world, and yet no two populisms are exactly alike. Populism spans the political spectrum. It emerges in urban, suburban, and rural settings. It can be mobilized against any number of social ills (such as crime or corruption), and it can take aim at any number of targets (e.g., dictators, liberal elites, corporations, immigrants). Populism can be tethered to a range of economic programs, and it is usually championed by a cross section of social classes. Charismatic leaders often arise, and yet there are scores of populist movements without any discernable head. To complicate matters further, most populist movements undergo profound transformations over the course of their lifetime.

Populism is the political equivalent of a shape-shifter. How do you approach a phenomenon that is fundamentally protean, that is seemingly everywhere and nowhere? For a long time, an answer eluded social science. Some scholars even questioned the concept's utility. In this way populism resembles another elusive subject—totemism. During the early twentieth century, totemism was everywhere. Comparative ethnologists found symbolic practices that assimilated humans and nonhumans among indigenous peoples the world over. The profusion of examples posed a definitional problem because no two totemisms were alike. This fact eventually led scholars to doubt its very existence. By the time that Claude Lévi-Strauss revisited the problem in 1960, totemism had become an anthropological footnote.[31]

I mention totemism because the tools of structural linguistics that Lévi-Strauss applied to the problem also unlock the riddle of populism. According to Lévi-Strauss, many of the practices clustered under the umbrella of totemism were organized by a pattern of symbolic thinking in which animals, plants, and natural phenomena came to stand in for relations between people. There was no a priori connection between, say, bears and the Bear clan or crows and the Crow moiety. Totemism was improvisational. It drew on the materials at hand to express abstract social relations. The same is true of populism. Its symbolic material is a patchwork of grievances both real and imagined. A list of such grievances might include crime, corruption, unemployment, immigration, racism, gender bias, sexual stigma, political marginalization, or the loss of certain privileges. Like totemism, the content of populism is constantly in flux. Where populism differs from totemism—what makes it an observable phenomenon rather than a figment of the anthropological imagination—is that all populist grievances are staged in the name of the people.

"The people" is the absent presence at the heart of every populist movement. All populisms claim to represent the will of the people as an insurgent force that rights wrongs and restores the political order.[32] The power of the people, in turn, is predicated on the doctrine of popular sovereignty. Government of the people, by the people, for the people is the common denominator of all populist movements. It is also democracy's starting point. There is, quite literally, no democracy without the demos. Whereas liberal democracy shackles the principle of popular sovereignty to a series of bureaucratic apparatuses and techniques of representation, populism promises to set it free.[33]

In its celebration of the people and the popular will, populism is as literal as it is militant, and this fetishlike attachment is its telltale sign. Like "the nation" or "the public" or "the social," invoking "the people" entails a kind of symbolic logic or magical thinking that bridges the gap between actual persons and their imagined communities. We are dealing with a species of political fiction, not in the sense that "the people" is unreal but that its reality is predicated on practices of signification. For "the people" to exist, it first must be invoked.[34]

Media play an underappreciated role in discursive practices of "people making," or what Laura Grattan pithily calls "peopling."[35] Later chapters focus on three such practices that were originally identified by Ernesto Laclau.[36] Here at the outset it may help to outline them briefly. The first of these practices is the articulation of shared discontent. Populist movements coalesce when otherwise unaligned persons begin to recognize a sense of shared frustration with the state or other powerful institutions. These disparate actors are likely to have dissimilar demands. What they have in common—and what serves as the basis for a collective identity—is the recognition that their demands have not been met. Shared frustration with the state allows otherwise heterogeneous demands to "articulate" or link up in a way that establishes a congruous source of incongruous grievances, or what scholars call "chains of equivalence."[37]

The second discursive practice essential to the formation of populist identities is the polarization of politics into warring camps. Populism divides the political field into a contest between friend and foe, "Us" (i.e., those who have been wronged) and "Them" (i.e., those responsible for the wrongdoing). This Manichean logic is essential. Before a populist identity can emerge, a common adversary must be identified.

The third and final discursive operation is the emergence of empty or charismatic signifiers. For a populist movement to emerge as a political force, one or more of the aforementioned grievances must come to stand for all the rest. This is what Ernesto Laclau, borrowing from Lévi-Strauss, calls an "empty signifier."[38] It is "empty" not because it is without meaning but because it is pregnant with possibility. The empty signifier can represent the entire constellation of demands because it is flexible enough to reflect multiple interests. For example, in Venezuela demands for security made in the name of crime victims appear to represent a common problem even though crime victimhood has vastly different meanings for elites and the urban poor. The ultimate empty signifier is the populist leader who is all things to all people (or, at least, all of the people who are part of the movement). That said, populist movements do not begin with charismatic leaders, nor must one emerge for them to have political success. If the empty signifier is the most charismatic element of a populist movement, its configuration is also the most unpredictable.

More essential to my analysis than any one of these practices or operations is the fundamental unit of analysis—the demand or grievance. Before some semblance of the popular will can crystallize, an otherwise diffuse series of demands must go unanswered by those in power. Ernesto Laclau explains as much in the following scenario:

> Think of a large mass of agrarian migrants who settle in the shantytowns on the outskirts of a developing industrial city. Problems of housing arise and the group of people requests some kind of solution from the local authorities. Here we have a *demand*, which is perhaps only a *request*. If the demand is satisfied, that is the end of the matter; but if it is not, people can start to perceive that their neighbors have other, equally unsatisfied demands— problems with water, health, schooling, and so on. If the situation remains unchanged for some time, there is an accumulation of unfulfilled demands

and an increasing inability for the institutional system to absorb them in a differential way and an equivalential relationship is established between them.[39]

Media play an important role in crystallizing these demands. This is precisely what I witnessed day in and day out on the Caracas crime beat through the practice of denunciation. By following the journalistic use of denuncias, it is possible to glimpse how specific demands move beyond their immediate context. In this way, mass mediated denuncias allow us to observe how the popular will is formed from the ground up. As with Laclau's hypothetical city, denunciations of crime and insecurity in Caracas did not function in a vacuum. They were powerful only when they referenced other denuncias, when they linked together an entire chain of perceived failures. The experience of crime victimhood in Caracas provided just this kind of recurring problem, and it was through the journalistic articulation of such grievances that insecurity emerged as a rallying cry for popular mobilization.

Media, Populism, Popular Culture

Mass media and mass movements go hand in hand. Tabloid newspapers and a crusading style of journalism were instrumental to the rise of populism in the United States during the late nineteenth century. Radio played a similar role in the populist movements that spread across Argentina, Brazil, Mexico, Peru, and Venezuela during the 1930s and 1940s. Today, cable news and social media are the leading edge of populist insurgencies worldwide. The link between media and populism—as intimated in the previous section—is popular sovereignty. Media are one of the main channels through which claims to represent the will of the people are made. Such claims are totalizing. Populist rhetoric asserts the unmediated unity between the popular will and a multitude of individual demands; in this way, it attempts to bridge the gap between discrete persons and collective subjects. This gap is internal to popular sovereignty, and it is reminiscent of a problem that haunted Christian monarchies, exemplified by the legal fiction of "the king's two bodies."[40]

In England, Spain, and much of Europe, the king was imagined as a dual entity.[41] One of the king's bodies was mortal ("the body natural"), the other divine ("the body politic"). The body natural was the flesh-and-blood person of the king. The body politic was more expansive. It was imagined as a corporate entity that extended through time and space to encompass everything within the realm. For a visual analogue of the royal body politic, think of the famous frontispiece to Thomas Hobbes's *Leviathan* in which the king's head sits atop a torso composed of smaller individual bodies.[42] By the end of the eighteenth century, this configuration of sovereignty was on its way out. The wars of independence cut off the head of the king and vested sovereign power in the multitudinous hands of the people. However, the fiction of the king's two bodies did not die; it was transposed onto the fledgling republics of the nineteenth century, albeit with a twist. Like the king, "the people" had two bodies.[43] The immortal body politic remained in many respects the same. The body natural was another matter. Whereas the king's body natural was located in his person, the people's body natural was only accessible through representative practices.[44]

If it is no longer fashioned in the likeness of the king, then what gives the contemporary body politic its shape? This question is at the heart of media studies. There are several ways to go about answering it.[45] One approach focuses primarily on the political economy of media and its conditions of production, consumption, and circulation.[46] A second looks at the interface between users and the physical infrastructures of communications technology.[47] This book takes a third tack. It looks at the relationship between political discourse on the body politic and everyday practices of mediation. This is a performative or praxis-based approach to media and politics, which pays close attention to the categories of political thought and the pragmatics of their use. It assumes that the will of the people is not something that exists in the world, as does a table or a rock; rather, it is something essentially asserted and contested—in a word, mediated.[48]

The people or the popular (from the Latin *populāris*, "of the people") is just one way of imagining the body politic.[49] Others include the public, the social, the masses, the multitude, the nation, the community, the population, the network, the crowd, and the common. Each of these concepts has its own particular genealogy; each imagines the body politic in subtly different ways; and each makes certain normative presuppositions. An ethnographic approach to media and politics begins by observing the categories that are in use. Do our interlocutors address the body politic as a public? A mass? A multitude? If so, then theories of the public sphere or the silent masses or the multitude are apropos. If not, then we risk speaking over our subjects when we impose such frameworks. My research suggests that the popular is the category that has greatest salience for media studies in Latin America.[50] That is certainly the case with crime news, which is a textbook example of popular culture.

No concept in media studies is more misunderstood than "popular culture," and like populism, it demands disambiguation. Two definitions should be flagged from the outset. The first is a market-based definition that equates popularity—of news, movies, music, fashion, art, and so forth—with sales. What is "popular" about popular culture is its mass appeal. A second, older understanding of popular culture defines it as the authentic folk culture of a people; it is the expression of a customary way of life embedded in everything from arts and crafts to food and clothing. Taken together, these two definitions begin to give us a sense of why popular culture is simultaneously celebrated and reviled. But neither explains why popular culture is so closely linked to populist movements. For that we need to recognize a third definition, which associates popular culture with the popular classes.[51]

North American audiences often overlook popular culture's implicit socioeconomic connotations. That is not the case in Latin America. To invoke *el pueblo* is to invoke the popular sectors, which include a mix of subaltern groups, most notably the urban masses and rural campesinos.[52] In Caracas, the persons most closely associated with the popular classes are residents of the city's informal settlements, or barrios. These neighborhoods are, in turn, associated with urban poverty as well an influx of rural migrants.[53] Since the 1920s, the urban popular sectors have been a powerful force in political struggles throughout much of Latin America. During the interwar period, mass migration from rural villages to cities such as Caracas made Latin America the second most urbanized region in the world.[54] The wave of populist movements that began to emerge in the 1930s incorporated these new urban popular sectors, and mass media—especially radio, tabloids, and film—played a crucial role in channeling their demands.

Does popular culture go hand in hand with populism because it is a direct expression of the popular sectors? This is a common but erroneous assumption. It is sometimes embraced by scholars who see the popular classes as an exclusively positive force for change. However, history has shown that shared socioeconomic conditions do not guarantee shared political consciousness. The popular classes can be constituted as a revolutionary force for social and economic justice. They can also be constituted as a force against it.

Popular culture is better described as a terrain of struggle. It is, as Stuart Hall argued, a site where different actors claim to represent "the people" for different political ends.[55] This terrain is constantly shifting. New articulations emerge. Others recede. One moment crime may be the primary grievance through which a political bloc is constituted; the next it might be corruption, joblessness, or immigration. The precise configuration of the popular will is constantly in flux. The one constant is popular sovereignty.

Popular sovereignty is the underlying principle that connects populism, the press, and popular culture. Like any other ideology or belief system, the power of popular sovereignty is predicated on its ritual reaffirmation. In the Americas, the staging of "we the people" is carried out in schools, courts, hospitals, and places of worship; it is at the heart of every protest, every demonstration, and every revolution; it is written into constitutions and enacted (sometimes feebly) through elections. The repetitive invocation of popular sovereignty is both constant and subtle, and no site of this ritual staging is more crucial than the media.[56]

Journalists take it for granted that their work is fundamental to democracy. Under normal circumstances, this faith is expressed in talk of civil society, the public sphere, the marketplace of ideas, and the fourth estate. In times of popular upheaval, however, the discourse on journalism shifts to a more radical register. News outlets refashion themselves as the unmediated voice of the people, the last defenders of democracy. This insistence on immediacy is what differentiates populist rhetoric from other expressions of popular sovereignty. Populism disavows the representative dimension of democracy by erasing the distinction between the people's two bodies. Pundits, journalists, demagogues, and ordinary citizens all claim to speak directly to the people and directly for the people. The urgency of populist rhetoric is not, as some observers would have it, irrational. It is grounded in grievances that are both real and imagined. We may sympathize with some of these grievances. We may adamantly oppose others. Refusing to recognize them, however, is a methodological and a political mistake.

Which brings me back to crime journalism and the Caracas crime beat. Time and again my interlocutors told me that crime news was the most popular news genre because it was the most "real." I take this to mean that crime news conveys the immediacy of violence and victimhood in a way that few other genres do. Where the immediacy of crime news intersects with the immediacy of populism is in the body of the victim. These bodies are both the irrefutable "fact" of crime and *el cuerpo del delito*, or "the body of proof," of crimes against the Venezuelan people.[57]

Shock Therapy

The crime beat was considered a proving ground for rookie journalists. If you could cover crime in Caracas, you could cover anything, or so the logic went. It was not so much the danger to one's person or the difficulty of finding material that made the crime beat challenging. Rather, it was learning to manage the emotional impact—the shock—of human suffering. Like any other rookie, my initiation into the Caracas crime beat consisted of a series of shocks. During the first few months, I became intimately familiar with crime scenes, corpses, funeral parlors, grieving relatives, accidents, morgues, hospitals, and seemingly endless stories about death. The crime journalists gauged my response to every new experience or situation; when I did not seem sufficiently moved, they made sure to reinforce the gravity of what I was witnessing.

Shock is the currency of journalism in general and crime journalism in particular. There is an affective intensity in images and stories of violence that is only rivaled by (and often equated with) pornography. The implicit relationship between shock and crime news is signaled by the term *sucesos*, which literally means "events" or "happenings." In the context of Latin American journalism, *sucesos* refers to news of violent events, specifically crimes or fatal accidents.[58] The word suggests a sudden, bodily shock. It is the kind of experience that theorists have linked to both trauma and mass mediation.[59] Crime journalists are in the business of mediating the most shocking of events; they are in the business of affect management.[60]

It is precisely the shocking or affective quality that has led many commentators to condemn crime news for its morbid sensationalism. Such a stigma might say more about our own cultural sensibilities than about representations of violence or popular culture. Taboos on shocking, affect-intensive stories and images are linked to political ideals that date back to the Enlightenment, in particular the elevation of reason above emotion.[61] If the former represented the height of human achievement, then the latter was a base animal instinct, a holdover from some prehistoric age. Irrational, unchecked emotion was associated with women, children, "savages," and the urban masses.[62] What makes crime news vulgar—what separates it from, say, a medical or criminological textbook—is its appeal to the emotions.[63]

Journalists on the Caracas crime beat were all too aware of the stigmas that followed them. Theirs was the dual burden of witnessing countless traumas and being secretly associated with them. In the preface to *Our War* (*Guerra nuestra*), his collection of crime chronicles written for the newspaper *El Nacional*, the former crime reporter José Roberto Duque confronted this stigma head-on: "The chronicles that appear in this book are fundamentally sensationalizing. Consequently, so is their author." Reviled though they may be, Duque insisted that he and his fellow "Draculas of the back page" served a higher purpose. Only by exposing the sordid details of human suffering could they draw attention to an urgent situation. Sensationalism was necessary, "otherwise the denuncia would fall on deaf ears."[64] Duque's defense of crime journalism underscored how he and many of his colleagues justified the use of affectively charged material. Denuncias redeemed their work, transforming it from morbid voyeurism into a form of social activism.[65]

The ethical dilemmas of crime journalists echo those of ethnographers who write about violence. But what about those of us who stand in judgment—that is, those of us who write about the writers, the photographers, the pundits, and the artists? Scholars often adopt a universalizing stance on representations of violence characterized by a kind of life-affirming parochialism, which asserts that "to represent violence is to reproduce it." Perhaps. And yet crime news is more than mere prurience. Rather than condemnation or praise, this ethnography of crime journalists aspires to a situated realism that is positioned in the world rather than above it.[66] The merits and failings of the journalists who covered the Caracas crime beat deserve to be understood on their own terms, from a vantage point that appreciates their social, historical, and political context. Theirs was an urgent situation. A young reporter once commented, offhandedly, that for all of her life Venezuela had been in a perpetual state of emergency.[67] It was under these exceptional circumstances that crime journalists came to champion the victims of violence, to channel their denuncias, and to mobilize popular opinion against crime.

Overview

This book makes three ethnographically grounded observations about the relationships among populism, the press, and the politics of crime in Venezuela. First, crime news creates crime victims. I mean this, of course, in a discursive sense. Crime news reproduces the figure of the innocent, suffering victim. In Caracas, even the most causal news consumer encountered this figure on a daily basis. The newspapers and television programs were replete with stories about good kids, hardworking fathers, and beloved mothers, all murdered for no reason at all. Critical scholars interested in mass mediated representations of crime have looked almost exclusively at the figure of the criminal. As a result, we have a very good idea about where the category of the criminal leads—to the bodies of young men who are marked by their poverty, their race, their ethnicity, their religion, their sexuality, or some combination of these factors. With an eye toward this finding, this ethnography poses a different albeit related question: What can we learn by following the category of the crime victim?

Second, crime victims became legible to themselves and to others through practices such as denunciation. We tend to think of crime victims as mute, passive objects; however, in Caracas, victimhood was anything but silent. To the contrary, victims were active performers who spoke their rage, their grief, and their tragedy. Denuncias permitted a whole spectrum of actors to assert their victimhood in the most public fashion.

Third and finally, denuncias made in the names of crime victims formed the building blocks of what I call "the will to security," and they created the conditions of possibility for a right-wing populist backlash. Studying anticrime and prosecurity denuncias allows us to observe how the popular will is produced in conjunction with a particular strain of populism that calls for more police, bigger prisons, and harsher punishments. Examples abound. Beginning with the grievances of crime victims gives us a granular understanding of how right-wing populism operated both in the Venezuelan context and more generally in the early twenty-first century. Too often populist movements are reduced to pitchfork-waving mobs and opportunistic demagogues. Denuncias allow us to look at the mechanisms and micropolitics—the logic—of right-wing populism. They provide insight into how the popular will is reproduced as a will to security and how the will to security can become the centerpiece of an oppressive solidarity.[68]

Readers will find the bulk of this argument concentrated in the book's later chapters. Ethnographic theory, however, demands ethnographic context. For that reason, chapter 1 provides an introduction to crime, journalism, and the politics of security during the Chávez era. Chapter 2 takes readers through a day on the Caracas crime beat to explain the practices, institutions, and social structures that shaped the production of crime news from the inside out. Chapter 3 extends this analysis by examining the stories that were published the following day. Specifically, it looks at the geographic references—the tacit cartographies of crime—written into crime news.

Chapters 4 and 5 take up the relationship between the practices of crime journalists and the construction of crime victimhood. Chapter 4 describes the sorting of victims into two categories, malandro (shady, suspicious, criminal) and sano (wholesome, innocent, pure), which map onto overlapping structures of inequality in Venezuela. Chapter 5 continues this theme albeit with a twist. In addition to the categorization of victims according to their assumed guilt or innocence, it describes how the construction of crime victimhood reflects the polarizing dynamic of populism. To this end, the chapter looks closely at the still unsolved murder of crime photographer Jorge Tortoza, who was killed on April 11, 2002, during the failed coup against Chávez.

Chapters 6 and 7 turn to the journalistic practice of denunciation and its relevance to the ethnographic study of populism. Chapter 6 provides the historical and theoretical background necessary to understand the relationship between press-fueled denuncias and populist mobilization in Venezuela during the 1980s and 1990s. It argues that the press created the conditions of possibility for the movement that eventually crystallized around the figure of Hugo Chávez. This background, in turn, sets the stage for chapter 7, which shows how crime reporters used denuncias to make sense of their work and to draw attention to the problem of insecurity. What emerges from this description is a larger argument about how denuncias made in the name of crime victims functioned as the building blocks of the will to security. It brings Laclau's concept of "chains of equivalence" into conversation with theories of performativity to explain how the popular will is formed from the ground up.

Chapter 8 shows how denuncias are similarly useful for explaining the relationship between the press and popular protests in Caracas. Rather than beginning with "rights," the insurgent force of democracy is propelled by "wrongs." How those wrongs are articulated has everything to do with the path that any populist project takes. This discussion leads to the book's concluding chapter 9 and the early years of the presidency of Nicolás Maduro. Just a few months after Hugo Chávez's death in March 2014, his successor performed an abrupt reversal on the subject of crime and insecurity. Prompted by the murder of the beauty queen and telenovela star Mónica Spear, President Maduro took up the metaphorical "iron fist" (*mano de hierro*) of security. He launched a series of punitive campaigns, including one called Operation Free the People, that have targeted the very sectors that chavismo once defended. How do we explain this seismic shift? I contend that struggles to contain the will to security allow us to understand how a project predicated on the rejection of neoliberalism ended up repeating one of its most egregious sins.

ONE

Politics in the Chávez Era

La Torre de David, or the Tower of David, is a half-finished skyscraper in downtown Caracas that became a metaphor for the Chávez era. Construction on the forty-five-story building began in 1989 as part of an ambitious project to create a financial complex in the heart of the city. Just a few years later it was abandoned amid economic turmoil and the death of its main backer, David Brillembourg. The structure sat vacant for years. In 2007 squatters took over with the tacit approval of the Chávez administration. The residents were eventually relocated, but not before they had built a city within the city. At its apex, there were more than 4,400 people and 1,100 families living in the complex.[1] The central tower was settled up to the twenty-eighth floor. In addition to personal habitations, the tower also contained a church, a hair salon, a basketball court, and several bodegas.[2]

I first learned about the Tower of David from a pair of journalists who described it as a criminal enclave. They told stories of armed guards, kidnapping rings, and dismembered bodies thrown from the rooftop.[3] This was the Tower of David that appeared in an episode of the television series *Homeland* and served as the central figure in Jon Lee Anderson's 2013 retrospective on the Chávez era. For Anderson, Caracas was "a failed city," and the Tower of David was "the ultimate symbol of that failure."[4] But like everything else in Venezuela, there was a second, more hopeful version of the story; it envisioned the Tower of David as the vanguard of a new urbanism, a testament to the ingenuity and resilience of the urban poor. This was the Tower of David studied by Urban-Think Tank, which made it the subject of a book, a documentary film, and an award-winning exhibition at the 2012 Venice Biennale for Architecture. Rather than a criminal underworld, they discovered a tightly organized community that "turned a ruin into a home."[5]

The Tower of David was typical of Caracas in the Chávez era. There were two versions of Venezuela's capital city, which was alternately represented as a radical utopia and a failed metropolis. Reconciling these competing visions was the greatest challenge of doing research in Caracas. My fieldwork plumbed the depths of what one urbanist called "Caracas the horrible."[6] There was, however, another version of the city that served as an inspiration for progressive politics worldwide. To deny the promise of the Bolivarian Revolution would be as misguided as denying the numerous problems besetting it. This chapter provides an overview of the politics of the Chávez era as it pertained to journalism and security. It is a brief primer to the complicated landscape that crime reporters navigated on a daily basis.

The Journalistic Field

Much of the international reporting about Venezuela in the Chávez era focused on the issue of press freedom or the lack thereof. Take, for example, the nongovernment organization Freedom House, whose annual study of press freedom was widely cited as evidence that press freedom in Venezuela was under assault. Starting in 2003, Freedom House categorized Venezuela as "not free," the same designation given to Iran, North Korea, and Russia. The irony of this designation was that most Venezuelans, regardless of their political allegiance, disagreed with this assessment. Moreover, "press freedom" was widely recognized as an expression of partisan struggle. To claim that press freedom was under assault was to assume an explicitly antigovernment stance. Denying that there was any problem meant assuming a progovernment stance. Given this polarizing rhetoric, I found that it was best to eschew debates about the relative freedom or unfreedom of the press and to focus instead on the journalistic field and the conditions of news production in Venezuela.[7]

Few cities in the world rivaled Caracas for the volume and diversity of its journalistic output during the Chávez era.[8] Print journalism was ubiquitous. More than a dozen newspapers served the Caracas metropolitan area, and at least four of these papers circulated nationally. Upward of 90 percent of these newspapers were sold at the kiosks that dotted all corners of the city.[9] Unlike in North America and Europe, the newspaper industry in Latin America was booming, and everywhere you turned in Caracas, the evidence was on display.[10] Television and radio news were equally robust. According to Andrés Cañizález and Jairo Lugo-Ocando, in Venezuela there were "more users and subscribers for television and radio per capita than in either Brazil or Mexico," Latin America's two traditional broadcast media powerhouses.[11]

Venezuela was also a regional leader in digital communication. By 2011 more than 40 percent of residents had internet access; cell phone penetration hovered around 100 percent; and Venezuelans ranked among the top five users of Twitter in the world.[12]

In contrast to global trends, the ownership of Venezuela's private press was also remarkably decentralized. For a variety of reasons, Venezuela resisted the consolidation of mass media empires so common in the United States and much of Latin America.[13] Even the mighty Gustavo Cisneros— one of Latin America's wealthiest and most influential media moguls— controlled only one major news property in Venezuela. During my fieldwork in Caracas, there were four important private television stations, three radio networks, and four major newspaper empires. All of them were owned and controlled by different groups.

What made Caracas truly extraordinary, however, were the three distinct sectors that made up the journalistic field: the private press, the state press, and the community media movement. The *private press* was old, well established, and widely viewed as the opposition's most potent tool. It consisted of several dozen privately owned and privately operated media outfits.[14] Some were massive, for-profit corporations with national distribution— for example, the television station Venevisión, the radio circuit Unión Radio, or the newspaper *El Universal*. These huge entities overlapped with regional newspapers, local radio stations, special interest magazines (e.g., sports, economy), a couple of privately funded news outlets, and a growing number of news websites. The *state press* was a rapidly expanding media empire under the control of the Chávez government. In 2002 there were just three state-owned, state-operated news outlets.[15] By 2012 the state press had ballooned to include more than a dozen media outfits across the print, broadcast, and digital spectrum.[16] The *community media movement* consisted of a loose network of grassroots media activists that won legitimacy under the Chávez administration. Across Venezuela there were hundreds of community radio stations—both authorized and unauthorized—perhaps one hundred community newspapers, and nearly forty community television stations.[17] Although most stations received support from the government in the way of equipment, the community media movement predated President Chávez by several decades.[18] Important community media outlets such as Catia TVe were independent outfits that had a complex relationship to the state.[19] Although there were important points of overlap between these sectors of the journalistic field, especially between the state press and the community media, they functioned independently and had their own spheres of influence.

In most contexts it makes sense to talk about the journalistic field as a single, discernable sphere of cultural production.[20] However, the struggle between the Venezuelan government and the opposition divided the journalistic field into two camps that were increasingly autonomous. This rift was evident from the perspective of news content. The private press and the state press followed news agendas that were so radically different it was as if they were reporting from altogether different countries. Many Venezuelans were in the habit of shuttling back and forth between the private press and the state press to try to "triangulate" the truth of any news event. This schism was even more apparent from the perspective of journalists. By the end of my fieldwork, two separate professional tracks had emerged, and it was increasingly difficult to move between the state press and the private press.[21] Although older generations of journalists had long-standing relations with their colleagues on both sides of the metaphorical aisle, most of the younger reporters and photographers were cut off from their fellow professionals. The decision to work in the state press could potentially exclude one from employment in the private sector and vice versa.

Later chapters detail the history behind this split, which was tied to the outsize role that the private press played in Venezuelan politics. While there is nothing unusual about the media playing the part of watchdog, news outlets in Venezuela acted more like political parties. They were not simply mouthpieces for the opposition; they *were* the opposition. Or at least that was how most Venezuelans viewed the matter. The ascendance of press power was the result of a series of corruption scandals during the 1980s and 1990s, when journalists helped expose wrongdoing at the highest level of government. Mass mediated denuncias led to the impeachment of Venezuela's president, and they helped thoroughly discredit the country's two main political parties, Acción Democrática (AD) and Partido Sociál Cristiano, known as COPEI. A power vacuum ensued. Many of the prominent reporters and news outlets that had crusaded against the old political parties stepped in to fill that vacuum. Journalists went from ostensibly reporting the news to openly shaping it. They also paved the way for a new series of political movements, most notably the Bolivarian Revolution.

Key figures in the private press helped elect President Hugo Chávez, but the relationship between the press and the president soured in little over a year. What transpired between 2000 and 2005 might be the most dramatic example of a media war in recent history. The private press was at the forefront of a failed coup d'état against Chávez (2002), a three-month oil strike (2002–3), and a presidential recall referendum (2004). Calls to oust Chávez dominated the news media. Aside from a pair of newspapers (*Últimas*

Noticias and *Panorama*), the president and his supporters had few defenders in the private press. That role fell primarily to an anemic state press and an insurgent network of grassroots media producers. As the president and his supporters began to bounce back from political defeat, they channeled resources to news outlets sympathetic to their position.

During President Chávez's second term in office (2006–12), the balance of forces in the journalistic field shifted in favor of the government. The administration's objective was "communicational hegemony," which would pave the way for its progressive sociopolitical agenda.[22] To that end, the state press was transformed into a veritable media empire that included six national television stations, three national radio networks, a press agency, and three Caracas-based newspapers.[23] The project of communicational hegemony also included sustained attempts to convert, co-opt, or censor oppositional elements within the private press. What was undoubtedly the most controversial move during this period was the government's refusal to renew the broadcasting license of Radio Caracas Television (RCTV) in 2007. This move effectively removed Venezuela's oldest and most popular private television station from the airwaves. The case of RCTV illustrated the selective enforcement of broadcast laws in ways that favored the Chávez government. Similar tactics were used against Globovisión and a number of radio stations, including Circuito Nacional Belfort (CNB), or the Belfort National Circuit. These were major developments that shook the journalistic field and provoked international condemnation. However, private press did not disappear, nor did it go silent.

Despite the rapid expansion of the state press, during the period of my fieldwork it was still dwarfed by the private press in terms of audience share. Take the case of television. By the end of 2010, private broadcast television stations commanded just over 61 percent of the national audience; cable and satellite television had approximately 33 percent of the national audience; and state television accounted for a little less than 6 percent of the total national audience.[24]

Perhaps the most important development during the second half of the Chávez era was the renewal of political pacts. Venezuela's media traditionally had been kept in check by a series of informal pacts between political elites and media owners.[25] If many of these pacts disintegrated during the 1980s and 1990s, the middle of the first decade of the twenty-first century witnessed their resurgence. The best example would be the pact between media mogul Gustavo Cisneros and the Chávez government. Cisneros's flagship television network, Venevisión, was one of the key actors behind a coup d'état that nearly ousted Chávez (as will be discussed further in chapter 5). When it became clear that the president was back in power, he and the media mogul struck a deal behind closed doors. Although the specifics of the deal were the subject of rumor, the existence of this pact was common knowledge. As a result, Venevisión shifted its editorial line in a direction favorable to the government. A number of other media outlets opted for a similar path. While there was massive and vocal opposition to the Chávez government at the beginning of the decade, the tone of news coverage in the private press was considerably muted by the end of the decade. This was not an outright conversion. The private press remained the focal point of oppositional politics in Venezuela, but most high-profile pundits, editors, and media owners were convinced or coerced to moderate the tone of their coverage.

The Politics of Security

Whereas there were varying opinions concerning press freedom, everyone agreed that crime was out of control. Consensus only made the issue more volatile. It took an unsettling conversation with the man who sold me the morning newspapers to help me realize this. Like most people in Caracas, I bought newspapers from a kiosk near my home, and I frequently talked politics with the *kiosquero* who sold them. A few months into our relationship, I asked him why Caracas had such high crime rates. His answer surprised me. "Too much democracy," he said, and went on to trace the current crime wave to the fall of the Marcos Pérez Jiménez dictatorship in 1958. Democracy had come at a price, and that price was public order, he contended. The newspaper vendor was a mild, grandfatherly type. A self-identified chavista, he usually sported a red baseball cap and liked to read the progovernment newspaper *Diario Vea*. And yet he was quite critical of the president on the subject of insecurity. Chávez was soft on crime, he told me. The country needed to return to the heavy-handed policies of old. As I discovered, he was not exceptional in his beliefs. Indeed, many of the president's most committed supporters favored openly repressive security measures.[26]

It was no secret that violent crime was the Chávez administration's Achilles's heel. From 2006 to 2013, Venezuelan voters ranked insecurity as the country's number one problem, ahead of unemployment, political instability, corruption, and the economy.[27] Growing concerns about crime coincided with a measurable increase in the rates of violence, but they also reflected booming oil prices and improved economic conditions for the popular classes. For many observers, violent crime symbolized the failure of the Venezuelan state to capitalize on its good fortune. Nowhere was this failure more evident than in Caracas.

In Caracas, violent crime disproportionately affected the president's political base among the urban poor. It represented the one issue that could potentially drive a wedge between Chávez and his supporters. For opposition leaders, including key figures within the private press, "insecurity" presented an important political opportunity. Strategists and politicians were alert to the possibilities of an anticrime, prosecurity platform. Many of these leaders believed that in the hands of the right candidate, a tough-on-crime approach could unseat Chávez.

No political figure embodied the anticrime, prosecurity platform better than Leopoldo López, the charismatic mayor (2000–2008) of Chacao, the city's smallest and wealthiest municipality. López established his reputation as a law-and-order candidate by transforming Policía Chacao into a model municipal police department. When I met López at a press conference in late 2007, he was positioning himself for the next step in his political career. Ostensibly, the purpose of the press conference was to announce the municipality's favorable end-of-year crime statistics, but it was also an opportunity for him to tout his new "Plan 180: A Proposal for Justice and Security in Venezuela." Plan 180 promised to turn insecurity around 180 degrees in 180 days, by reforming the justice system from the bottom up. The proposal included everything from programs for at-risk populations to suggestions for transforming the police, the courts, and the prison system.[28] With López at the helm, all of Venezuela would be just like Chacao.

López's track record in Chacao and his fiery rhetoric made him one of the president's most formidable political adversaries. It was no coincidence that in late 2008 he was barred from running for political office by a dubious court ruling.[29] Although the ban stretched through 2014, López nonetheless went on to establish a new political party, Voluntad Popular (Popular Will). He also explored a 2012 presidential run. As in 2008, security was at the center of López's political platform. In an op-ed piece for the newspaper *El Nacional*, he wrote, "There is no concept that better describes the desire of Venezuelans than that of security. This country's path to peace, well-being, and progress that we will build starting next year will guarantee a territory that is secure for living, secure for working, secure for studying, secure for investing, secure for progressing."[30] Over the years López's message remained remarkably consistent. Even the 2014 protests in Caracas—which marked the beginning of López's transformation into an international poster boy for human rights—were inspired by demands for security that held the national government responsible for the overwhelming levels of violent crime in Caracas.[31] For crime to diminish, chavismo had to go.[32]

Unlike the opposition, President Chávez rarely spoke about violent crime, and his relative silence on the issue was the subject of much speculation. When forced to confront the rise of urban violence, Chávez consistently emphasized social and economic exclusion as the root cause. The best way to go about solving the problem of insecurity was to attack poverty, inequality, and marginalization, he asserted. Take the following excerpt from an interview from his first presidential campaign: "For example, public insecurity: how are you going to fight it? With more police, more patrols, more searches, more guns on the street? No. Not without fighting the root [of the problem]—hunger, unemployment, abandoned children, and that has to do with the social and economic model and the role of the state."[33]

More than a decade later, Chávez continued to insist that crime would diminish only if the structural roots of the problem were addressed. He was similarly consistent in his public repudiation of "the repressive model" of security. Chávez regularly criticized the *mano dura* (literally, "hard hand"), or heavy-handed vision of security, even though it was popular with his political base. Instead, he declared himself in line with "humanist," "preventative," or (much later) "socialist" ideals of public security. Despite a growing crisis and accusations that his government had no interest in protecting its citizens, Chávez remained steadfast on this point, much to his credit.[34]

When I began fieldwork in 2007, intense pressure to solve the crime problem was starting to transform the government's security policies from the inside out.[35] Around this time, a series of highly publicized crimes galvanized popular opinion in Caracas and other cities.[36] In response to this crisis, the Chávez government adopted an incongruous mixture of progressive and heavy-handed policies. The most hopeful programs were implemented under the auspices of the National Commission on Police Reform. The commission promoted a model of policing in line with the humanist vision of security that Chávez touted publicly. It intended to weed out corruption, curb the indiscriminate use of force, foster respect for human rights, and create closer ties between officers and communities.[37] However, the same period also witnessed the gradual spread of "broken windows" campaigns—such as Plan Secure Caracas (Plan Caracas Segura), and Plan Secure the Homeland (Plan Patria Segura)—that projected the spectacle of order through the use of brute force.[38]

During the final years of the Chávez era (2009–13), the president continued to insist that crime would diminish only if the structural roots of the problem were addressed, but his repudiation of the punitive model of se-

stopped repudiating punitive paradigm

curity gradually waned. Instead, he turned his attention to controlling perceptions of crime. Anytime Chávez broached the subject of urban violence, he inevitably focused on the news media and how they created a sensation of insecurity. These observations were always unflattering. Chávez accused crime journalists of everything from morbid voyeurism to insurrectionary propaganda. He also spoke about the political threat posed by news coverage of crime. In this charged environment, stories and images of crime were more than just information. They were tools of political struggle, weapons in a battle of ideas.

Although Chávez never publicly embraced the punitive paradigm, by the end of his presidency, many of the government's policies were drifting in that direction. When Nicolás Maduro assumed the presidency in March 2013, he swiftly adopted the language of *mano dura* and zero tolerance. There are some analysts who see Maduro's policies as merely a continuation of those implemented under Chávez, and it is true that the militarization of policing was already under way. However, the continuity argument overlooks two key points. First, there was a pronounced shift in presidential discourse on security; whereas Chávez was always circumspect in his rhetoric on crime and public safety, Maduro openly embraced language normally associated with right-wing populism. Second, this rhetoric justified the use of deadly force against the urban popular sectors, which made up much of the government's political base. Under President Chávez, police violence against the popular sectors was never condoned. In contrast, under President Maduro, programs such as Operation Free the People (OLP) openly targeted the urban poor.[39] This represented a dramatic transformation of the Bolivarian Revolution's approach to crime and the politics of security, the implications of which are still unfolding.

Roots of Urban Violence

What about crime itself? What was responsible for the crisis of urban violence in the first place? Scholars have offered several explanations for Caracas's exceptionally high homicide rate, including political polarization, the rise of narcotrafficking and organized crime, the extractive logic of neoliberalism, and the abject failure of the police, the prisons, and the legal system.[40] All of these factors contributed to a dire situation, and they all shared a crucial albeit usually neglected point of convergence—the profound impact of urban restructuring on Caracas. To understand the spiraling homicide rates in Venezuela's capital, it helps to understand changes in the fabric of the city itself.

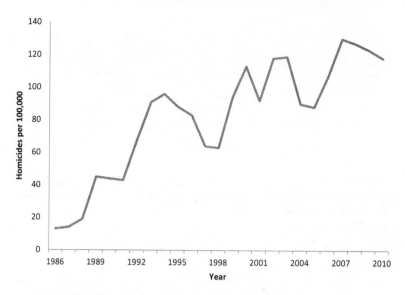

1.1. Upward trend in homicide rates for Caracas. Note the major upticks that occur in 1989, 1992–93, 2000, and 2007. (From PROVEA/Cuerpo de Investigaciones Científicas, Penales y Criminalísticas [CICPC].)

Caracas's crime problem predated chavismo.[41] It became most acute during the late 1980s and early 1990s, a period that witnessed the simultaneous expansion of political rights, neoliberal economic policies, and violent crime (see fig. 1.1).[42] This is a familiar story in many respects. The twin expansion of democracy and neoliberal economic programs transformed cities across Latin America.[43] In Caracas, neoliberalism transferred the fiscal responsibility for the city away from the central government to the state and municipal levels, resulting in the privatization of services. At the same time, democratization meant that citizens with the socioeconomic means to organize were able to reshape the city's political geography from the ground up. What Evelina Dagnino calls the "perverse confluence" of democracy and neoliberalism in Caracas gave rise to a number of unanticipated results, including the further consolidation of wealth enclaves, the decimation of public services, and the widening of socioeconomic inequality.[44] By the turn of the millennium, Venezuela's capital was politically fragmented, unevenly serviced, and socioeconomically segregated.[45]

The reforms that further fragmented Caracas and led to rising levels of violent crime had their roots in the crisis of the Venezuelan petrostate.[46] Since the early twentieth century, Venezuela has been one of the world's leading oil exporters, and in 1960 it became one of five founding members of the

Organization of Petroleum Exporting Countries (OPEC).[47] Oil money produced miraculous feats of urban development in Venezuela's capital and spurred a massive rural-to-urban migration. During the 1950s, 1960s, and 1970s, Caracas was a boomtown. Among caraqueños, this period is nostalgically remembered as a golden age when theirs was the most modern city in South America, equal to the capitals of Europe and North America. Caracas was safe. Caracas was clean. Caracas was prosperous.

If oil made Caracas a world-class city, like many single-export commodities, it proved to be an unstable economic foundation. The first sign of the larger crisis came on February 18, 1983, a day remembered in Venezuela as Black Friday. Despite an unprecedented spike in oil prices in 1973 and again in 1979, the Venezuelan government was forced to downgrade its currency to service its foreign debt. As oil prices plummeted throughout the 1980s, Venezuela's pacted democracy began to crumble under the combined weight of economic and political expectations. Foreign lenders pushed the country to adopt plans for structural adjustment, plans that included the privatization of the national oil industry, but talk of austerity was highly unpopular among Venezuelans. In December 1988, the charismatic former President Carlos Andrés Pérez was elected to his second term in office on a platform that explicitly rejected such measures. Within days of assuming office, he did an about-face and announced a series of shock adjustments. When the president raised the price of gasoline, the city's bus drivers responded by raising fares. Residents of Caracas, already pushed to the brink by a decade of economic stagnation,[48] exploded into protest. President Pérez's response was to call out the National Guard. Hundreds, probably thousands of civilians were killed between February 27 and March 3, 1989, in what were the largest, most violently suppressed urban protests in Venezuelan history.[49]

The Caracazo, as it came to be known, was a watershed event in Venezuelan and Latin American history.[50] Internationally, it was the first popular uprising against neoliberal austerity measures. In Venezuela, it represented the beginning of the end of Venezuelan exceptionalism and the two-party rule of AD and COPEI.[51] Seen from Caracas, the protests and their violent repression marked the escalation of urban violence.

The precipitous rise of violence in Caracas since 1989 has been attributed to a number of factors. Ana María Sanjuán describes it as part of a crisis of legitimacy facing the Venezuelan state. This crisis "affected the guarantees of universal access to essential public health services and judicial order" and "eroded [the state's] ability to maintain a legal monopoly on violence." Roberto Briceño-León characterizes urban violence as the result of a ruptured social pact between elites and the popular classes, which was sustained by the promise of oil rents. After those rents dried up, Briceño-León observes, the pact was broken and "criminals as well as common people felt more at ease with using violence." Susana Rotker suggests that the problem was a lack of empathy for the popular classes: rather than recognizing the suffering of the urban poor, the media portrayed them as the barbarians at the gate, further justifying their violent oppression.[52]

These explanations all suggest that crime rates in Caracas soared at the very moment that neoliberal policies and democratic reforms segregated the city into an uneven patchwork of economic, political, and social territories. The overall effect of urban restructuring was to further exacerbate already pronounced inequalities. Rather than strengthening civil society, the confluence of neoliberal policies and democratic reforms produced new enclaves of privilege and zones of abandonment throughout the city.[53]

The splintering of law enforcement serves as a prime example of the fragmentation of Caracas, and one that allows us to understand struggles over the securitization of Venezuela's capital city. Between 1990 and 2006, more than one hundred new state and municipal police departments were created in Venezuela.[54] By the time that I began my fieldwork, Caracas was patrolled by no fewer than thirteen independent law enforcement agencies. These policing agencies operated under the auspices of eight municipal, state, and national entities, many of which were openly hostile to one another. From a policing perspective, the city was a chaotic patchwork of jurisdictions that overlapped with a proliferation of private security enclaves, autonomous zones, and zones abandoned by police altogether.

During the Chávez era, a new pattern of urban segregation was superimposed over the old one. In addition to partitioning the city down racial and socioeconomic lines, large pockets of the city were identified as "turf" for either chavismo or the opposition. The western half of the city was identified with support for Chávez while the eastern half was opposition territory. Rather than coordinating efforts across the five municipalities, struggles for political control of the capital held the entire metropolitan area hostage.[55]

The upshot of these processes was that all of the thirteen aforementioned police forces were associated with separate political factions. These were not simply servants of the state but rather armed urban militias whose allegiances were dictated by a larger struggle for control of Caracas. Take the former Metropolitan Police (Policía Metropolitana, or PM), which was eventually dismantled and merged into the National Bolivarian Police (Policía Nacional Bolivarana, or PNB). When Chávez first came into office in 1999, the PM was by far the largest police force in Venezuela. Control of the PM fell to the metropolitan mayor, Alfredo Peña, a onetime Chávez associate who became an outspoken critic. Peña enlisted William Bratton—the renowned champion of zero-tolerance policing—to reform the Metropolitan Police, a move that was strenuously opposed by the president. The controversy boiled over during the 2002 coup d'état that briefly deposed Chávez. Within chavismo, it was widely believed that the PM actively participated in the plot to overthrow the government. For the president and his supporters, the Metropolitan Police functioned as an armed wing of the opposition. Reasserting control over the police force became one of the government's explicit objectives, and all of the reforms that followed were carried out with an eye toward larger geostrategic implications. These reforms included transferring authority over the agency, promoting a new cadre of leaders, retraining its officers, and eventually dissolving the PM into an ostensibly new agency (the PNB). A similar dynamic was at play in reforms to police departments citywide so that assuring the loyalty of any given police force often took precedence over problems of corruption and criminality.

Policing was just the tip of the iceberg. The courts were largely ineffective. The prisons became incubators for organized crime. Firearms were readily available. Narcotrafficking was a growing menace. Vigilantism was on the rise. Given this state of affairs, it was little wonder that the problem of violent crime spread during the Chávez era. The rise in violent crime was especially pronounced on a national level (see fig. 1.2).[56] There is a great deal of controversy surrounding the calculation of homicide rates in Venezuela; however, there is no question that they climbed precipitously under the Chávez administration.[57] According to the official police statistics, there were 4,550 homicides nationwide—or 20 per 100,000—in 1998, the year before Chávez took office.[58] By 2008, that official figure more than tripled, to 14,500 homicides nationwide—or almost 52 per 100,000.[59] The situation did not improve under the administration of President Maduro, and it may have even deteriorated. For 2016, Venezuela's Ministerio Público reported 21,000 homicides and an annual homicide rate that spiked to 70 deaths per 100,000 inhabitants, although unpublished internal police records indicate a lower figure of around 16,000 homicides, or a rate of approximately 53 per 100,000.[60] Either way, the situation is dire. In 2016 the global average for homicides was estimated at just over 5 per 100,000, and the regional average for South America was estimated at slightly over 24 homicides per 100,000.[61] That same year, the FBI reported 17,250 homicides in the entire United States (which has a population ten times larger than Venezuela's). The only countries in the world with comparable rates of homicide and violent death were El Salvador, Honduras, and Syria.[62]

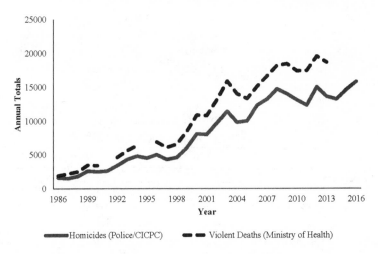

1.2. Two measures of lethal violence in Venezuela. (Data courtesy
of Dorothy Kronick; figure from CICPC and Venezuelan Ministry of Health.)

Under these circumstances, the backlash against crime in Caracas
seemed all but inevitable. That backlash, concentrated in the second half
of the Chávez era, made Caracas an especially good location to observe
the relationship between populism and the politics of security. During this
period, we can observe how demands for security were staged in the name
of the Venezuelan people as well as the Chávez government's halting, provisional, ultimately unsuccessful attempts to turn back the tide. Eventually,
crime as an object of popular mobilization came to dominate Venezuelan
politics at both the urban and national scales.[63]

TWO

Crime Beat

We were lost. Our news van had been circling the western edge of Caracas for nearly two hours searching for the scene of a double homicide.[1] The bodies would be long gone by now. Before giving up the search, we tried one last time. Rolling down the window, the driver asked a pedestrian how to get to barrio Alfredo Rojas. The woman shrugged uncertainly. "There was a murder," he explained, "just off the third turn on Atlantic Avenue." She thought for a moment and then pointed back in the direction from which we had come, toward the superblock towers that marked the neighborhood 23 de Enero. Among caraqueños, "El 23" was infamous as a hotbed of political radicalism, a semiautonomous zone policed by armed collectives.[2] Staring out the back window, Cesar, a longtime photojournalist, nudged me. "That place is dangerous [candela], you know." His partner, Jenny, sitting in the front seat, snapped back that this was total nonsense. El 23 was only trouble, she assured me, for those who came looking for it.[3]

Danger was a recurring topic in Caracas, and not just among crime journalists. Everyone in Venezuela's capital city had deeply felt beliefs about what places were more or less treacherous and what routes were more or less secure. One's sense of danger corresponded to one's understanding of urban space and one's place within it. Crime journalists had a particularly acute awareness of crime's sociospatial dimensions. Before they learned anything else, they learned to navigate Caracas and its dangers, both real and imagined.

Making sense of crime meant making sense of the city. For rookie journalists, the Caracas crime beat was a dizzying chaos of place-names. The city appeared to be a haphazard collection of streets, corners, buildings, neighborhoods, and municipalities all stitched together by threads of violence. For veterans, crime reporting mapped emergent geographies of violence.

It outlined the contours of security and made danger legible. In this respect, the production of crime news coincided with the production of urban space; or, to be more precise, it coincided with the production of secure space, insecure space, and the boundaries between them.[4] This is not to say that there was consensus among crime journalists about the ever-shifting frontiers of security in Caracas. However they did share mutual practices and routines that generated a common image of the city.

This chapter and the next follow a day on the Caracas crime beat. Attending to the routines of crime reporters provides a behind-the-scenes account of the cognitive maps written into crime news.[5] It reveals tacit knowledge about social geography, knowledge that informed narratives of crime and shaped the public image of Caracas. Two aspects of the city's social geography were particularly notable: the association of crime with the poor, informal settlements, known as *barrios*, and the association of crime victims with the city morgue. For crime journalists and their readers these locations encapsulated key features of Caracas's crime city image. For our purposes, they illustrate a dynamic whereby urban space is politically encoded (see fig. 2.1).

Monday, February 25, 2008

Monday, February 25, 2008, was an eventful day on the Caracas crime beat. It included trips to most of the major sites that the crime journalists routinely visited, starting at their unofficial headquarters in downtown Caracas and continuing on to the city morgue, to a crime scene in one of the poor barrios, and to a press conference with a government minister. It also involved encounters with all of the main sources of crime news, including relatives of victims, crime scene eyewitnesses, government officials, and police informants. At the same time, the day was sufficiently ordinary to give readers a sense of how the beat functioned on a regular basis and to glimpse the everyday spatial practices that shaped crime reporting.

7:00 a.m.—Meet the Power Rangers

Weekday mornings the bright orange booths of Il Subito café in downtown Caracas were filled with half a dozen crime reporters drinking coffee, trading gossip, and sharing notes about the spiral of violence that had this city on edge. Just two doors down from the old press offices of the investigative police (CICPC),[6] Il Subito looked out over a neighborhood collapsing under the weight of neglect. Once upon a time this was the center of crime reporting in

Caracas. That was before January 2003, a moment of extreme political tension in Venezuela when the government took the extraordinary step of closing the press offices. They never reopened. However, the crime journalists kept coming back for reasons of convenience, camaraderie, and sheer force of habit.

Thanks to a friendly agreement with the café's owners, the two booths closest to the street were reserved for the reporters who began trickling in as early as 7:00 a.m. The crime reporters who gathered every morning were predominantly women, and they worked the crime beat as a team despite being employed by competing news outlets. Collectively, they exercised considerable influence on the field of crime journalism in Caracas. For a time they even jokingly referred to themselves as "the Power Rangers," after the children's show featuring a team of superheroes dressed in kitschy, multicolored uniforms.

Sandra Guerrero was the unofficial leader of this crime-writing team. One of the most influential reporters on the crime beat, she had covered crime in Caracas since the 1980s. Most of her career was spent at the newspaper *El Nacional*, where she earned a reputation for spartan prose and meticulous attention to detail. Like most beat journalists, Sandra had a routine that she liked to follow:[7]

5:30 a.m. Sandra's mornings began with the early news programs on Radio Caracas Television (RCTV) or Globovisión. These shows gave her a sense as to the stories that other news outlets were covering and what she needed to pay attention to during her rounds.

7:00 a.m. By this hour Sandra was on the phone with her editors and her sources. If there was important breaking news, she might head directly to a crime scene or a press conference. Otherwise she walked a few blocks from her apartment in the middle-class Candelaria neighborhood to Il Subito café in Parque Carabobo. There she waited for the team to assemble, making more phone calls and staying on the alert for anything newsworthy.

8:00 a.m. Sometime between 8:00 and 8:30, Sandra left for the city morgue, riding in an unmarked SUV that belonged to *El Nacional*.

8:30 a.m. At the morgue Sandra interviewed the families and friends of homicide victims, a process that often took upwards of an hour on busy days. Depending on what she found, Sandra would decide whether to follow a story, visit a crime scene, attend a press conference, or continue waiting at the morgue.

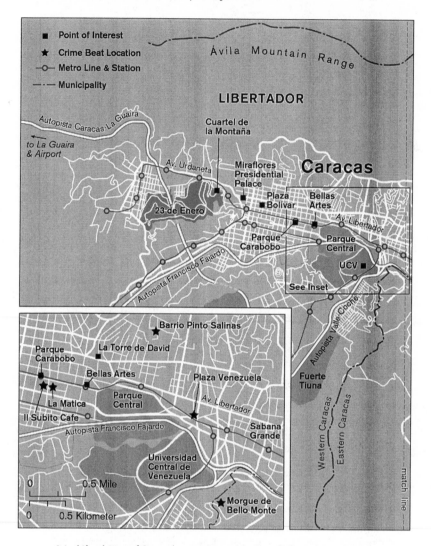

2.1. (*Above*) Map of Caracas's western municipality of Libertador, with inset map of crime beat locations described in this chapter. (*Opposite*) Map of Caracas's four eastern municipalities, with inset map showing Venezuela in regional perspective. (Maps by Ben Pease, www.peasepress.com.)

11:30 a.m. On a good day, Sandra had all of her stories in hand before regrouping with the rest of the team at Il Subito just before noon. Back at the café the reporters pooled their notes, checking to make sure that everyone agreed on the key facts (names, ages, places, and so forth). If one reporter had received a tip from a source, visited a crime scene, or attended a press

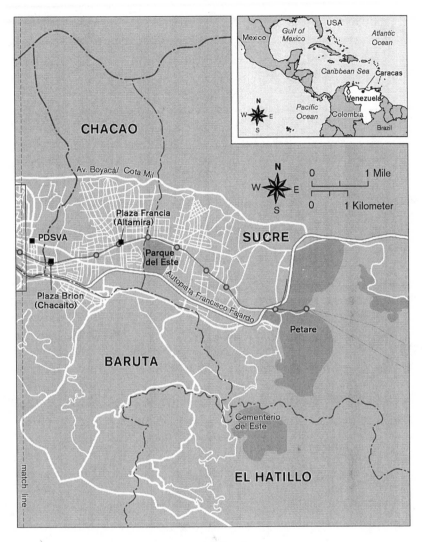

2.1. (*continued*)

conference that the others missed, that reporter was expected to dictate his or her notes to the rest of the team.

12:30 p.m. Sometime between noon and 1:00 p.m. Sandra headed back across town to the offices of *El Nacional*, where she reported to her editors. Based on the number of stories that Sandra and her colleagues collected as well as the amount of space that needed to be filled, the crime desk editor created a page layout.

5:00 p.m. The remainder of Sandra's afternoon was spent at her desk, where she quietly went about the business of writing two, three, sometimes as many as four articles per day. Like most reporters, she had to work fast to meet the 5:00 p.m. deadline.

Of course, journalists' routines were constantly subject to change. Although most Monday mornings Sandra was seated at her usual spot, on this particular day she was working on a special about a plane crash in the Andean state of Mérida.[8] In her place was Thabata Molina, the youngest reporter from *El Nacional*, who was tapping away on her smartphone. Beside her at the table were two of the most veteran members of the team, María Alejandra Monagas (*Últimas Noticias*) and Felicita Blanco (*El Carabobeño*). The pair was smoking and chatting over a makeup catalog. All three greeted me with a warm shower of hellos, and Felicita asked with mock seriousness, "What should I go with, Robert? The coffee or the caramel base powder?"

Sitting down at the booth, I busied myself with the morning papers, handing a copy of *Últimas Noticias* to María Alejandra and *El Nacional* to Thabata. Yesterday's big news was the bizarre conclusion to a string of bombings in the city by a group calling itself Frente Venceremos.[9] Sandra had called at 7:00 a.m. the previous day to inform me that one of the bombers tripped his own explosive device and met an untimely end outside of the Federated Chambers of Commerce (Fedecameras). Interested to know more about the case, I inquired whether there were any updates.

"Was the bomber really carrying police credentials?" I asked, incredulously.

"What do you think?" Thabata said, darkly.

"How weird," was all I managed to say, not sure what Thabata was getting at.

"It is not weird at all," one of the other reporters replied. "They've been arming the barrios for years. Frente Venceremos is just a bunch of *malandros* [thugs]."

Barely eight o'clock and I had already stirred up a political hornet's nest. I tried to steer the conversation in another direction, but Thabata just chuckled. "Malandros," she said decisively. As we were talking, three more members of the team arrived: Efrén Pérez Hernández (*Diario El Siglo*), Sabrina Machado (*Panorama*), and Altagracia Anzola (*Diario La Voz* and *El Nuevo País*). There were more greetings all around. I got up to buy a round of coffees. When I returned, the group was preparing to leave for the morgue.

8:30 a.m.—La Matica

While the reporters gathered at Il Subito, the photographers, cameramen, drivers, and all the journalists who were not affiliated with the Power Ranger clique congregated at a nearby street corner known affectionately as *la matica*, or "little shrub." Named after a cluster of small, squat trees that grew up out of the sidewalk, la matica offered a good view of the old investigative police building and the surrounding area. It was not a particularly attractive location. One side bordered an abandoned strip of dirt, and another side sat adjacent to four massive dumpsters whose contents usually overflowed into the street. However, it was a convenient place to park the news vans.

The photographers, cameramen, and drivers who worked the crime beat were all men, most of them in their fifties and sixties, and la matica had a men's club atmosphere. Between assignments they passed the time with practical jokes, sports talk, salsa music, and admiring "compliments" directed toward unaccompanied women. These daily sessions started around 6:00 a.m. Since many of the men lived in barrios or working-class neighborhoods on the outskirts of the city, that meant leaving the house long before dawn and waiting patiently for the reporters to arrive. Every now and then they rushed off to early morning assignments—a body in the street, an accident on the highway, a shoot-out with the police. However, between bursts of activity they spent long stretches of the day watching and waiting.

Early on, I wondered about this gendered division of labor. Why were so many crime reporters women? Why were all of the crime photographers men? The answers that I received from editors and directors were telling. Women made good crime reporters, they reasoned, because they were better equipped to create rapport with the victims of violence. They were more adept at drawing out testimonies and soliciting denuncias. However, the same gendered politics that made them suitable for crime reporting also marked them as potentially vulnerable when venturing into poor barrios or covering tense protests and demonstrations. My first interview in Caracas was with a section editor who expressed no small concern for the safety of two young women in his care.[10] One of the tacit assumptions was that working-class men were better equipped for the dangers associated with the crime beat, particularly the risks associated with taking photos and being visibly marked as a journalist in neighborhoods that were strongholds of support for President Chávez. So while the women worked to create rapport with the victims of violence, the photographers doubled as scouts and quasi bodyguards tasked with protecting the vulnerable female body.

Once upon a time, crime reporting was an exclusively male domain. How-ever, the profile of the ideal crime reporter changed with the exigencies of the Caracas crime beat. The masculine image of crime-reporter-as-detective was predicated on the close association between journalists and the police.[11] Un-der ordinary circumstances, the police and the judiciary are the best sources of information for crime reporters.[12] In Caracas, however, the official channels of communication between the police and the journalists were more con-strained, in part because of the closing of the press offices of the investigative police in 2003.[13] Although veteran reporters still had unofficial police sources, crime journalists became increasingly reliant on the testimony of victims of violence. As their sources changed, the crime reporter began to be associated with another figure, that of the victim. Women reporters were charged with channeling victimhood in their reporting. As it stood, the gendered division of labor on the crime beat was linked to the growing importance of victims' testimonies and their emphasis on denunciation.

The Power Rangers were running late and la matica was almost empty. Just two men were standing under the trees, their cameras hanging loosely around their necks. One of them, a photographer with cropped gray hair and wearing a light blue guayabera, shouted playfully, "Look! They finally rolled out of bed!" Thabata smiled and Felicita yelled back with feigned indignation, "Ay, Boca!"

Alex Delgado, alias Bocanegro, was one of the most senior photogra-phers on the crime beat. He had worked for El Nacional since 1977 when he got his start in the newspaper's darkroom.[14] Slender and graceful, Alex played Puck to Sandra's Oberon: he was an impish prankster who was fond of loud jokes, parties, and the occasional drink. None of this got in the way of his skill as a beat photographer. Alex was quick with the camera and constantly looking for a distinctive shot, one that escaped the other photog-raphers. Sandra trusted him completely, as did Thabata. One of the secrets to his longevity on the beat was probably his comfortable working relation-ship with Sandra and the other crime reporters at El Nacional.

An occupational hierarchy set reporters above photographers and cam-eramen, and it was a hidden source of tension on the crime beat.[15] This hierarchy was reflected in the pay scale. Reporters were often paid 20, 30, even 40 percent more than photographers. It was reflected in terms of "cul-tural capital." Reporters were generally accorded greater respect within the journalistic profession. Finally, and most crucially, it was reflected in the working relationship between reporters and photographers. While they were together, the reporter was the boss. On more than one occasion I heard reporters refer to their colleagues as "my photographer" or "my driver" despite the fact that these men were often thirty years their senior.

Alex, like many of his colleagues, referred to himself a "graphic reporter" rather than a photographer. This was a conscious attempt to legitimize his labor, to draw out its informative content, and to set it on an equal plane with the written word. Many of the self-identified graphic reporters on the crime beat had achieved some degree of professional parity thanks to their long tenure on the beat and their status within the profession. Along with Alex, men such as Fernando Sánchez and Luis Vallenilla—the president and vice president, respectively, of the National Circle of Graphic Reporters—managed to establish themselves as crime journalists in their own right.

Although Alex did not call the shots, he was taken seriously as a fellow journalist. The front seat was always reserved for him just in case he saw a photo opportunity. On days like this one, it was hard not to envy him. Since there were only two cars, six of us crammed into the *El Nacional* vehicle. It was a tight fit, but no one complained. For freelancers and journalists from small newspapers, transportation was one advantage of teamwork.[16] Although the television channels and the big Caracas papers provided their reporters with cars and drivers, news outlets with fewer resources expected journalists to find their own means of transportation. If not for the Power Rangers, these reporters would have struggled to do their jobs.

9:00 a.m.—The Morgue in Bello Monte

After official access to the investigative police was cut off, the city morgue came to serve as a kind of surrogate press office for one simple reason: sooner or later every homicide in Caracas passed through its doors. Housed in the sagging remains of the old Pampero Social Club, the morgue sat up in the hills of Bello Monte, just southeast of the city's center (fig. 2.2). A low, rectangular building divided into two wings, the morgue was visually nondescript. The only thing that gave away the building's purpose was an overpoweringly thick and sickly sweet smell, which filled the air like a miasma. Today it was particularly bad. Stepping out of the car, I saw Thabata pass her hand in front of her nose, warding off the initial shock. From the front seat, Alex mischievously waved a yellow tin of tiger balm at me. The photographers sometimes applied a dab of it to their upper lips to counteract the smell, although in my experience this remedy was as uncomfortable as the affliction and not particularly effective. I grinned back at him and hopped out of the car, trying not to hold up traffic on this narrow road.

2.2. Families and journalists gather outside the morgue
in Bello Monte. (Photograph by author.)

The morgue was not originally designed for forensic work, which was evident from its location. Although there were a few office buildings in the neighborhood, Bello Monte was almost exclusively a residential enclave, and a fairly well-to-do one at that. The nearest Metro mass transit railway stop was well over a mile away. Getting to the morgue without a car meant catching a private bus or taking a taxi. Other than a few newspaper kiosks, there was nowhere to eat, rest, or pass the time; and since there was no waiting room inside the morgue, families and friends clustered around the front of the building. Anyone who could bear the smell sat in the fixed green waiting chairs that lined the front patio (fig. 2.3). The journalists often preferred to hang back a short distance from the main entrance, not just because of the smell but also to survey the scene.

It was a Monday, and the morgue was packed. The small carport was even more cramped than usual, and the narrow street that ran in front of the morgue was lined with cars on either side. The patio was filled to capacity, and clusters of people spilled out onto the low, stone walls fronting the building. Across the road, the newsstand was doing a steady business selling drinks and snacks, as were its proprietor's two competitors, who had set up shop on either side with coolers and coffee thermoses.

Scattered among the crowd were nearly two dozen journalists from most of the major news outlets in Caracas. We spotted a group of photographers in the shade of the newsstand, cameras slung loosely around their necks, leaning against a high retaining wall that held back the steep hillside. Alex popped out of the front seat and headed over to the group with me in tow. The fraternity greeted us warmly. "Hey, Bocanegro, we thought you were lost," one of them chuckled before turning to greet me with a wide-eyed smile. "Oh, it is Pollo Crudo!" Such names were teasing, affectionate, and often tinged with racial humor. Dark-skinned Alex was sometimes referred to simply as *el negro*, and after a couple weeks on the beat I was baptized "raw chicken" (*pollo crudo*) in reference to both my pale coloring and my rookie status (after further seasoning, I eventually graduated to "fried chicken").

The friendly banter continued as Alex pulled a cigarette from his breast pocket. "So what have we got today?" he asked one of the other photographers who was fidgeting with his camera. Without looking up, the photographer replied softly, "A guy that disappeared last week and a double from Filas

2.3. Crime journalist working outside the morgue. (Photograph by author.)

de Mariches. The double is over there by the front entrance." Then to me he said, "Stand still," and fired off half a dozen shots of a cluster of people, using my body as a shield to conceal the telephoto lens.

Across the street the reporters had stationed themselves near the mouth of the carport, quietly surveying the scene. Picking out potential stories took a discriminating eye. Usually, it was the reporters who were tasked with reading the telltale signs of victimhood. On a day like this one, when the morgue had nearly one hundred visitors, it took a keen observer to distinguish who was here and for what purpose. The clues were subtle, but after a few years on the beat, most of the reporters could pick out the relatives of homicide victims with remarkable accuracy.

Class was the first and most important marker that reporters registered. Experienced crime reporters often told me that they could distinguish the families of homicide victims based on what they were wearing: "If they look disheveled, like they do not care about their appearances, like they just rushed out the door, then they are probably here because of a murder." Appearances indicated much more than the proximate circumstances, however. In Venezuela—a country renowned for producing beauty queens—appearances were everything. Along with skin complexion, a quick glance at a person's clothing, hairstyle, makeup, cell phone(s), and accessories was almost always sufficient to make a judgment about class position and more. These judgments were then refined during the interviewing process.

If identifying the families of victims took a matter of seconds, getting them to talk could be much more challenging. On this particular day, Efrén and Sabrina had the delicate task of initiating contact. Notepads and smartphones at their sides, the pair drifted toward two women seated near the front entrance of the morgue. One of the women, in her early twenties, sported a long black ponytail and white pendant earrings, which give her a schoolgirl air. The second woman was much older, with blocky glasses and a dome of curly black hair framing a weathered countenance. Efrén took the lead, addressing the elder woman in a respectful tone. "Excuse us. Are you relatives of someone killed in an act of violence?" The grandmotherly woman glanced over at the younger one who nodded, "Yes, my brother." Efrén murmured his condolences and continued.

"Where did it happen?"

"In Filas de Mariche," she said, a grieved look on her face.

"You were with him?" Efrén asked, gently easing the girl toward an interview.

"No, I was at home. He was there with friends." The girl's voice was filled with emotion but her response was positive and engaged. The reporters took this as a good sign. Raising her smartphone, Sabrina inquired, "When was this?" Efrén also had his notebook in hand and was writing rapidly.

Within a matter of minutes a small crowd of reporters had gathered around the two women. The story that began to emerge was horrible even by their standards. There was a party that was brutally interrupted by gang violence. The gang arrived uninvited, turned off the lights, yelled "surprise," and opened fire on everyone inside. According to the sister's testimony, the police refused to enter the zone for lack of reinforcements. The older woman, who turned out to be a member of the local communal council, talked about the outbreak of violence in the neighborhood and the absence of the police. While the reporters were busy asking questions and scribbling notes, the photographers stalked the edges of the circle looking for a good angle, sometimes jostling one another or gently pushing the reporters to one side or another. As the details of the story emerged in full, the television reporters waved the cameramen over. The television cameramen came last because their presence made people uncomfortable and it often shut down interviews. In this case the young woman seemed unfazed by the attention. At one moment I counted eighteen reporters, photographers, and camera-men clustered around her. The scrum was so dense that her neighbor had to duck her head awkwardly to avoid being suffocated by microphones. Even-tually the spectacle peaked, the cameramen and photographers got their images, and the reporters got their quotes. As the journalists were slowly drifting away, I overheard one comment, "This is a good one."

9:45 a.m.—The Bloodhound's Call

The Power Rangers were still going over their notes when a sudden flurry of activity captured their attention. All the television crews were rushing toward their trucks and in a matter of seconds RCTV, Televen, Globovisión, and Canal-i had cleared out of the morgue. Thabata and María Alejandra were immediately on their smartphones trying to figure out what just hap-pened, when Altagracia got a call. She reported that there was a shoot-out in the barrio Pinto Salinas involving the investigative police. "Gustavo is there," she added. The reporters quickly weighed the information. While Felicita and Efrén elected to stay behind at the morgue, the rest of us dashed to our cars.

The mention of Gustavo Rodríguez meant that most of the journalists were bound to follow this story. Gustavo was the senior crime reporter for the newspaper *El Universal* and the one reporter whose renown equaled or ex-ceeded Sandra's. At the time of my fieldwork, he had been reporting on crime in Caracas for some twenty years. Unlike most of the other journalists, crime was the only beat that Gustavo had ever worked. It was the only beat he ever wanted to work. As a student of journalism at the Central University of Venezuela, he realized that while politics, economics, culture, and even sports were all coveted assignments, crime had a bad reputation, and the quality of crime reporting suffered as a consequence. He set out to change that.[17]

Gustavo's dedication to the crime beat earned him the reputation of being "a bloodhound." Completely bald, with light brown skin and perpetually squinted blue eyes, he carried himself with an air of tragic aloofness as if he had just stepped out of a 1950s film noir. Along with his journalism degree, Gustavo had a master's degree in criminology and had trained with the investigative police. He was comfortable at a crime scene and on familiar terms with many of the officers in the CICPC. Among crime reporters he was revered for his knowledge of forensics and his willingness to follow a case wherever it might lead. Gustavo routinely went to places that most of the other reporters were leery of setting foot, such as prisons, hospital morgues, and the barrios. Predictably, the bloodhound worked alone. Although he may not have had the broad agenda-setting capacity of the Power Rangers, editors from rival news outlets paid close attention to what he published. If Gustavo was covering a story and all the television stations had that same story, then the Power Rangers were more or less obligated to cover the story, too.

10:15 a.m.—Barrio Pinto Salinas (Official Sources, Part 1)

Barrio Pinto Salinas was located near the city center, in the shadow of the Ávila mountain range that formed Caracas's northern boundary. At the time, Pinto Salinas had earned a bad reputation for violent crime owing to rumors about Los Capriceros, a gang that became notorious for filming a string of murders and posting the videos online. Driving into the sector, Alex took the lead, leaning out the front window, asking for directions, and looking for the scene of the shoot-out. He and the driver both lived in the aforementioned barrio 23 de Enero, and they were visibly more at ease in this environment than the reporters were. Whenever the team from *El Nacional* headed into the city's poor, populous neighborhoods, Alex played the local guide shielding his charges. It was a role to which he had grown accustomed.

Thanks to Alex's efforts, we found the right street without much trouble. The caravan parked under a gnarled tree whose roots buckled the pavement. Our destination was a five-story tenement building that rose up above rows of redbrick shacks. To get there we passed through a narrow opening in a chain-link fence, across an empty parking lot to the back of the building, and then circled around to the front entrance. A crowd of maybe thirty people had gathered near a small convenience store that flanked the stairwell. We spotted a couple of reporters just inside the building and followed them up to the third floor.

The hard, concrete stairs of the building were slippery and congested with journalists. As we rounded the corner to the third-floor landing, a woman on the second floor emerged with a bucket of water that she was using to rinse blood out of the hallway. The reporters were bunched together against the far wall of the third floor. One was talking quietly with an officer wearing a bulletproof vest, while the cameramen and photographers were focused on the closed door of one of the apartments.

Mixed in with the journalists were about half a dozen heavily armed agents from the investigative police. Despite the government's decision to close the press offices, they had not completely severed the ties between crime reporters and CICPC agents. For many of the veteran reporters, their careers were intertwined with the careers of the CICPC brass, whom they knew from a lifetime of covering the beat. For many of the younger journalists, their careers depended on fostering such connections.

Before the era of political polarization, reporters were privy to all manner of off-the-record information. In turn, they fed leads from their own investigations to CICPC agents. Many of the reporters and agents could be found eating or drinking together downtown. In fact, the relationship between crime journalists and the CICPC was so close that some journalists earned the reputation of being "half cop, half reporter."[18]

Conflicting political allegiances of both the press and the police brass caused the relationship to cool considerably during the Chávez era. The Ministry of Interior and Justice's appointees to head the CICPC—men such as Marcos Chávez (2003–8) and Wilmer Flores Trosel (2008–11)—vowed to make it loyal to the Hugo Chávez administration. As a result, officers who were otherwise sympathetic to the crime reporters were not keen on being seen with them in public. Still, the press had its uses. The CICPC regularly fed reporters basic information in return for positive news coverage. Given the avalanche of bad news and mounting pressure to show reductions in violent crime, the CICPC was eager to publicize any kind of success—gangs dismantled, arms decommissioned, hostages rescued, drugs seized. If the cozy relationship between the press and the investigative police was no more, there was still a good deal of give and take, both on and (mostly) off the record.

Nevertheless, this particular gathering was unusual. Generally, encounters between reporters and the CICPC took place in police stations, at staged press conferences, or over the phone. While there were always three or four officers from the CICPC at the scene of a crime for purposes of forensic analysis, the men in this hallway were not here as part of the postmortem. When I asked what was going on, one of the journalists told me that this was a potentially big story about the gang Los Capriceros.[19] It was not the shoot-out that interested them so much as the search being conducted behind closed doors. There was speculation that the infamous murder tapes could be inside this apartment.

As the group milled about, one of the neighbors pushed through the journalists, hand in front of her face. Before the reporters even registered her presence, she said angrily and to no one in particular, "You may not interview me," before disappearing into her apartment. The woman one flight down was more willing to talk, but only on the condition that the reporters would not take her photo or publish anything that she said. She chatted with them briefly, bucket in hand.

After about ten minutes of waiting, the official story emerged wearing a navy blue suit and a dark tie. Captain Alfredo Montero explained that his officers tracked members of the gang to this apartment and that they shot one Leinad Oswaldo Blanco who was resisting arrest. Surrounded by microphones and cameras, he calmly fielded the reporters' questions. No, he was not here during the shoot-out. Yes, they had reason to suspect that tapes of the murders might be inside. No, the subject did not die inside the apartment but rather en route to the hospital. The camera lights were bright in this dim hallway, and the captain was in control.

After the cameras went off, the reporters lingered a little longer to speak with the captain. One of the women from a rival clique of reporters complimented him on his suit. They continued back and forth for a few minutes, alternately flirtatious and serious. As the police started to trickle out of the building, we followed them. Months before, on my first trip into the barrios with the crime reporters, Sandra explained, "When the police go, so do we."[20]

11:00 a.m.—Meet the Minister (Official Sources, Part 2)

Although the press conference with the new head of the Ministry of Interior and Justice (MIJ), Ramón Rodríguez Chacín, was scheduled for 11:00 a.m., the Power Rangers were no hurry to get there. "This is politics, not crime," said one in a defiant tone. "I'm not going." The rest of the reporters were undecided. For many news outlets, press conferences with the MIJ bordered a gray zone. On one hand, the ministry was in charge of all things having to do with crime and policing, including the CICPC and the Metropolitan

Police. On the other hand, the ministers were, first and foremost, political appointees of the president. Ultimately, the decision about whether or not the crime reporters covered a particular press conference was up to their editors. Although it was clear that no one wanted to go, about half of the group grudgingly made their way to the designated location in Plaza Venezuela.

We arrived in Plaza Venezuela to find it decked out for the day's affair. Two large white tents billowed gently in the breeze. The first tent was enclosed on three sides by white canvas walls. Inside, a small lectern was flanked on either side by two large television screens, a pair of microphones, and a wall of posters displaying crime rates for Caracas and Venezuela. The stage was set so that television cameras could capture both the speaker and these wall-size display charts. The second tent was an extension of the first, and it was filled with row upon row of white plastic chairs. There were, by my count, 180 seats set out for this press conference.

Official press conferences were one of the only situations in which the crime journalists, who worked almost exclusively for privately owned media outlets, came into contact with their peers from the state press. While we waited for the minister to arrive, I spoke with a cameraman from Venezuela Television (VTV), the oldest and most influential of the state television channels. There were also journalists from two newly created state television stations, Vive TV and TVes, as well as representatives from ABN (the state press agency) and RNV (a state-owned radio station). These journalists mingled with half a dozen press officers from the MIJ, who dressed in matching red jackets and badges. However there was minimal interaction between these representatives of the state press and the crime journalists. They formed two separate spheres of influence. Although a few members of each group greeted friends and acquaintances on the other side of the political divide, the separation was unmistakable.

For almost an hour, the two factions of journalists milled about the tents chatting, checking their smartphones, making phone calls, examining the posters, and munching on pastries. It was a lively scene. Between the private press, the state press, and a handful of representatives from community media outlets, there were almost eighty journalists on hand, representing more than three dozen outlets across the print and broadcast spectrum. Rather than join the proceedings, most of the Power Rangers opted to wait in their cars until the minister arrived.

Around noon the minister roared into the plaza atop a black Yamaha motorcycle accompanied by four other bikers. Dressed in all black from helmet to boots, he appeared on the scene like a rider out of some postapocalyptic fantasy. For a fleeting moment, I had a vision of Mad Max. That vision was dispelled when the black helmet came off to reveal a bespectacled bureaucrat with protruding ears and thinning hair.

Ramón Rodríguez Chacín was a former naval officer and an intelligence specialist. He was also a longtime friend and ally of President Chávez who served two terms at the helm of the MIJ, first in 2002 and then again in 2008. His second stint as the minister of interior and justice had gotten off to a rocky start. Just over a month after taking office, he announced that his new "Plan Secure Caracas" had reduced homicide rates in the city by more than 60 percent. Plan Secure Caracas was initiated right after the Christmas holidays, which is the worst time of the year for violent crime. Homicide rates regularly doubled during this period. Celebrating a 60 percent decrease in homicides since Christmas as evidence of the success of an anticrime program was a bogus claim, and the press attacked him for it. As one reporter told me, it was like claiming that declining consumer sales after Christmas provided evidence of a recession. Even a staff member close to the minister acknowledged, privately, that this had been a tactical error on the ministry's part.

Taking the podium, Rodríguez Chacín reluctantly admitted that his earlier claims were erroneous, but he still insisted that Plan Secure Caracas was producing results. The program's success was the theme of the press conference. "During the first eight weeks of 2008," the minister began, "we have cut the average weekly homicide rate in Caracas by more than 40 percent." In 2007 there were an average of fifty-two homicides per week in Caracas. During the first weeks of 2008, that figure had fallen to an average of thirty-one.[21]

The minister's remarks stretched for just over half an hour. Near the midway point, I looked up and realized that I was the only person taking notes. Most of the reporters looked on dully, with glazed eyes. This attitude only changed near the end of the press conference when Rodríguez Chacín turned his attention to the recent spate of bombings by Frente Venceremos. At this point, everyone started writing furiously. According to the minister, the man who died in the explosion early Sunday morning was one Héctor Serrano. Although he carried police credentials, Serrano was not an officer of the Metropolitan Police but rather an official informant. Rodríguez Chacín described the members of the group who carried out the bombings as "terrorists" and "anarchists" possibly linked to a militant faction of the opposition known as Bandera Roja. He was careful never to use the name Frente Venceremos, despite the fact that this name appeared on all of the leaflets associated with the bombings.

After Rodríguez Chacín concluded his remarks, the ministry staff led a carefully staged question-and-answer session. The only questions permitted were those vetted ahead of time. A total of eight reporters took turns approaching the microphones, including reporters from the four private news networks: Televen, Globovisión, Venevisión, and RCTV. The vast majority of the questions concerned the bombings and Frente Venceremos. One reporter asked if all police informants carry credentials. Another asked about alleged ties between Héctor Serrano—who lived in 23 de Enero—and the armed civil defense group Tupamaro, known to operate out of this area. A third wanted to know how the police ascertained that all four bombings were connected. The minister seemed relieved to talk about something as tangible as an ongoing investigation. He answered all of the questions crisply, confidently.

As the question-and-answer session wrapped up, the television crews hurried back to their respective studios. The Power Rangers headed back to their vehicles. On a normal day, they would all meet back at Il Subito café in Parque Carabobo. Because of the press conference, though, they were running behind schedule, and so most of the reporters and photographers made their way back to their respective newsrooms.

1:00 p.m.—Teamwork

Back at Il Subito café, a handful of crime reporters reviewed the morning's events. One journalist was missing notes about the shoot-out in barrio Pinto Salinas. Another skipped the press conference with the minister and needed a quick overview of what transpired. Everyone knew the drill. For the next half hour, the journalists took turns dictating from their notes while the rest of the group wrote down the details.

Sharing notes was a common practice among reporters on the Caracas crime beat. Everyone helped out colleagues with the expectation that the favor would be returned. What separated the Power Rangers from the rest of the pack was the way that they synchronized their reporting. Not only did they share notes, but they also worked to establish an official version of the story. Without the police to act as the source of crime news, seemingly simple details became objects of contention. The Power Rangers solved this problem by pooling their notes and coming to an agreement on such key facts as the time and place of the crime, the names and ages of the victims, potential motives for the crime, important witnesses, and essential quotes. They decided which sources were reliable, which details were too sensitive to publish, and which stories were most important. What made their collaboration especially powerful was that the Power Rangers represented perhaps half a dozen news outlets. By synchronizing their work, the group had an agenda-setting power that even editors had to respect.

There are those who see "pack journalism" as anathema.[22] It homogenizes news coverage. It discourages investigation. It produces complacent reporters and predictable stories. Many journalists privately criticized the dynamic of the crime beat. One reporter described the Power Rangers as a journalistic cartel, a kind of crime-writing syndicate. Another reporter who preferred to work alone remarked, pointedly, "where there are journalists, there is no news" (*donde hay periodistas, no hay noticias*). Editors were similarly critical of the cozy relationship among reporters from competing news outlets. They encouraged their journalists to distance themselves from this kind of reporting, albeit with mixed results. After all, the Power Rangers were the ones who did all the on-the-job training, and most journalists who worked on the crime beat were beholden to them in one way or another.

Cooperation on the crime beat served an important function. Beat journalists were underpaid and overworked. Most of them had little chance of professional advancement. Although they viewed their job as a vocation, most of the veterans rightfully insisted that their labor was abused by their editors and by media owners. During my fieldwork, I observed no fewer than three major strikes by journalists' unions. If many of the crime reporters were unsympathetic toward chavismo, they were equally critical of the elites who owned and operated the private press. It was not just their labor but also their ideals that were often compromised by the demands of media owners and editors. By working together, they created a community of professionals who were powerful in their own right. They also created a common cartography of crime, which shaped the ways in which they represented Caracas, Venezuela, and the problem of urban violence.

As soon as the journalists had their notes and photographs, their videos and sound bites, they made their way back to their respective newsrooms scattered across the city. By 1:00 p.m. the television crews were already back in the studio. Those few reporters who were still at Il Subito would have to scramble to make their end-of-day deadlines. The news-gathering portion of the day was complete. The next chapter turns to the stories that were produced.

THREE

Crime City

One of the peculiarities of crime news is its tendency to jump scale. Journalistic depictions of urban violence shuttle back and forth between intimate snapshots of tragedy and sweeping panoramas of crisis. One moment we are alongside grieving relatives at a particular site in a particular neighborhood. The next moment we are being drawn toward conclusions about the city or the country as a whole. Following crime news means following a moving object. The conditions of its circulation are tied to its ability to imagine crime at multiple scales.[1]

Coverage of crime in Caracas was a case in point. The image of the city as crime-ridden dystopia was tied to a series of synecdochic substitutions: certain areas were made to stand for Caracas's crime problem, which came to stand for Venezuela's crime problem. These substitutions were not mere abstractions. They grew out of the lived experience of violent crime and its aftermath, but they were mediated by the social geography of those who reported it. Consequently, how crime scaled up was tied to the ways in which journalists imagined Caracas.

The crime city image of Caracas reflected two complementary sociospatial patterns. The first was the partitioning of urban space, which was pronounced in journalistic depictions of the barrios. Reporters' outsider status vis-à-vis the barrios coupled with their limited resources for investigation ended up reproducing conventional maps of security in which crime became synonymous with social marginalization. The second sociospatial pattern was the articulation of grief and grievance, which was epitomized in spaces of mourning, protest, and contention. Journalists' estrangement from the police and dependence on victims had the effect of orienting crime news toward expressions of victimhood that were concentrated in places like the morgue in Bello Monte. Together, the barrios and the city morgue acted as key coordinates for the mental maps that guided the routines of crime journalists. More broadly, they provide an understanding of a dialectical relationship that drives both the politics of security and the production of urban space.

A brief analysis of news coverage from February 25, 2008 (published on February 26) demonstrates how these complementary understandings of urban space were written into crime news. This reading is based on the three major Caracas newspapers: *Últimas Noticias,* a popular tabloid with a reputation for balanced news coverage as well as the highest circulation numbers in Venezuela; *El Nacional,* a liberal broadsheet with a long history of investigative journalism and oppositional politics; and *El Universal,* a conservative broadsheet and the longest-running newspaper in Caracas. What follows is not a content analysis per se but rather a broad textual reading informed by an insider's perspective on how these texts were produced in the first place.

The Barrios

A pair of stories dominated the crime pages on February 26, 2008: an airplane crash in the Venezuelan Andes that killed forty-six people and the death of the bomber from Frente Venceremos. Both of these stories were deemed extraordinary by the private press. The airplane crash was first reported on February 21, and five days later the causes were still unclear. The string of bombings by Frente Venceremos dated back to December and represented an even greater mystery. Both stories received extended coverage from all of Caracas's major news outlets—not just periodicals but also the broadcast and digital news outlets. The press dissected the possible causes of the airplane crash and speculated about the motives behind the mysterious bombings. These lead stories contrasted markedly with those that were deemed more everyday occurrences. Such stories were usually treated as one-offs. They contained perfunctory details about the time and place of a crime, its modus operandi, its victims, and the reactions of those it affected. Sometimes they even supplied information about potential suspects. However, the motives behind any specific incident of urban violence were either opaque or thinly explained. In most cases, journalists had neither the time nor the resources to investigate individual crimes. Instead of definitively spelling out the reasons that led to a violent act, they used other means to hint at its probable causes.

Location was key. Where a crime took place mattered because it indexed an entire set of social, political, and material relationships. As Charles Briggs has demonstrated, the temporal aspects of crime news lend it a sense of immediacy, an on-the-scene quality, which makes crime news the ultimate reality genre.[2] In order to interpret this reality, audiences depended on shared understandings of place. The location of a crime spoke volumes about the position of the people involved and possible explanations about why it happened. Moreover, the location of a crime allowed readers to gauge its proximity to their own lives. Was this a near and present danger or was it someone else's problem?

No location figured more prominently in the cognitive maps of crime journalists and their audiences than the barrios. Barrios were synonymous with crime, as well as with poverty, the popular classes, and a lack of state services (e.g., policing, electricity, running water, and trash removal). When explaining the motives behind crimes that took place in the barrios, reporters often resorted to shorthand. The most commonly reported reasons for violent death were "a settling of scores," "a shoot-out between gangs," or "resisting arrest." Rarely did the explanations go beyond terse one-liners. Rarer still were those stories deemed worthy of investigation. Since crime in the barrios was considered ordinary, only the most shocking incidents had news value. Take, for example, the tragic double homicide described in the previous chapter. All of the major print and broadcast news outlets in Caracas carried stories about the incident. *Últimas Noticias* published a short, two hundred-word article.

Two dead in shoot-out at a party in Mariches

Caracas. A party culminated in shots in the predawn Sunday morning in the sector Caballo Mocho, Vuelta del Mango at kilometer 14 of Filas de Mariches. In total there were two dead, seven wounded.

The victims were identified as Luis Miguel Vels Acosta (21), a construction worker, and Yorgenis Astudillo Flores.

Vels Acosta lived close to Terminal de Oriente [bus station]. His relatives explained that shortly before 1:00 a.m. on Sunday the lights were turned out in the house and shots were exchanged by rival gangs. The youth, who was near the [ground floor] talking with other boys, took two bullets and was stripped of his Puma shoes and belongings.

His sister, Carolina Vels, explained that upon learning what occurred, they went to help him in a taxi. In light of the fact that there was still confusion in the zone, they solicited help at the PM [police] module in Valle Fresco, "but they told us that they could not do anything because only two police officers were present."[3]

If this was gang violence, then what provoked it? Was the young man in one of the rival gangs? Was he an intended target of the shooting or an innocent bystander? None of these questions were answered in the article. In place of motives, we have social geography. The shootings happened in Filas de Mariche (Mariches for short), a district located on the eastern periphery of Caracas, past the sprawling megabarrio of Petare at the far edge of the Sucre municipality. Most audiences familiar with Caracas would recognize it as a district populated by poor and working-class residents. More discerning readers might also draw a connection to the ongoing influx of rural populations from the Colombian countryside. These associations were spelled out explicitly in the version of the double homicide story that was published by *El Universal*. The sensational headline—"they turned off the lights at a party and murdered two youths"—was immediately followed by a description of the crime scene. According to *El Universal*, the killings took place in "a shack [*rancho*] in barrio Caballo Mocho off the Petare-Mariches highway."[4] *El Nacional* also opened by emphasizing the horrific circumstances of the shooting. "Two peopled killed at a party. The murderers arrive at the celebration, turned off the house lights, and opened fired against everyone present." According to one of the victim's relatives, the area was so dangerous that even the police avoided it: "The police are afraid of the malandros, it seems, because they never come where they're really needed. They refuse to go any further than the lower part of the barrio where people think it is safe."[5]

Geographically, the barrios were associated with the hills surrounding and interspersed throughout Caracas. Greater altitude connoted greater distance from the city proper. This contrast between the informal hillsides and the formal city, in turn, structured the imagination of crime and insecurity (see fig. 3.1). It was epitomized by talk of a not-too-distant future in which the hills would come down and swallow the city. Part barbarian invasion, part natural catastrophe, this apocalyptic vision was in tension with ideals espoused by President Hugo Chávez. For Chávez and his supporters, the barrios represented the vanguard of a new, revolutionary struggle. At its most utopian, chavismo proposed to solve urban violence by incorporating the barrios into the city. However, the government had to contend with widespread perceptions of the barrios as the epicenter of the crime problem, perceptions held by both its supporters and opponents.

The preponderance of crime news reproduced this image of the barrios as a looming threat. It reproduced what Janice Perlman has called the "myth of marginality"—the persistent belief that the barrios represent the margins of Latin American cities when in fact they are socially, economically,

3.1. The formal/informal divide. (Photograph by Lurdes R. Basolí.)

and often geographically central to the functioning of these cities.[6] In most crime reporting, the barrios of Caracas were shunted from the city proper and exiled to a discursive periphery. Such depictions of marginal barrio dwellers clashed with reality. More than 40 percent of Caracas's population lived in areas described as barrios.[7] Even the most affluent neighborhoods, places such as Altamira and Las Mercedes, contained pockets of informal settlement, so that it was difficult to say with any precision where the barrios began or where they ended. If barrios were marginal, then the margins shot through the entire city, and danger was potentially everywhere.

Since the threat of the barrios was ubiquitous, crime news reasserted the appearance of order by reinscribing the imagined frontier between the formal and the informal city. Nowhere was this split more apparent than in articles that analyzed larger patterns of urban violence. Take the following piece, which appeared in *El Universal* just above the story of the double homicide. The subject was crime in El Valle, a district in south-central Caracas with a social geography that straddled the formal and informal city. *El Universal* dedicated a half page of newsprint to making legible the dangerous barrios and their effects on the rest of the district. The article begins with a murder that transpired during a gang-imposed curfew.

In El Valle the underworld ravages neighbors
and police alike

When the "azotes" [scourges or delinquents] of barrios Bruzual and La
Ceiba came across their neighbors from El Valle parish on Friday the
15th of February, they knew that curfew had started because the police
were fleeing their post at the foot of the hill.

At the doors of the morgue in Bello Monte, Juan González explained, "'Lights out' started at nine in the evening, and as always,
none of the gang members were killed. This time it was my nephew,
Jhonathan González's turn [to die]. He was a young man working as
a motorcycle-taxi driver so that he could raise his one-year-old son."

González said that on Saturday morning, neighbors knocked on his
door to let him know. "We don't know when it happened. In La Ceiba
we hide ourselves when the delinquents confront each other."

The night of the shoot-out, the neighbors sent an emissary to plaza
El Valle to ask for help from the officers who spend the night there in a
campaign tent. They never obtained a response.

"You sometimes realize that these guys, the police, have to sleep on
the floor. The delinquents are better armed, and when they rev their
motorcycles, they [the police] go running. It is a shame that this is happening in the country. The [government's] operation Secure Caracas is
pure propaganda. The underworld keeps killing," said González.[8]

The article goes on to suggest that insecurity was spreading outward from the
barrios to encompass the entire parish. Although it is ornately written, the
story provides no explanation about what was going on in these barrios, why
González was killed, how the curfew operated, or who was doing the shooting. What it does provide is a very detailed series of spatial references, including the following call-out box placed at the center of the page:

ATTENTION

Dangerous Gangs: According to neighbors they are from the sectors
Veulta el Beso, Nueva Tacagua, Cajigal, Los 70, San Antonio, El Loro,
Bruzual y La Invasion, and La Ceibita.

The Aggrieved: [Bus and taxi] drivers who cover the route El Valle-
Bruzual-San Andrés ascertain that an average of five robberies are committed every day; what's more, [the drivers] are often attacked.

Instead of investigative reporting, crime journalists relied on folk geography. They equated insecurity with informality and mapped crime onto the barrios. Dominant assumptions about social space replaced a more nuanced analysis of crime in Caracas for a variety of reasons. There was the issue of time and resources. Reporters were under enormous pressure to produce large quantities of news content every day. What is more, the sheer number of cases that reporters encountered on a daily basis overwhelmed them. Following even a fraction would have been impossible for reasons of time alone. There were also issues of personal safety. Most journalists only ventured into the barrios on the rare occasions that the police were there. Finally, there was the socioeconomic position of reporters themselves. They were professionals with college degrees and a substantial amount of cultural capital. Although many of them empathized deeply with crime victims, there was a good deal of social distance between the reporters and the people that they encountered on a daily basis. For all of these reasons, reporters relied on dominant understandings of danger and marginality to explain the circumstances of a violent crime, discourses that tied urban violence to conventional understanding of urban space.

This link between the barrios and criminality is unsurprising, but in Venezuela's charged political atmosphere it assumed an additional layer of meaning. To understand its significance, let me refer back to the previous chapter and those superblock towers that marked the neighborhood known as El 23 de Enero. Cesar said that El 23 was "hot" or dangerous. Jenny remonstrated him for talking nonsense. Much was at stake in claims about the relative danger or safety of any given place, especially this one.

El 23 de Enero was Venezuela's most iconic barrio. Its fame as a hotbed of radicalism and popular urban struggles was established long before Hugo Chávez arrived on the scene. During the Chávez era, however, its importance was magnified. El 23 came to symbolize the popular movements behind the Bolivarian Revolution. It was their mythic point of inception, their spiritual home, and their guardian presence. When Chávez was momentarily deposed in April 2002, residents from this neighborhood mobilized and marched on the presidential palace demanding his return. At the time of his death in March 2013, Chávez's legacy was so closely tied to El 23 de Enero that it became his final resting place.[9]

To associate El 23 with danger and criminality was to associate chavismo with danger and criminality. In Caracas the standard discourse that demonized the poor, the deviant, and the racially marked—in short, the barrio dweller—was complicated by the fact that the so-called dangerous classes were also the standard-bearers of the revolution. The barrios were *el pueblo* (the people). They were both the heroic force of a new political project and looming presences that threated to upend the selfsame project.[10] As a result, the Chávez government faced a conundrum: criminalizing the barrios eroded its own legitimacy, but so did failing to control them.

Crime journalists paid close attention to El 23 de Enero because it revealed constituent tensions within the Bolivarian Revolution. Of particular interest was the relationship between the police and the "collectives," or civil defense groups. For much of my tenure on the crime beat, El 23 was considered a no-go zone for police agencies. Several high-profile shoot-outs between the police and the civil defense groups made it clear that police presence was unwelcome, so that the Chávez government was compelled to grant the neighborhood a kind of provisional autonomy. For the reporters and their audiences, this standoff was a source of constant speculation. Were the collectives revolutionaries or were they common criminals? Did they represent the interests of El 23 de Enero and its inhabitants? If so, did their resistance to the police signal a weakening of the bond between chavismo and the popular sectors? Was this a revolution within the revolution? Or was it merely a turf war?

If crime news often linked barrios such as El 23 to criminality, then the politics of the Chávez era opened up a universe of alternative readings. Instead of lawless zones, the barrios became workshops of the revolution; instead of crime dens, they were sites of popular struggle. Given this state of affairs, easy assumptions about crime and social geography came unmoored. Questions multiplied. Doubts proliferated. One thing was certain. The barrios were dangerous: but was this danger criminal, political, or something else altogether?

The Morgue

The second distinctive feature of the news stories published on February 26 was their basis in what we could provisionally call the space of victimhood. Along with the imagined threat of the barrios, these articles highlighted the presence of victims and the absence of police. Stories about the double homicide and the feature on crime in El Valle were based entirely on interviews with crime victims and their relatives. Journalists paid close attention to what these victims had to say about the lack of police response. Indeed, every article that appeared on this particular date was framed around the narrative of police neglect, which was not a coincidence.[11]

Among reporters, the failings of the police were viewed as one of the principal reasons for high crime rates in Caracas. This theme was central to the Frente Venceremos story, in which the dead bomber was carrying police credentials. All the newspapers converged on the narrative thread of police misconduct. *Últimas Noticias* reported, "Government has nabbed all of the bombers. Subject who died was an officer of the DISIP [secret police] and they are searching for two PM [Metropolitan Police]."[12] *El Universal* led with a full-page story on the front page of the city section, stating, "Ex-DISIP died in explosion. [. . .] Ex-officer was carrying a Glock pistol, radio, and motorcycle of the PM."[13] The headline in *El Nacional* read, "Authors of explosives placed in Caracas identified. The subject who died carried credentials from the intelligence network of the PM."[14] Police officials were fully aware of the bad press. Indeed, this was the likely motivation for inviting reporters to the scene of a police shoot-out in Pinto Salinas and for the press conference with the minister of justice.[15]

This thematic focus on failed police was enabled in part by the growing importance of victims' testimonies. Crime journalists were increasingly less beholden to police sources, which made the Caracas crime beat exceptional. Modern policing focuses explicitly on controlling perceptions of crime and law enforcement. Police press offices are the key sites where informal control is exercised. This is true in cities across North America and Europe. It was also true in Caracas before 2003. The absence of these offices meant that the police had considerably less influence over crime reporters than is normally the case. Little wonder journalists were relatively uninhibited in their critiques of the police. What they lost in terms of insider information was compensated by a greater degree of journalistic license.

The morgue in Bello Monte symbolized the shift toward crime victims as news sources. For journalists and their audiences, the morgue was a metonym for crime city. It epitomized everything gone wrong with Caracas. Its infrastructure was crumbling and antiquated. The facilities were overcrowded. There were far too few forensic pathologists for the scores of cases that it handled every week. It was difficult to access. Information was highly restricted. Bodies arrived late. There were rumors of low-level corruption. The place was unsanitary and it smelled of putrefaction. Despite all of these problems, no one was accountable, and nothing ever seemed to get better, least of all the violence. In an essay titled "The City of Crimes," David González, a former crime reporter for the newspaper *El Nacional*, used the morgue to sum up his experience on the crime beat.

If I were to choose one site in the city where the marks of violence are most concentrated, I would choose the morgue in Bello Monte. It is an old building. The pipes and wires show signs of failure. It is on a quiet street that straddles the municipalities of Libertador and Baurta, and there are days when the smell of death lingers outside. Lined up outside are the relatives of victims. I have spoken with hundreds of them about their family members and the circumstances in which they died. Students. Workers. Fathers. Athletes. Artists. From the most distant corners of the city, they all ended up there.[16]

González's description reveals the sociospatial contours of victimhood. The morgue was the symbolic heart of crime city where victims from all parts of Caracas converged. In contrast to journalistic treatment of the barrios— which were predicated on their differentiation from the city proper—the morgue was a space of concentration and articulation where socioeconomic distinctions came together in an imagined unity. In this way it resembled what social movement scholars call a "space of contention."[17]

Historically, there is a close correlation between mass movements and the ordering of urban space.[18] Key to this history is the contentious relationship between crowds and the police. Policing is predicated on separation, distance, and boundary maintenance. It orders urban space by keeping people and things in their place. The crowd is the great force of urban disorder; it is a concentrated mass of humanity that is not easily predicted or contained. Studies of policing show that the problem of unruly crowds helped precipitate the formation of modern police forces beginning in the late eighteenth century.[19] Under normal circumstances, police are charged with breaking up crowds and neutralizing popular uprisings. What stands out about the work of crime reporters in Caracas is how their use of space partially inverted this paradigm.

Rather than running from the police, crime journalists sought them out. In this way they shared a close affinity with activists who organized protests, marches, demonstrations, and vigils in the name of security. These crowds used crime victimhood to call for more and better police even as they clashed with them. No place symbolized this strategy better than the morgue in Bello Monte. It was the perfect location to stage prosecurity, anticrime demonstrations because it allowed people to congregate at a police facility under the protective aegis of crime victimhood.

As a space of contention, the morgue challenges conventional wisdom about crime and urban space, a relationship that is almost exclusively conceptualized through the distancing prism of fear. Scholars have been conducting research on fear of crime for more than half a century now. This research is guided by three assumptions: (1) people are afraid of crime; (2) fear is something negative that can be dispelled by expert knowledge; and (3) fear of crime can be separated from the objective reality of urban violence.[20] It is not my intention to dismiss any of these claims. People are afraid of crime, and that fear often has negative consequences. Yet the scholarly fascination with fear may conceal as much as it reveals about how the politics of crime shapes urban space.[21]

Fear of crime is usually associated with a retreat from public space and a distrust of strangers. At its most extreme, fear creates a world in which decent people hide behind locked doors, too timid to venture out after dark. A visitor to Caracas would, no doubt, observe these behaviors. I certainly did. However, foregrounding the distancing dynamic of fear means downplaying the link between crime victimhood and geographies of political insurgency. Violence brings people into proximity with one another, and that proximity creates the conditions of possibility for political mobilization. Crime journalists relied on this proximity in their coverage of denuncias, protests, demonstrations, and political rallies. No place was more important for bringing crime victims together than the morgue in Bello Monte, and everyone in Caracas knew it. Rather than a paranoid, paralyzed city, the morgue revealed a side of Caracas in which crime was linked to a dynamic of social concentration and mobilization.

Dialectic of Dystopia

If urban space is written into crime news, then the cartographers of crime city relied on two essential reference points. The first reference point, the barrios, marked places that reporters avoided. Danger was represented as a kind of blank space on a map that was riddled with blank spaces. For crime journalists and their audiences, these cognitive maps of Caracas outlined no-go zones and secure sites in a way that mirrored the separation between the formal and the informal city. In contrast, the second reference point, the morgue, stood as a testament to what happened when these boundaries were crossed. More than any other site in Caracas, the morgue blurred the lines between safety and danger, innocence and guilt, sacred and profane. Unlike the barrios, the morgue was where journalists spent long stretches of time, and they made it the center of their symbolic universe.

These reference points, the barrios and the morgue, reflected two complementary logics of security. The former, the barrios, represented the work of sociospatial segregation by which vulnerable populations were marginalized; this was the same logic that created privileged enclosures that were walled off from the rest of the city. The latter, the morgue, represented the work of spatial concentration through which victimhood became a shared grievance with explosive potential; this was the same logic that fed a series of anticrime, prosecurity mobilizations in Caracas.

Critical studies of crime and security usually emphasize the logic of spatial segregation. Practices of gating in and walling out reproduce a dynamic in which the partitioning of space is tied to accumulation by dispossession. One can read violent dispossession on either side of the wall as the crime that takes away property or the crime that creates it in the first place. And yet common space does not disappear entirely. It remains a promise, often a deeply held conviction. Even as caraqueños retreated from common space, they reimagined and reinvented it. Here we might be reminded, albeit somewhat obliquely, of E. P. Thompson's writings on bread riots and the moral economy of the English crowd.[22] A people who has the commons violently dispossessed, nonetheless resists. Whereas the moral economy of bread riots in eighteenth-century England revolved around the demand for fair prices, the moral economy of anticrime mobilizations in Caracas was qualitatively different. It revolved around demands for justice, punishment, revenge, and protection that were made in the name of crime victims.

This dialectic of distancing and concentration is evident in one of the most influential works on crime and urban space in Latin America, Teresa Caldeira's *City of Walls*. In it, Caldeira describes how "talk of crime" affected the built environment of the Brazilian megacity, São Paulo, resulting in a retreat from public space, the creation of private enclaves, and the further segregation of the city along socioeconomic lines. She shows this dynamic at work in an extended interview with an upper-middle-class woman who blames the rise of violent crime on the growth of favelas and an influx of poor rural migrants. Caldeira's analysis of this interview focuses on the racism that criminalizes an entire class of people and leads to the decimation of public space. Where her analysis stops short is the way in which victimhood becomes the grounds of a collective identity that pretends to bridge racial and class divisions.[23] We observe this process at work in the interview itself. Throughout their conversation, the interviewee is trying to recruit her listener. She does this by universalizing her own experience of crime: "Here in Moóca [a district of São Paulo] there isn't a person who hasn't been robbed." Crime affects everyone, she argues—rich and poor, light-skinned and dark-skinned, longtime residents and recent arrivals: "Nobody goes out anymore, nobody wears a necklace, anything." To make matters worse, filing a police report is useless. This perceived absence of the state leads the woman to advocate a kind violent solidarity: "I'm going to tell you right away: I'm in favor of the death penalty for people who deserve it. Here in Moóca we're in favor of the death penalty." Shortly after making this pronouncement, she enlists the maid to help argue her case.[24]

Caldeira's interview illustrates how narratives of crime configure urban space dialectically. In addition to segregation and retreat, crime news is linked to processes of spatial concentration, which in turn create the conditions of possibility for popular mobilization. This dynamic can be observed in the way that testimonies of crime victims jump scale. They articulate the particular and the universal in such a way as to create an imagined community of sufferers. That was certainly true in Caracas. The testimonies favored by crime journalists were those that encompassed the largest possible audience by making totalizing distinctions between a victimized "Us" and a predatory "Them." These twinned identities of victim and perpetrator structured the mental maps written into crime news, and they begin to explain how spaces of victimhood became the nexus of an oppressive solidarity.

FOUR

Malandro/Sano

The converted station wagon hearse limped through late afternoon traffic. A light drizzle accompanied our funeral caravan on its way toward Cementerio del Este, a massive necropolis on the southeastern edge of Caracas. Margarita was in the front seat, squeezed between her husband and the funeral driver. We rode in the back, hunched uncomfortably beside the coffined remains of her eldest son, José Luis. As the rain subsided, a thunder of motorcycle engines roared up along either side of the hearse, stereos blasting. Two loud thumps reverberated against the roof, followed by a piercing scream. Visibly agitated by the commotion, Margarita flung herself out of the car, yelling, "I told you to behave!" Seconds later she returned with her damp, slightly inebriated son Ricardo in tow. The front seat was now impossibly full. Margarita looked sternly ahead. Ricardo fidgeted in awkward silence.

My most intimate experience of crime victimhood was a one-hour odyssey trapped beside a coffin. On that particular day a friend invited me to tag along while she photographed a *homenaje*, or homage ceremony, in one of the barrios (fig. 4.1). Homenajes of this sort were public spectacles that paid tribute to people who died violent deaths. In the popular imagination they were associated with gangs, guns, and vendettas. My friend, a Catalan photojournalist, had already been to half a dozen of these, and she assured me this would not be that kind of homenaje. The man was from a good family. There would be no gunplay. We would be safe.

We met Margarita and Ricardo earlier that day at the funeral home where the wake was being held. I paid my respects to a closed casket. It was closed because José Luis was shot thirteen times in El Carpintero, one of Caracas's poorest barrios. The motives behind his murder were unclear. When we asked Margarita about what happened, she told us that there was no reason for the shooting and that it must have been a case of mistaken identity, but

4.1. The *homenaje* (homage ceremony) for José Luis winds
through the barrio. (Photograph by Lurdes R. Basolí.)

even she seemed unconvinced. When we asked Ricardo, he talked at length,
not about his brother's death but about his own feeling of impotence in
the face of injustice. "It's hard to walk a straight line in a place where the
delinquents and the police are likely to take whatever you earn or leave you
lying face down on the street. Why buy a motorcycle? Why buy a car?" As he
talked, someone passed him a bottle of Santa Teresa rum. He splashed some
on the pavement before taking the first of many drinks.

Few beat reporters would follow a story like this one in which the details
surrounding the death were so opaque, but follow it we did, all the way to
the dead man's home in Petare and then to his final resting place in Cementerio del Este. On the first leg of the journey, we rode with Ricardo and his
siblings on a bus that the family had rented. They watched over us as the
coffin was paraded through the old neighborhood, people pouring out of
their houses to stream alongside it. In the midst of the homenaje, as José
Luis was making one last tour of the basketball courts, the sky opened up
and rain came down in torrents. The streets became creeks. When we looked
up, the bus was gone (perhaps it floated off, I thought) and all that was left
was the back of the hearse.

Riding with the coffin, we were at the epicenter of the funeral procession,
tucked in beside its object of mourning and celebration. Even after Margarita

corralled her youngest son, the thumps continued. They reverberated through the hearse, hailing the dead man and mingling with the beat of Reggaeton. As we neared the cemetery, the motorcycle brigade pulled up alongside us again, blasting the popular Wisin and Yandel song "Ya me voy" ("I'm Leaving").

Ya me voy	*I'm leaving now*
Si me pasa algo	*If something happens to me*
Cuida a mis hijos	*Take care of my kids*
Hubo un mal entendido	*There was a misunderstanding*
Reventaron a mi amigo	*They took out my friend*
Ahora tengo enemigos	*Now I've got enemies*
De frente y solo	*Straight up and solo*
Exploto la guerra	*Blow up the war*
Si me pasa algo	*If something happens to me*
Cuida mis hijos	*Take care of my kids*
Exploto la guerra	*Blow up the war*
Cuida mis hijos	*Take care of my kids*

Upon registering the song, Ricardo became agitated. Lurching toward the driver's-side window, he yelled hoarsely, "Turn it off! Turn it off! My brother was not a malandro! He was not a malandro! He was not a malandro!" over and over until his mother took him by the elbow and shook him forcefully (fig. 4.2).[1]

Ricardo's words still ring out all these years later. I recall them here because they speak directly to one of the two binaries that structured depictions of crime and victimhood in Caracas—the distinction between the sano and the malandro. *Sano* means "healthy," "wholesome," or "clean." It is a word with sanitizing overtones. Applied to a person, it indicates that he or she is pure, innocent, within the moral order. *Malandro* is somewhat more complex. The root is *mal*—evil or bad—and, as one commentator points out, the second part resembles *ladron*, the Spanish word for "thief."[2] However, a malandro is not exactly a criminal or even a delinquent. Instead, he (or, infrequently, she) is a shady character who inhabits the fringes of the moral order.[3] Malandros are assumed to be the physical and metaphysical opposite of the sano. Whereas the sano is pure, the malandro is dangerous, deviant; in a word, *dirty.*

The binary sano/malandro was part of a symbolic universe that was so akin to the one described by Mary Douglas in *Purity and Danger* that it is

4.2. Ricardo's grief over his brother's death is visible. (Photograph by Lurdes R. Basolí.)

worth recalling her argument at length. "Dirt," Douglas tells us, "offends against order. Eliminating it is not a negative movement, but a positive effort to organize the environment." She explains:

> If we can abstract pathogenicity and hygiene from our notion of dirt, we are left with the old definition of dirt as matter out of place. This is a very suggestive approach. It implies two conditions: a set of ordered relations and a contravention of that order. Dirt, then, is never a unique, isolated event. Where there is dirt there is system. Dirt is the by-product of a systematic ordering and classification of matter, in so far as ordering involves rejecting inappropriate elements. This idea of dirt takes us straight into the field of symbolism and promises a link-up with more obviously symbolic systems of purity.[4]

These are tidy observations when they are limited to such phenomena as religious rituals, public health practices, or the organization of one's domicile. The implications are more ominous when applied to categories of people. Those deemed impure are usually the most vulnerable members of society. Study after study has shown that the kind of purifying efforts described by Douglas criminalize the poor, the foreign, the queer, the black, the brown, and so many others. Their vulnerability is transformed into dangerousness and used to justify their violent oppression. Crime journalism reproduces this pattern.

It would be convenient to leave it at that, to argue that in Caracas crime news reinforced social stigmas, which in turn oppressed an entire class of persons. More often than not, such was indeed the case. Reducing the politics of security to symbols, structure, and the mechanical reproduction of oppression, however, is to trivialize it. The sano was a political category, and claiming victimhood reflected, in Douglas's words, a "positive effort to organize the environment." Which is not to say that claims of victimhood were good (or bad, for that matter) but that they were incredibly productive. In later chapters I describe how the category of the crime victim was mobilized at the national scale. This chapter is concerned with a more intimate level of activism: the work of classifying people like Margarita, Ricardo, and José Luis. I begin with a description of how journalists judged crime victims and their families before presenting two examples that allow us to see these categories at work.

Judging the Dead

As I have explained, crime reporters in Caracas were increasingly reliant on the testimonies of crime victims and those of their family and friends. Despite this reliance, the relationship between crime journalists and the victims of violence was tenuous at best. Reporters and photographers showed up at times of intense personal grief, a group of strangers with cameras who asked people to perform their pain. Some found the experience of being photographed and interviewed cathartic. Some found it intensely alienating, demeaning, or disrespectful. For crime journalists, managing these various responses was part of the job. To lessen the shock of the encounter, they developed an informal interviewing etiquette—approach people delicately and not en masse, respect the wishes of those who do not want to speak or be photographed, keep the tone of the questioning gentle and sympathetic, and avoid interviewing the same person repeatedly. Yet even the most seasoned approach could not mitigate the discomfort of these encounters, the sense that the journalists were intruding into the sacred space of mourning and death. Nor could it overcome the deep distrust of journalists that many relatives of homicide victims harbored.

There were good reasons for the relatives of victims not to trust crime journalists. The way that the reporters told it, partisan politics were to blame. It was true that political differences often exacerbated tensions, particularly

among staunch government supporters who perceived journalists as opera-
tives of the opposition, a point that I will return to shortly. However, such
an explanation also had the effect of downplaying the inequalities between
crime journalists and the victims of violence. These interactions often (although not always) involved people from different class backgrounds with
vastly disparate access to the means of representation. An identifying quote,
a revealing photograph, or an erroneous detail hardly affected the journalists. For the victims and their relatives, however, it could have serious consequences, including violent reprisal. Standing before a crowd of reporters
and photographers, they were vulnerable and they knew it. Take the following example from my field notes:

> *April 20, 2009*: It is a busy Monday at the morgue. While a group of us are
> standing just outside the front door, one of the reporters strikes up a quiet
> conversation with a round woman in a sweat suit who looks to be in her early
> thirties. She [the reporter] is taking notes and asking a few gentle questions.
> The answers are short, but forthcoming. I overhear snippets of a conversation
> about a husband killed by a stray bullet while playing a game of dominos in
> barrio Julian Blanco (Petare). The two are speaking for scarcely two minutes
> when an older woman, probably the victim's mother, loudly interrupts, end-
> ing the conversation midsentence:
>
> "What are you doing talking to the press? You know what they're going
> to say. They're going to say that he was a delinquent. It's obligatory for them.
> Everyone who dies in the barrios is a malandro."
>
> The chastened wife falls silent and the (presumed) mother walks off leav-
> ing the rest of us to sit in awkward silence. A little bit later another veteran
> reporter tells me that the woman's outburst against journalists was politically
> motivated. "Chavista," he shrugs.[5]

Perhaps the woman was a Chávez supporter. I never found out. Regardless of her political allegiances, what stood out to me was the misrecogni-
tion on the part of the journalist. Rather than acknowledging the power
imbalance between journalists and the victims of violence, he attributed the
woman's outburst to partisanship on the part of a chavista. This misrecog-
nition was all the more telling because it elided the central question that
drove every interview with the relatives of victims—the question of guilt or
innocence.

One of the key tensions in encounters between crime journalists and
the relatives of victims concerned the categorization of the dead. Reporters
were constantly looking for clues that would help them ascertain the dead

person's moral status and where he or she fit within the binary sano/malandro. Although it was never explicitly stated, one question always hung in the air: Was the victim a sano or a malandro, a good kid or a good-for-nothing? For the relatives, this tacit inquiry represented an interrogation of their own moral status and the status of their loved ones. For the journalists, it was an equally complex process of trying to detect and judge the circumstances surrounding a violent act.

Detecting the moral status of a victim required journalists to search for any number of clues, starting with the comportment of the victim's family and friends. How were they dressed? How were they holding themselves? Did they seem upset or indifferent? This issue of moral status was not simply a question of rich or poor but of aspiration. Initial impressions were refined or reworked during the interview with the relatives. Was this a good family? Was the victim a child, a student, or a worker? Did the victim have children or a heterosexual spouse? Was the victim involved in the community? Reporters also search for clues in the details of the autopsy. When, where, and how was the person killed? Did the evidence point to an accidental death, a random act of violence, a crime of passion, or a targeted killing? The impressions that reporters gathered from these interviews were, in turn, weighed against conversations with informal police sources as well as conversations among reporters. Journalists spent a great deal of their time trying to determine the relative guilt or innocence of homicide victims. Whereas the murder of an "innocent" victim was a tragedy that often warranted an extended retelling, the death of a malandro was just a fact of life and, perhaps, a justified fate.

Depictions of victims were laden with assumptions about masculinity, youth, and violence as well as racial and economic stereotypes. Unless otherwise stated, it was assumed that the perpetrators of violent crime were men—poor, ethnically marked men. If the victim was also a young man in his teens or twenties, as was usually the case, audiences suspected that the attack was an *ajuste de cuentas* (settling of scores) between malandros.[6] Women, children, and the elderly were generally assumed to be innocent victims,[7] although from time to time a feminized malandro, *la malandra*, made her appearance.[8] Similarly, young men from middle-class or well-to-do backgrounds were partially shielded by their social status. All of this disparity in treatment was closely related to the way in which Venezuela's explicit racial and economic hierarchies, which imagined affluent persons of European descent to be more civilized than those of African American or indigenous descent, intersected with questions of gender, sexuality, and kinship under late capitalism.[9] Which is not to say that every poor, dark-skinned young man was assumed guilty, but the closer a victim was to the stereotypical figure of the malandro, the heavier the burden of proof. Crime journalists were aware of this fact. Some were critical of it. As one of the younger crime reporters confessed:

> We have this faulty vision, Robert. When we go to the morgue and they tell us that a seventeen-year-old boy was shot fifteen times, we all go "Ahhhh." To us it appears like a death that is not newsworthy because we assume that the kid was involved in some kind of trouble. We assume that he killed someone or that he was trafficking drugs or something. This is the shortsighted vision of the police. These are police guidelines, but we are not the police. Sometimes a kid who was shot fifteen times, the only thing that he did wrong was to refuse to loan his motorcycle to a malandro, and that was enough for them to kill him.[10]

Proof of innocence, at least in homicide cases, often depended upon the willingness of family and friends to testify on behalf of the victim. Crime journalists favored stories told by relatives who openly shared their grief and outrage, who showed up at the morgue with photos of their loved ones, who divulged details about their life and the circumstance of their death, who gave reporters their phone numbers and agreed to do follow-up interviews (sometimes in their own homes). Such testimonies were usually interpreted as a sign of innocence and victimhood. In contrast, journalists often assumed that those who were not willing to testify had something to hide. Even though they were acutely aware of the manifold reasons for victims and their relatives to avoid the press—including the fear that their own testimonies could make them the next victim—silence was incriminating. On several occasions I was told that persons who flatly refused interviews were "probably the relatives of malandros."

This dynamic goes a long way toward explaining journalistic representations of urban violence. While film, fiction, and the true crime dramas that circulated in Venezuela often provided rich visual and linguistic depictions of the malandro, in the news the perpetrators of violent crime were shadowy presences that rarely had faces (they are always covered), names (they often go by aliases), or anyone to speak on their behalf. From time to time journalists would do a piece about a notorious gang or an infamous criminal. More often than not, though, dangerousness was territorialized. Crime news represented the malandro not so much through depictions of these "shady" characters but through sociospatial references to particular neighborhoods and through the forensic details of death.[11]

In contrast to these spatial and corporeal depictions of danger, crime journalism portrayed innocence in biographical terms.[12] The more the victims and their relatives fit the profile of a sano, the more likely they were to feature in the news. Images of innocent victims regularly appeared in the press, often from an old photo or a copy of an identification card. Along with these visual descriptions, the papers regularly published their full name, the names of their family members, descriptions of their accomplishments, stories about their life, and poignant reflections on their dreams.

Stereotypical markers of race, class, nationality, gender, sexuality, age, and aspiration were mobilized in depictions of malandros and sanos. It would not be difficult to demonstrate that, in Caracas, the poster child of innocence was a fair-skinned young girl from a "good home" or that malandros were assumed to be poor young men from the barrios. It would be a mistake, however, to assume that the portraits of victims circulating on television and in the newspapers were homogeneous. Quite the opposite. Persons from all social strata appeared in crime stories—rich and poor, young and old, women and men, dark and light complexioned. Judgments of innocence and guilt were situated within a constantly evolving chain of signification. It mattered how victims represented themselves to crime journalists. Similarly, it mattered how journalists represented victims to their editors and producers, how editors and producers arranged the stories for consumption, and how particular audiences interpreted these stories. At every turn the question of innocence or guilt, sano or malandro, was posed anew.

Portraiture

The newspaper series "Portraits of Violence" was a good example of how media outlets depicted the figure of the sano. A weekly feature in *El Nacional*, the series profiled families struggling with the aftermath of violence.[13] These profiles were based on lengthy interviews that focused on the suffering of survivors and their memories of the dead. As the name suggested, photography occupied a place of prominence. "Portraits of Violence" regularly paired pictures of grieving relatives with old photos of their loved ones. Taken together, the photographs and interviews created a series that was part crime story, part obituary, and part denunciation.

In July 2009, I accompanied a reporter–photographer team on assignment for "Portraits of Violence." We traveled all the way to El Junquito to meet a woman whose nineteen-year-old son was murdered outside a dance club. En route we reviewed details of the case. Aarón Medina was shot late Sunday night defending his twin sister, Génesis. The murder took place in the affluent Las Mercedes neighborhood at a club the twins frequented. A few weeks earlier a group of young men had harassed Génesis while she was on the dance floor. Aarón interceded. There was a confrontation; however, Aarón retreated from the fight and the twins thought that the matter was resolved. It wasn't. The night of Aarón's death, the twins were at the same club and they had the misfortune of running into the same group of young men. Another confrontation ensued. This time it ended in gunplay. According to Génesis, the men attacked their group in the parking lot as they were leaving the dance club. Aarón and a friend were rushed to the hospital. The friend pulled through. Aarón did not.

When scrutinized, the circumstances of this particular homicide were ambiguous. A nineteen-year-old man involved in a late-night shooting at a dance club—even one located in an affluent section of town—raised questions. The genius of the "Portraits of Violence" series was that it directed attention away from the crime event to concentrate instead on the suffering of family members, especially mothers.

Mothers occupy a privileged place in the pantheon of victims, especially in Latin America. No one has greater moral authority in matters of life and death. From the late twentieth century forward, the symbolic power of grieving mothers was channeled by a series of social movements that reshaped the fabric of Latin American politics. Groups like Madres de Plaza de Mayo in Argentina and CoMadres in El Salvador were at the center of rights-based struggles that pitted victims of state violence against military dictatorships and the apparatuses of state terror.[14] These movements drew their symbolic force, in part, from Roman Catholic theology and the place of the Virgin Mary in the Spanish-American religious tradition. Equally important was the changing political economic place of women, especially among the urban popular sectors where mothers functioned simultaneously as the primary breadwinners and domestic heads of families.

"Portraits of Violence" drew heavily on the theological and political economic symbolism of maternal grief in its portraits of victims and their families. Tahís Mendoza—Aarón Medina's mother—embodied maternal suffering. As a stranger, I felt uncomfortable, even voyeuristic, in her presence. I tried to distract myself with note taking. My jottings from this encounter mostly concerned the outward signs of status, a string of judgments that began with a sketch of her brother-in-law, who met us at a nearby café: "He drives us to the house in Blue Chevy Aveo. In jeans and a yellow polo. Very respectable." I also noted my first impressions of the house: "Door opens into kitchen. What's on the television: RCTV. Pink and blue paint. Brownish orange tiles. Dark brown wood paneling. Marble dinner table." About the grieving mother, I wrote quite a bit, starting with her appearance: "She is in black and gold velvet tracksuit. Not wearing jewelry or make up. A solidly middle-class citizen." About her faith, I underlined a statement that she herself emphasized: "I am a Catholic, very Christian." When the reporter asked for a photo of the twins, I noted that there were stacks of albums hidden neatly inside a bench seat. About the photo itself, I wrote, "Lovely kids. She's in graduation regalia and made up like a Venezuelan beauty—bright eyes, glossy lips, freckles, straightened hair. He's respectable in a sweater over oxford in nice jeans. Hair short and slicked."

My field jottings go on, intermingling observations about the interview with learned hierarchies of race, class, gender, and sexuality. For the crime journalists, such signs were second nature. They formed part of a shared, nonverbal lexicon that operated at the level of the political unconscious.[15] I draw attention to them here because they were tied to questions that confounded me from the start. What made a person a sano? How did crime journalists recognize a "good family"? What were the outward signs of innocence that made a victim's story worth retelling? Abstractly one can surmise the answers. Learning to actually recognize and interpret the signs of innocent victimhood, however, takes practice. One must be fully immersed in a web of significations to be able to read taken-for-granted hierarchies and subtle gradations of social status. My hasty jottings from the interview give some sense as to what signs stood out in this particular case.

As I was busy noting the signs of bodily and spiritual comportment, the journalists were working to paint a sympathetic portrait of a family victimized by urban violence. To do so, they needed quotes, stories, images, and anything else that could convey the experience of maternal suffering. Much of the interview involved biographical questions about Tahís Mendoza, her children, and their life together. Equally important were questions that elicited her emotional response to the tragedy. The interview also returned, repeatedly, to broader themes of violence, justice, and social decline. All of these elements were threaded together in the article that appeared several days later.[16]

"Catch the people who killed my son"

Crime: Aarón Medina was a nineteen-year-old student of Auto Mechanics.
Tahís Mendoza, the mother of the youth murdered leaving a club, fears for
the life of her daughter

Portraits of Violence: Aarón and Génesis. Those were the names that Tahís Mendoza gave her twins nineteen years ago. She says that the people who killed her son took half of her life and she describes being overwhelmed by a profound sense of impotence.

"This is karma. All I ask is that they catch the people who killed my son. I know that this won't return him to me, but at least they should pay for what they have done," says Tahís Mendoza.

Many of her reasons for living were snuffed out the evening of Sunday, July 12, when she arrived at hospital Miguel Pérez Carreño and her daughter told her that Aarón had died.

"My son was the 49th [body] in the morgue that weekend, because they killed him late at night. It shows how they kill people in this country. It was one of my sisters who first told me that he had been shot, because my daughter called her aunt. When my sister called she only said that he was wounded," recalled Mendoza.

The young man's mother believed her children were safe because they were always together. "Those two never did anything alone. They were good kids [*muchachos sanos*] who never went looking to get into it with anyone. They followed each other everywhere. At every party if one of them left, then the other would leave, too. If he didn't want to go, she would wait for him or look for him later, but they were always together," Mendoza said. [. . .]

The article—part eulogy, part cry for justice—occupied half a page of newsprint above the fold. Under the aegis of maternal suffering, Aarón Medina's death became an object worthy of collective mourning. Two photographs illustrated this dynamic. One was the aforementioned graduation photo in which the twins presented a picture of respectability. The second, placed directly above the first, was a portrait of their tearstained mother. The selection and arrangement of these portraits of suffering and respectability reflected just one tactic for conveying innocent victimhood.

Ordinarily, these photos and their accompanying narrative would be enough to redeem the dead man. Tahís Mendoza's maternal grief, however, did not exist in a vacuum. This particular portrait of violence was complicated by a sidebar in the top right corner of the page. According to the police, the culprits had been identified. Moreover, Aarón Medina's assailants were not the only ones shooting. The victim was also armed. Even readers skeptical of the police account were left to wonder, all over again, about the dead man's moral status. Was he a good kid shot down in the prime of his youth or someone involved in shady dealings? This final detail serves as a reminder about the complex and unceasing work of judgment that weighed on both the living and the dead. It also points to other dynamics that influenced the framing of crime victimhood, including crime journalists' relationship with police sources and the broader political significance of violent crime in Caracas.

To imagine crime news as nothing more than a contemporary morality play would be naive. Crime journalists were right to say that their interactions with crime victims were thoroughly colored by partisan politics. "Portraits of Violence" was a good example. The series appeared in *El Nacional*, a newspaper closely associated with the opposition. Its purpose went beyond humanizing crime victims. It also attempted to link their suffering to a critique of insecurity and the Chávez government. Tahís Mendoza, and anyone else who agreed to do an interview with reporters from *El Nacional*, was well aware of the paper's editorial slant. Over the course of the interview, the reporter offered Tahís Mendoza a series of subtle cues, which would have allowed her to denounce the Chávez government were she so inclined. She was not. This was a deliberate choice, and one that left her political allegiances open to interpretation.

Representations of crime victims drew on an entire chain of judgments. Assumptions about guilt and innocence, malandro and sano, rested on a series of deeper assumptions about race, class, gender, sexuality, and more. These assumptions were, in turn, shaped by a political calculus, which revolved around the binary of chavista/opposition. This calculus was implicit in the Aarón Medina case. It was explicit in the next one, the death of former crime reporter Javier García.

Exposé

Jenny was livid. "That macabre bitch! They should take away her journalism license for publishing this shit." The "shit" to which Jenny referred was an interview with the man who murdered their friend and colleague, the television reporter Javier García. The interview pulled back the covers on something that she and her fellow crime journalists had desperately tried to conceal: Javier García was gay.[17] Weeks earlier, after the former reporter was found dead in his apartment, the journalists collectively agreed not to publish details about his sexual life. Now the dead man was out of the closet. Worse still, another reporter was responsible. "Why would you make a denunciation against one of your own?" one of the other reporters fumed. "It doesn't serve any purpose. So why denounce him like that?"[18]

When the news of García's death was first reported, there seemed little reason to interrogate his sexuality. A noted reporter for one of Venezuela's oldest and most venerable television stations, RCTV, García enjoyed the minor celebrity status of a local news presenter. His death provoked an outpouring of grief as colleagues, friends, and family grappled with their loss. During my tenure on the crime beat, no other case hit home like this one. I still remember the distress it caused one journalist, who subsequently took a leave of absence. Although reporters were accustomed to dealing with death, this case was like waking up and "seeing blood seeping under your own front door." Sexual orientation was the furthest thing from my mind when I wrote these field notes.

Monday, June 16, 2008: The morning papers all carry short articles about a television reporter from RCTV who was found stabbed to death in his own home. It is only when I meet up with the crime reporters at the morgue that I realize the enormity of the news. Javier García was not just any reporter: he was a former crime reporter and a close friend to many of the journalists on the Caracas crime beat. His death comes as a tremendous shock.

García's body was only discovered late last night, and the details of the case are still trickling in. As of now we know that he was stabbed multiple times; that his apartment shows no sign of forced entry; that he was last seen at an upscale restaurant in the eastern part of the city; that friends in the newsroom became alarmed when he did not show up to work on Saturday morning; and that a potential suspect was seen leaving the apartment with a suitcase.

The reporters discuss, in hushed tones, facts and theories about the case, even as they try to comfort each other and the victim's family. Then, the interviews begin. One after another, journalists step in front of the news cameras to talk about García's life and death. They describe him as a caring friend, an excellent reporter, and a generous colleague. To a person, they all tie his death to the larger problem of crime and insecurity in Caracas. One of García's closest friends at RCTV, Jose Pernalete, expresses his hope that the police will capture the culprit. To him the murder is just more proof of a terrible societal illness in which people have lost all respect for the sanctity of life.[19]

Only a fraction of what crime journalists know about a case ever makes it into the news. Like Ernest Hemingway's iceberg, most of the story is submerged below the surface of the text, a looming presence whose outlines can only be surmised. Audiences know this. When perusing the crime pages or watching the afternoon news, they do not simply read between the lines—they read under them. It is hermeneutics with a forensic twist. The submerged story, in this case, was the fact of García's sexual orientation. All of the crime journalists knew that he was gay. As it turned out, so did much of their audience.

Despite their careful attempts to steer around the subject of García's sexual orientation, the clues were there for the interpreting. García was thirty-seven years old, unmarried, well groomed, and living alone. He was stabbed in his own apartment, which is a modus operandi commonly associated with intimacy and masculine violence. In a city like Caracas where crime news was both popular and tragically plentiful, a discerning audience quickly picked up on these details. The fact that people were reading the case in this light snapped into focus for me the following morning. My field notes again:

> *Tuesday, June 17, 2008*: When I pick up the daily papers at my usual news kiosk, my friend Mendoza is upset about what he sees as prejudice in the Javier García case. He tells me that people are saying that the dead man was gay because he lived alone. Mendoza protests that a single man living in his own apartment is not necessarily gay. "After all," he shrugs, "I lived by myself for awhile. Now I am married." I try to point out that the problem is not García's sexual orientation, but the fact that it is being used against him. "Does it make his death any less tragic?" I ask. Mendoza nods politely, but I get the feeling that we are talking past one another.[20]

The first person to publicly suggest reading sexuality back into the García case was none other than Mario Silva, the Chávez government's pundit-in-chief. Scarcely twenty-four hours after the story broke, Silva was dissecting it on his popular late-night television show, *The Razorblade*. Seated in front of a psychedelic mural of leftist leaders living and dead, he started on a note of conciliation: "No one's death is cause for celebration. All human beings have the right to live." Silva paused before wading in further: "But to me it seems risky on the part of Globovisión and the Inter American Press Association, to me it seems risky to call this a problem of insecurity." Another dramatic pause, then Silva leaned into the camera and said, "Let me explain something." He then proceeded to review the facts of the case point by point—the lack of forced entry, the details of the crime scene, the man with the suitcase—all of which allowed him to come to a rather simple conclusion: this was a crime of passion. "Nobody is pleased about anyone's death. Much less with anyone's murder," Silva continued. "But you cannot connect this case to insecurity. No one refers to a traffic accident, a heart attack, or a crime of passion as 'insecurity.'"[21]

According to Silva's reasoning, García's murder was not a murder at all. It was an accident, an act of nature, something outside the realm of the political. Absurd as this sounds, it was not an idiosyncratic position. Days earlier the minister of justice made a similar argument about the death of a young taxi driver. According to the minister, the murdered taxi driver did not deserve to be counted as a victim of insecurity because he was a malandro and because disputes between malandros had no impact on the lives of ordinary citizens.[22] Unlike the minister of justice, who was roundly criticized, Silva knew that he was treading on eggshells. Every one of his statements was qualified. At no point did he explicitly state that García was gay. However, no one watching the program could miss the innuendos. While paying homage to the sanctity of life, Silva was trying to diminish the political importance of García's death. He said as much: "With all due respect to the family, enough already. RCTV and Globovisión are using the death of a person—they are using what one comrade called journalistic necrophilia—to try to create a matrix of opinion that can be converted into an act of protest."[23] It was protest that worried Silva. The last thing that Silva or anyone else in the government wanted to see was a high-profile murder transformed into a cause célèbre.

Something like a protest indeed took place the following Sunday, when several hundred mourners and an equal number of curious onlookers converged on Plaza Brion, a shopping district in the east of Caracas. Women wearing black congregated in front of a hastily erected stage that was decorated like a church altar. White orchids, white lace, and silver candlesticks rested atop a simple wooden table; behind it stood a lectern, and behind that a triptych of two saints framing a white cross. The stage had been set, quite literally, by García's former employer, RCTV, which had organized the event and taped it from start to finish.[24]

To understand this gathering, it helps to locate RCTV within the landscape of national politics. Up until the summer of 2007, RCTV was the largest and oldest television station in Venezuela. It was also the main mouthpiece of political opposition to President Hugo Chávez. Of all Venezuela's media outlets, none had been more vocal or intransigent in channeling antigovernment sentiment than RCTV. In retaliation, the Chávez government refused to renew RCTV's public broadcasting license. This legal maneuver effectively shuttered the station. Mass demonstrations followed, but it was too little too late. A much-diminished RCTV vowed to carry on its fight against the government as a cable access channel.[25]

Showing up at anything organized by RCTV was a self-conscious statement of opposition to the Chávez government. This final homage to García was a mixture of mourning, protest, and televised spectacle. Once again, friends and colleagues spoke dolefully about what they had lost and insisted that this death was part of a much larger problem plaguing Venezuela.

Crime was out of control. The overwhelming fact of insecurity touched everyone, embittered everything. There was no need to mention who was to blame. If you had to ask, then you did not belong there in the first place.

Crime journalists say that recognizing a story is a matter of instinct. "The nose knows." My instincts told me that García's murder was a big story. I fully expected that the crime journalists would continue to follow the case and that it would be one of the major stories of my first summer on the crime beat. Instead, it disappeared. The protest-cum-memorial service in Plaza Brion was the last public event that I witnessed in honor of García. One week later, *El Universal* published its bombshell interview. It alleged that the man who murdered García had been his lover for going on eight months. The journalist who filed the interview faced the wrath of her colleagues, who attempted to disbar the offending reporter. A line had been crossed. Even after the professional proceedings had run their course, the outrage and grief over García's death continued to linger among the journalists. However, on the airwaves and in the print, the case was left behind. Six months later, when newspapers including *El Nacional* and *La Voz* published retrospectives about the major crime stories of 2008, they made no mention of the former crime reporter.

Victimless Crimes

When is a murder victim not a victim? For a young man in Caracas—and poor men made up the overwhelming majority of the city's nameless, faceless homicides—it was when he had tattoos or a police record. When he lived in a poor, supposedly dangerous neighborhood. When he was killed late at night on a street with a bad reputation. When he was a dark-skinned immigrant. When he was a hip-hop artist. When he had dreadlocks. When he worked in an AIDS clinic and did not have a wife or children. When he could be associated with drugs or was alleged to be in a gang. When he was both out of school and out of work. When he drove a motorcycle. When his body had been shot multiple times and the police claimed that he was killed in an act of vengeance. When the police killed him. When his relatives refused to be interviewed by the press or when journalists looked at the relatives and assumed that they were not worth interviewing. In short, a murder victim was not a victim when there was any reason to suspect that he was matter out of place or that death might have put him in his place and restored the order of things.[26]

In Javier García's case, sexuality was the basis on which his innocence was called into question. When it came out that his male lover killed him, the case suddenly receded from the public eye. There was more to this story than just heteronormative bias, however.

The García case was situated at the intersection of two political dynamics. What I have described in this chapter was the familiar dynamic of law and ordering. This dynamic distinguishes the sano from the malandro, the innocent from the suspicious, the healthy from the diseased, and so forth. According to normative ideals of Venezuelan society, García's sexuality made him suspect; however, given his standing as a journalist and a beloved public figure, it is not hard to imagine circumstances in which such judgments could have been suspended. His fellow crime reporters worked hard to do just that. Here was where the second political dynamic became important, something that I describe in the next chapter as *populist logic*. In Caracas, populist logic divided the world into two camps: those who were with the Chávez government and those who were against it. In life García was clearly identified with the opposition. In death he was pulled into the larger attempts to mobilize against the government in the name of security. Because García's case intersected with this second dynamic—because it was part of a larger political struggle that crystallized around the demands for security—it garnered intense scrutiny in a way that called into question his status as innocent victim. The next chapter takes up the story of another murdered journalist to explain the relationship between crime victimhood, populist mobilization, and political polarization in Caracas.

FIVE

The Photographer's Body

"Liars! Coup plotters! *Escuálidos!*"[1] What had been a slow Sunday on the Caracas crime beat was rapidly heating up. The woman shouting in our direction wore a bright red shirt, which identified her as a supporter of President Hugo Chávez. Our group of two dozen crime journalists was covering a press event near the capital. We were there to observe as investigators and victims reconstructed the tragic events of April 11, 2002, a day that mass protests in Caracas turned violent. Six years earlier, many of these same journalists witnessed the violence firsthand. They, too, had painful memories. On this very spot their longtime friend and colleague, the photojournalist Jorge Tortoza, was gunned down.

When we arrived at the reconstructed crime scene, it was sealed off by two hundred police in riot gear. Several official-looking men were taking measurements, snapping photos, and documenting the testimonies of victims. For about half an hour the journalists trailed the proceedings, waiting patiently for a chance to interview the victims and their relatives. Eventually, an interview opportunity materialized. One reporter struck up a conversation with a man who was shot by the Metropolitan Police. Removing his cap, he pointed to a mass of scar tissue just above the hairline. "It is a miracle that I am alive. That day, the police ruined my life." Standing beside him, a woman in red-rimmed glasses chimed in, "And it has taken so long to bring them to justice because of the lies of the media." I braced myself for an encounter, but the journalists took the accusation unflinchingly. The reporter closest to the woman made eye contact and nodded her head sympathetically. A second reporter added, "We are here today to tell *your* side of the story." A third reporter interjected with a follow-up question. "What do you hope that this reenactment will establish?" In a matter of moments, the journalists defused a volatile situation with practiced ease. However, there was always the danger that such an encounter could go wrong. When it did, journalists could find themselves in precarious positions.[2]

The polarization of Caracas during the Chávez era reflected the shared logic of populism. In this chapter, I detail how the antagonism between chavismo and the opposition was produced and policed. Doing so not only upends this divide's givenness, its ontological status, but also demonstrates how these two antagonistic identities share striking similarities at the level of political practice. The quickest, clearest window onto this observation, ethnographically speaking, is how representations of victimhood and suffering get articulated. It is with an eye toward the production of friends and enemies that I follow the death of the photojournalist Jorge Tortoza. Examining the events leading up to Tortoza's murder and the afterlife of the investigation allows us to glimpse the populist logic that animated politics in the Chávez era. In particular, I concentrate on the way that self-identification with victims provided the idiom for populist mobilization.

I first encountered Tortoza's story in January 2008 during the early months of my fieldwork. Among his fellow crime journalists, the case symbolized the turbulent political atmosphere that placed the press at the center of a fierce political struggle to determine the future of Venezuela. Killed during the failed 2002 coup d'état against President Chávez, both the opposition and chavismo adopted Tortoza as a martyr. This dual claim was possible because, like most photojournalists, Tortoza was a liminal figure. The polarization of Venezuelan politics is usually portrayed as a conflict between elites and the popular sectors. Photojournalists move back and forth between these worlds. In his professional capacity, Tortoza was associated with the opposition and cultural elites because he worked for the single most vocal anti-Chávez institution in Venezuela—the private press. However, strip away the camera and the press badge, and Tortoza was likely to be taken for a chavista because of his dark skin and working-class background, identities that are associated with support for the former president. The struggle over his memory illustrates both the importance of these political identities and the work that goes into maintaining the divide between them. Such Manichean distinctions between friend and foe, which become apparent in depictions of Tortoza's death, are also well-recognized hallmarks of populism.[3]

Treating populism as an object of ethnographic inquiry allows us to rethink contemporary Venezuelan politics, particularly the relationship between polarization and the formation of political identities. Populist movements are majoritarian in their appeals to the popular will, yet they bring together disparate constituencies with distinct, sometimes contradictory grievances. What holds these constituencies together and makes them internally coherent is the identification of a common enemy. This enemy serves as the negative backdrop against which the movement defines itself. Political antagonism is so crucial to the formation of populist identities that it trumps any ideological program. Indeed, the enemy is often more clearly defined than the movement itself. For this reason, critics often claim that populism is empty or incoherent. What these critics overlook is the shared sense of victimhood and the firm commitment to popular sovereignty that unites populist movements. Populism sets out to right wrongs in the name of the oppressed. If the enemy is the figure that articulates and justifies populist claims of sovereignty, then "the people" emerges as the victim of that enemy. In Venezuela, this dialectical relationship between the enemy and the victim is the grounds on which populist political identities are constructed.

Following the figure of the victim reveals an important similarity between chavismo and the opposition. For most of the Chávez era, Venezuela was home to two competing populisms. Scholars have paid close attention to the populism of Hugo Chávez, the best example of a charismatic Latin American leader since Argentina's Juan Perón. What has gone unacknowledged is that the opposition, and especially the private press, was also a case study in populist mobilization.[4] The parallels between the opposition and chavismo must not be overstated, for the two movements are not mirror images of each other. However, looking at the similarities between these two political blocs may help rethink the conceptual impasse that has led much of the scholarship to reproduce the chavista/opposition divide. To that end, the Tortoza case presents an excellent ethnographic example through which we can think about the construction of populist identities, the way that people try to negotiate these identities, and the tragic consequences when these negotiations fail.

The Life and Death of Jorge Tortoza

Jorge Tortoza was, by all accounts, a quiet man. For the better part of eleven years he covered the Caracas crime beat as a photojournalist for the newspaper *Diario 2001*. Colleagues remember him as a consummate professional, punctual and meticulously groomed. If the press office of the investigative police opened at 7:00 a.m., Tortoza would be there at 6:30, dressed in his trademark suit and tie, camera at the ready. His punctuality and his style earned him the nickname *el gallo*—"the cock" or "the rooster"—and from the handful of photographs that I have seen, the name fit the man: his square jaw, dark mustache, and small, expressive eyes all seem to radiate a mixture of virility and distance, a countenance more like a police officer than a journalist.[5]

"He was silent, he didn't talk much," recalled Fernando Sánchez, one of Tortoza's closest friends on the crime beat.[6] On that point everyone agreed. The phrase that repeated whenever anyone reached for a description was *muy callado*, "very quiet." Rarely would Tortoza indulge in the pranks or practical jokes that were the norm among most of the photographers who covered the crime beat, preferring to focus on his work. Tortoza was so reserved, in fact, that the other journalists knew very little about his personal life outside of a few details. He lived in Catia, a working-class neighborhood. He was divorced and had a young daughter. He enjoyed the occasional beer. He supported President Chávez, although he rarely, if ever, shared his political views. Beyond these scattered details, Tortoza's personal life was a secret, the man himself something of a cipher. As Simon Clemente, director of photography at *Diario 2001*, told me, "There was much I never knew about his life, and I did not push him to tell me anything. It wasn't any of my business."[7]

It is no small irony that a man so reserved in life became the center of so much attention upon his death. On April 11, 2002, Tortoza was covering the clashes between opposition marchers and government supporters near the presidential palace when he was shot in the back of the head and did an impossible somersault toward the pavement. Over the following weeks, photos and videos of his death were widely circulated, along with conflicting stories about what exactly happened that afternoon. Both sides of the political divide claimed Tortoza as a martyr for their respective causes. Editorials in opposition newspapers depicted him as a "defender of press freedom," a man whose commitment to journalism put him in the path of the government and its "savage hordes."[8] In contrast, government supporters, including Tortoza's own family, claimed him as a chavista hero and the victim of an opposition conspiracy. The controversy made Tortoza the most emblematic victim of the most emblematic event of the Chávez era, what became known as "the events of April," "the April coup," "the massacre in El Silencio," or simply (and most diplomatically) "April 11."

The curious case of Jorge Tortoza was tied to the coup d'état that briefly deposed President Chávez. In total, nineteen people died and scores were wounded on the afternoon of April 11, 2002, amid violent confrontations in the streets of downtown Caracas. Responsibility for the deaths was initially laid at the feet of the national government, and less than twelve hours after the shootings subsided, members of the armed forces escorted President Chávez out of the presidential palace. Barely halfway through his term in office, Hugo Chávez appeared to be finished. On April 12, the chairman of the national federation of private business chambers, Pedro Carmona, swore himself in as Venezuela's acting president on national television, dissolving the constitution, the National Assembly, and the presidential cabinet to thunderous applause. That evening most of the high-profile members of the old government were in hiding; however, a few of the president's most ardent supporters started a vigil around Miraflores. Despite a concerted media blackout, details of the situation began to leak out, and by Saturday afternoon, residents of the city's poor barrios had surrounded the palace demanding the return of their president. Behind closed doors, the new government was rife with division. The Carmona regime failed to gain the support of key figures within the military and came undone almost as soon as it was announced. On April 13, less than forty-eight hours after he was forcibly removed from office, Chávez made a miraculous return to power.[9]

It would be hard to overstate the symbolic importance of April 11 to politics in the Chávez era, and accounts of what happened that day bifurcated along political lines. Chavismo enshrined the coup as a mythical moment in which the will of the people triumphed over the machinations of the old regime. Supporters of President Chávez believed that this was a classic coup that involved a conscious conspiracy, one that was aided and abetted by the private press. The telling and retelling of the coup story reinforced the belief that, in the final instance, the government of Hugo Chávez was supported by popular mandate. In contrast, the Venezuelan opposition was openly skeptical of the coup narrative. A number of accounts suggest, convincingly, that there was not a deliberate strategy in place but rather a chaotic series of events that led to a temporary vacuum of power. These accounts tend to emphasize the size of the popular uprising against the Chávez government and the responsibility of the president and his followers for the initial outburst of violence. Between these two competing versions of the April 11 story there was little neutral ground. The vast majority of Venezuelans subscribed to one version of events or the other; trying to keep both in view was like suffering a bout of double vision.

As with the story of April 11, there were conflicting accounts of who killed Jorge Tortoza, and the identity of his killer remained an unsolved mystery. My purpose is not to get to the root of what happened that day by playing detective or teasing truth out of rumors. Instead, I am interested in the stories themselves and what becomes visible in their telling. In particular, I am interested in how divergent stories of Tortoza's death illustrated the work that went into maintaining the boundary between the chavista and opposition camps.

The Chavista/Opposition Divide

Photojournalists like Tortoza were liminal figures in terms of the boundary between antagonistic political identities. They illustrated the fact that, despite its rhetorical force, the dividing line between chavismo and the opposition was in no way self-evident, nor was it absolute. These two political identities subsumed preexisting racial, gender, and class divisions, which were bound up with deep histories of imperialism, colonialism, and revolutionary struggle in the Americas. If it was common to categorize these divisions in terms of their cardinal directions (e.g., "left" vs. "right" or "global south" vs. "global north"), then the enactment of political and social identity always exceeded such dichotomies the moment they pronounced them because as loose political coalitions, both chavismo and the opposition encompassed multiple, conflicting social identities so that internal divisions crisscrossed each coalition. The boundaries that defined these two alliances and that distinguished one from the other were all the more important because they were so porous. Indeed, the work of classifying politics into warring camps went on not despite such ambiguities but because of them.[10]

To paraphrase Ernesto Laclau, populist movements in Venezuela had no necessary class, race, or gender, yet their claims to represent the true voice of the people were predicated on the performance of such identities. Take chavismo. During the 1990s, the movement that crystallized around Hugo Chávez valorized *el pueblo* against a corrupt "oligarchy." In Venezuela, as in much of Latin America, the figure of *el pueblo* carried strong racial and socioeconomic connotations, which chavismo fashioned into a powerful, positive political identity. For chavistas, *el pueblo* was the masculine force of revolutionary, democratic change. As Luis Duno-Gottberg has argued, it was the insurgent threat that always hung over the city.[11] Yet, despite the explicit political equation of chavismo with the popular classes, it was not clear that the urban poor disproportionately supported the movement. Noam Lupu has demonstrated that support for President Chávez cut across socioeconomic divisions.[12] This finding suggests that chavismo did not simply "represent" the discontent of the popular classes but produced it as an expression of its own political mandate.

For the opposition, the performance of collective identity proved more challenging. Unlike chavismo, the opposition was not associated with any single person but rather with a heterogeneous collection of institutions, parties, and public figures. The opposition emerged as a political movement shortly after President Chávez came to power and gained momentum during the 1999 constitutional referendum. Although dominated by the owners of capital, it embraced a range of political positions—neoliberal, social democratic, even dissident Marxist—not to mention divergent networks of patronage. Along with the private press and the Catholic Church, the opposition included the two parties that ruled Venezuela for nearly thirty years (Acción Democrática, COPEI) and a handful of newer parties (Causa R, Nuevo Tiempo, Podemos, PPT), many of which were formerly part of President Chávez's political coalition. Conspicuously absent from this heterogeneous coalition was any form of ideological coherence. The only thing that held the opposition together was strident rejection of chavismo and its claim to speak out on behalf of "respectable citizens."[13] In many regards this valorization of respectability resembled the paternalistic populism of an earlier era, which imagined a tutelary relationship between enlightened elites and *el pueblo*.[14]

Both chavismo and the opposition drew on preexisting socioeconomic divisions that provided the idiom of political struggle. This struggle was couched in Manichean terms. Whereas *el pueblo* and "respectable citizens" were the positive, legitimating political identities that aimed to recruit the largest possible support base, the figure of the enemy was the negative category, a kind of scapegoat, against which each movement defined itself. There was no opposition without the "abomination" of Chávez and his supporters. Similarly, without the opposition of "escuálidos," the chavista movement would have quickly lost coherence. It was the perceived injustice, corruption, and wrongdoing on the part of these enemy others that formed the basis of both movements. This sense of victimhood and outrage was articulated in the language of race, class, and gender. From the perspective of many in the opposition, rightful authority had been usurped by a gang of poor, dark, and dangerous thugs; from the perspective of many chavistas, it had been stolen by the same effete, white elites that have exploited the country for centuries.[15] Either way, partisans of chavismo and the opposition saw themselves as victims mobilizing the force of popular sovereignty against the abuses of power.

Of course, not everyone in Caracas was a self-identified partisan. Through polling data, we know that a large swath of voters rejected both chavismo and the opposition.[16] Despite the presence of this third political bloc, the logic of populism insisted that everyone choose a side. As a result, the labels "chavista" and "opposition" were regularly imposed on people who resisted being grouped into one camp or the other.

This dynamic—whereby an absolute political identity was imposed from the outside—became dangerously apparent during the events of April 11 and was especially true for photojournalists like Jorge Tortoza who were precariously positioned between the two worlds. Although their professions linked them to the opposition and the elite world of cultural production, most of these photographers came from the popular classes and eked out a modest existence. Under normal circumstances, this in-between status gave them tremendous social mobility. However, in the context of April 11, their liminality became untenable. As battle lines were drawn, cameras took on the aspect of weapons, and photographers were transformed into friends or foes.

The News Coup

"Whoever killed Tortoza shot him because he was taking photos." Seated behind the editor's desk in the spartan offices of *Diario 2001*, Ricardo Mateus spoke with the authority of someone who was there. On the afternoon of April 11 he was working the crime beat just a few blocks from where Tortoza fell. For veterans like Mateus, Tortoza's name brought back memories of that fateful day, memories that kaleidoscoped with the unsettling awareness of their own vulnerability. Rather than disappearing into the background of the event that they were covering, journalists found that they were targets of attention on April 11—particularly the photographers, who stood out because of their equipment. "It was not a stray bullet," Mateus emphasized. "It was aimed at him."[17]

Tortoza died during the bloody finale of what was one of the largest political demonstrations in Venezuelan history. Despite a light drizzle, hundreds of thousands of anti-Chávez marchers gathered on the morning of April 11 demanding the president's resignation. The march was scheduled to snake across the affluent eastern districts of Caracas and to culminate in a rally at the steps of Petróleos de Venezuela, S.A. (PDVSA), the state oil company and the engine of Venezuela's economy. Around noon, incited by the rally, the marchers swung westward, crossing the invisible boundary that partitions the city down political and socioeconomic lines. Although the march permit only extended to the offices of PDVSA, there had been talk that the demonstration would continue all the way to the Miraflores presidential palace, more than eleven kilometers away in the heart of chavista territory. In anticipation, several thousand Chávez supporters had surrounded the palace. There was a general sense that if the two groups met, there would be bloodshed. Sonia Tortoza had said as much to her brother over coffee that morning.[18] Indeed, the march had been in the back of Tortoza's mind that morning when he chose to wear a photographer's vest and jeans rather than his traditional suit. The vest gave him more room to store additional lenses, and the jeans would make it easier to move quickly in case of trouble.[19]

It was the looming threat of violence that explains why crime reporters like Tortoza were covering a political rally in the first place. Earlier that morning, Tortoza and his colleagues made the trip to the town of San Francisco de Yare, nearly an hour outside the city, to cover the aftermath of a much smaller demonstration, in which a dozen opposition protesters sustained injuries. The trip was long and uneventful. As it turned out, the injuries to protesters were relatively light. Tortoza and his work partner, the reporter Jenny Oropeza, arrived back in Caracas around the same time that the opposition marchers were streaming toward the presidential palace. After following a false alarm to the Central University of Venezuela (Universidad Central de Venezuela, or UCV), the two journalists split up to cover the march. They would meet again an hour later on the edge of the conflict. Oropeza realized she that was a marked woman. Her stylish jeans sported an American flag design on the thigh. In the eyes of many caraqueños, this small symbol would have marked her as an opposition marcher. Fearing for her safety, Oropeza headed back to the newspaper while Tortoza elected to stay behind.

One of the last people to see Tortoza alive was his fellow photojournalist Henry Solórzano. The two met near the massive white stairs of El Calvario, just south of the presidential palace, and drifted a few blocks east to the corner known as La Pedrera on Baralt Avenue. This was one of the main corridors of the conflict, the site where the shootings were the most concentrated. Here they parted ways. Solórzano remembers glimpsing Tortoza one last time through the smoke and confusion, then moving up another block searching for a better angle. When he returned a short while later, Tortoza had disappeared. "People were shouting that a photographer had been shot. Seeing the body on the ground, I ran towards him shouting, 'Tortoza! Tortoza!'"[20] A few other journalists were around him, including Tortoza's close friend and fellow photojournalist Fernando Sánchez. It was Sánchez who had the presence of mind to convince a Metropolitan Police officer to use his motorcycle as a makeshift ambulance. The officer transported Tortoza to the Vargas hospital, where he died later that night.[21]

Journalists who covered the events of April 11 unanimously believed that Tortoza was intentionally singled out. It was not just Tortoza, though. Anyone who was carrying a camera or who looked like a journalist was a potential target. This is one of the few points of agreement that the many versions of the story share. No fewer than seven journalists were wounded covering the events of April 11. A total of six photographers or cameramen were shot, and one reporter was struck in the head with a baseball bat. Often added to this tally is an eighth victim, an undercover intelligence officer who was disguised as a photojournalist. Added to the list of injuries was a multitude of threats and near misses. Simon Clemente from *Diario 2001* was threatened with his life just north of Miraflores.[22] Alex Delgado with *El Nacional* remembered bullets whistling past his head in El Calvario.[23] Francisco Toro and videographer Megan Folsom were told by a mysterious stranger that they should leave immediately because the camera made them likely victims.[24] Rather than working under the aegis of neutrality and being allowed to fade into the background of events, photojournalists were treated as active participants during the events of April 11. The camera did not hide them or protect them. It made them immediately visible and therefore doubly vulnerable.

Tortoza's death came as tensions peaked between the private press and the Chávez government. There is quite a bit of irony in the fact that the private press became the president's most visible adversary. Throughout the political crises of the 1980s and the 1990s, key figures in the Venezuelan press promoted the popular movement that eventually brought Chávez to power, a story that I detail in the next chapter. The crisis forged an unspoken alliance between journalists and the city's popular sectors. During my interviews and conversations with veterans on the Caracas crime beat, many recalled the solidarity expressed by residents of the city's poorest neighborhoods during these turbulent times. After Chávez won the presidency in 1999, all of that would change.

Although key figures within the private press supported the candidacy of Hugo Chávez, within less than a year, all four of the city's major television stations and all but one newspaper adopted a stridently anti-Chávez editorial line.[25] The feud between the president and the private press became very bitter and very public. Chávez lashed out at his adversaries in the "media dictatorship" that was trying to usurp his government and the popular revolution.[26] In turn, the president was branded "a dictator," "a tyrant," "an autocrat," and another Fidel Castro in the making.[27]

Accounts of April 11 that are sympathetic to President Chávez—most famously the documentary film *The Revolution Will Not Be Televised*—argue that the Venezuelan media masterminded the coup.[28] Although this perspective tends to downplay the culpability of the president and his supporters, there is ample evidence that a powerful group of media owners, editors, and opinion makers helped set events in motion. In the months leading up to April 11, news coverage returned time and again to two subjects: the president's declining popularity and loud rumblings of discontent within the military.[29] Press elites fanned rumors of a coup, and in at least one important case these elites actively and intentionally planted them.[30] The press also played a pivotal role in promoting the march. The time and place of the demonstration were a relatively last-minute decision and it took a Herculean effort on the part of the private television and radio stations to get the word out. Without the massive pro bono publicity campaign, it is unlikely that anyone at all would have showed up on the morning of April 11. In addition to promoting the march, some of the more radical news outlets pushed it toward a confrontation. For example, on the morning of April 11 the headline of *El Nacional* read, "The Final Battle Will Be at Miraflores."[31] It is not simply that this headline used combative imagery. It seemed to publicly proclaim intent to violate the marching permit by crossing into chavista territory. When violence broke out, it was immediately interpreted as "a massacre" instigated by the president and his supporters. The best evidence of the massacre was video footage of government supporters firing from the overpass at the presidential palace. Although they were in a shoot-out with the Metropolitan Police, it was made to look as though they were firing on unarmed opposition marchers. Images and stories like this one gave the ensuing coup d'état a patina of legitimacy. Finally, on April 13, while a group of powerful media owners and directors met privately with Pedro Carmona, the rest of Caracas was experiencing a news blackout.[32] Journalist-turned-opposition-blogger Francisco Toro recalls searching the television and radio stations in vain for any kind of news. "If the anti-Chávez news media were not reporting, it must mean that the new anti-Chávez government was in trouble. By not covering the news they were, in effect, trying to prop up Carmona."[33]

Setting aside the question of responsibility, there was no doubt that Venezuela's main media outlets threw their weight behind the effort to oust Chávez. If the people driving these efforts were owners, high-ranking editors, and opinion makers, it was beat journalists like Tortoza who were literally and figuratively caught in the crossfire.

The Janus-Faced Martyr

In death, Jorge Tortoza became a political symbol, visible in a way that he had never been in life. Along with numerous obituaries and articles memorializing his career, Tortoza was honored with no fewer than four posthumous awards for journalism, including two national prizes.[34] The press office of the investigative police in downtown Caracas was renamed the Jorge Tortoza Press Office.[35] A commemorative plaque in his name was placed on the corner of La Pedrera "in honor of those who fell for the country."[36] His name was included on the Journalists Memorial in the Newseum in Washington, DC.[37] Each of these honors presented another opportunity to publish more articles about Tortoza and the circumstances of his death, articles that shrouded tragedy in the idiom of Christian sacrifice.

This sacrificial idiom was nowhere more apparent than in the images of the fallen photojournalist. Three photos of Tortoza, which were widely circulated, corresponded to three overlapping aspects of his posthumous identity as victim, hero, and martyr. There was the photo taken moments after he was shot. Tortoza was laid out on the pavement, his camera still lassoed around his neck, a trickle of blood pooling behind his head: Tortoza the victim. Then there was the photo taken years earlier by his friend Carlos Ramirez, in which the photojournalist was leaping off the roof of a news truck, surrounded by smoke, his camera in hand and his jacket billowing up like a cape: Tortoza the hero. The last photograph was the least spectacular, but it proved to be the one with the longest life span. It was a head shot of the photographer looking mournfully toward the camera, his white shirt unbuttoned, a cross dangling against his naked chest: Tortoza the martyr.

The opposition immediately appropriated Tortoza's sacrifice in the service of its cause. With one or two exceptions, the private press cast him as the victim of attacks on journalists that were incited by Chávez himself. Overnight, Tortoza became a symbol for resistance to government aggression, a man who put his own body on the line in pursuit of press freedom. His story merged with the larger narrative about April 11 as a massacre of innocent citizens at the hands of the president and his horde of followers. Prominent journalist Roberto Giusti summed up this view in a speech dedicated to his fallen colleague: "On April 11, Tortoza was turned into a symbol, an object of hatred owing to the government's criminal and irresponsible instigations against journalists. Tortoza did not die accidentally; they killed Tortoza for being a reporter, because his camera carried the proof of a massacre of which he ended up a victim."[38] Giusti's speech was delivered months after the failed coup, by which time it was widely known that Tortoza had been sympathetic to President Chávez, and yet this did not stop Giusti from framing the photographer's death as a selfless act of opposition against the government.

Although chavismo was somewhat slower in appropriating Tortoza's death, it was even more explicit in its use of the sacrificial idiom. The pro-government version of April 11 likened Chávez's calamitous fall and his miraculous return to the crucifixion and resurrection of Jesus Christ. Within this narrative, Tortoza and other victims of April 11 were adopted as martyrs who sacrificed themselves on behalf of the popular revolution. There were faint hints of this story in the private press. However, I found even clearer evidence of this perspective buried in Tortoza's old locker in *Diario 2001* in the form of a six-stanza poem, handwritten on a single sheet of white typing paper. Dated April 12, 2002, and titled "Homage to a great Hero," the poem was written by one Miguelina Campos, who "did not know you . . . / but felt a great pain / when I saw you fall / bathed in blood, sir." Campos's poem echoes the same tropes that we find in Giusti's speech. What is peculiar, though, is the fifth stanza: "You are, Tortoza, a great Hero / Of this great Revolution / With your death you helped / To free our Nation / From many things, Sir." The phrase "great Revolution" indicates that the poet, in all probability, identified Tortoza with chavismo.[39] Within weeks, the link between Tortoza and chavismo was strengthened as a result of the interventions of his family. Insisting that the fallen photographer had considered himself a chavista, the Tortoza family denounced the perversion of his death by the very institution that he had served in life. Like Chávez, Tortoza would come to be portrayed as the victim of media manipulation, a man whose legacy was scandalously appropriated against his own wishes.[40]

When the shootings stopped and the sharp pain of suffering was replaced by the pale fame of martyrdom, Tortoza was the one victim claimed by both communities of mourners. To which camp did Tortoza belong? That is, who could rightfully claim the victim's suffering, the hero's daring, the martyr's sacrifice? This was the question that confronted investigations into the photographer's death, yet this question obscured the underlying political dynamic. Rather than forcing us to choose a side, these mirroring images of Tortoza demonstrate how the legitimacy of both of these "sides" was reproduced through the sanctification of his death.

Victimhood, Sacrifice, and Populism

Through the idiom of sacrifice, the two dominant stories of Tortoza's death transformed his victimhood into a rationale for popular mobilization against an external enemy. This deployment of sacrifice was consonant with some of the characteristics identified by classical anthropology. Dating back to William Robertson Smith, studies of ritual sacrifice have traced a correlation between violence and the formation of collective identities.[41] Sigmund Freud, René Girard, and Maurice Bloch have all argued that self-identification with the sacrificial victim serves as a medium for group formation. For Freud, the victim of sacrifice was the father or alpha male, who was simultaneously an object of envy and reverence.[42] Similarly, Girard's scapegoat is a surrogate victim chosen from within the community.[43] Bloch is even more explicit about this self-identification with victims, placing it at the center of his analysis of ritual transformation from prey into hunter.[44] Every one of these accounts shows how the assertion of power—by the father, the king, the hunter, the state—derives legitimacy from its identification with the victim. Populist claims to represent the will of the people mimic a similar pattern.[45]

Self-identification with victims is a recurrent albeit underappreciated feature of populist movements. Time and again, scholars have described how the insurgent force of popular sovereignty grows out of a shared sense of injustice that pits righteous victims against the iniquities of the powerful. It is from this position of victimhood that populist movements assert themselves as the true and legitimate expression of the popular will. As with sacrificial rituals, suffering becomes the ground on which a collective identity is established and sovereignty is asserted. Such a dynamic was clearly present in the stories about Jorge Tortoza and the other victims of April 11. It was through their association with the victims of April 11 that both the opposition and chavismo portrayed themselves as the legitimate response to the illegitimate use of force. I do not mean to suggest that the sanctification of these victims was a conscious ruse to justify political action. Nonetheless, the act of mourning served as a powerful public spectacle through which both camps claimed the mantle of popular sovereignty against an external enemy.

In the turmoil that followed the failed coup d'état, the idiom of sacrifice acted as a privileged medium for the performance of popular sovereignty, a performance that simultaneously sanctified the victims and demonized their killers. The investigation into Tortoza's death was more than merely a quest for justice. It had the potential to become a search for scapegoats against whom popular outrage could be channeled. Through Tortoza both the opposition and the Chávez government attempted to portray themselves as victims, their opponents as murderers. Each coalition attempted to perform its own version of legitimate power by drawing a distinction between the righteousness of their cause and the wickedness of their political adversaries. One of the casualties of this struggle was the humanity of the victims.

Tortoza's fellow photojournalists did their best to extricate their friend from this posthumous predicament. Just a few weeks after his death, the National Circle of Graphic Reporters held a march under the banner *Tortoza somos todos*—"We are all Tortoza." Everyone wore white T-shirts with the slogan framing the mournful photo of the martyr. His mother, Rosa, was there along with his two-year-old daughter in pigtails and two hundred or so photojournalists. One of his colleagues told me that the purpose of the march was to repudiate the politicization of Tortoza's death, to call for national unity amid tragedy, and to urge for the speedy resolution of the case.[46] No politicians were allowed to join the procession, and the document that the photojournalists presented to the National Assembly asserted their political neutrality. "We do not opine, we do not interpret. We merely collect information, and that is the work to which we are dedicated."[47] It was to no avail. Their own newspapers and television stations continued to portray Tortoza as a freedom fighter. In the streets people continued to see the photojournalists as political partisans. And despite their efforts to reach out to Tortoza's family, the photojournalists found themselves the objects of suspicion.

Who Killed Jorge Tortoza?

Tortoza's death remained one of the unsolved mysteries of April 11. Despite numerous public declarations that the case was nearing its conclusion, no one was charged with the shooting. There were many hypotheses. Over the course of my research into the circumstances surrounding his death, I encountered perhaps a dozen versions of the story. Most of these versions belonged to what I call the *mainstream* political discourse, which read April 11 down partisan lines. On the surface, these mainstream accounts seemed to contradict one another. Some pinned Tortoza's death on chavista gunmen and set blame at the feet of the government, while others described it as part of an opposition conspiracy. However, all of the mainstream versions of the story agreed that Tortoza's murder was politically motivated and that his killers were responsible for setting in motion the chain of events that eventually led to the death of nineteen civilians and the ouster of President Chávez. In the mainstream political discourse, identifying Tortoza's killer meant assigning blame for what happened that day.

However, there were also two accounts of Tortoza's death that troubled the chavista/opposition divide. I call these *subaltern* accounts because they contradicted the dominant framing of April 11 and because they were formulated from a position of socioeconomic marginality. One of these subaltern accounts belonged to Tortoza's brother, Edgar. The other belonged to Tortoza's fellow photojournalists on the Caracas crime beat. Both refused to make Tortoza a martyr for chavismo or the opposition. Following the ways in which these stories diverged from the dominant discourse allows us to glimpse the dynamic that collapsed multiple accounts into a set of opposing narratives about Tortoza's death and, by extension, about who bore ultimate responsibility for April 11. These narratives also revealed how people struggled to forge their own identities in a highly polarized context. Like Jorge Tortoza, his brother and his colleagues were precariously positioned. Before describing their versions of events, it helps to briefly sketch the two mainstream versions that I encountered in my research.

The Mainstream Versions

The first mainstream account of Tortoza's death maintained that chavista gunmen killed him. Scrutiny fell on a group of armed civilians firing from the Llaguno overpass, a bridge three blocks north of where Tortoza fell. These suspicions were fueled by a video of the shooters captured by the television channel Venevisión and broadcast repeatedly by the private press.[48] Forensic evidence later dismissed the hypothesis that the Llaguno gunmen killed Tortoza and maintained that the shot was fired from close range. Seven months into the investigation, reports surfaced that the police possessed photographs of the presumed shooter, a man who was mingling with pro-Chávez demonstrators on Baralt Avenue.[49] Shortly thereafter, pictures were leaked to the press showing a wiry man in his late forties or early fifties, wearing blue jeans, a white oxford shirt, and a yellow baseball cap with a blue brim.[50] Although the investigative police originally confirmed that the man in the yellow hat was a potential suspect, they were never able to identify him and would later deny the validity of the photos altogether. Most of the crime reporters who were familiar with the case believed that this mysterious figure was responsible for the murder. From their perspective, the inability or refusal to find the man in the yellow hat smacked of a cover-up.

The second mainstream account tied Tortoza's death to an opposition conspiracy hatched within the military and tacitly supported by the press, the private sector, and the US government. According to this version, Tortoza was gunned down by hidden snipers who were planted by the coup plotters with the intention of creating a violent confrontation. The story's logic was baldly sacrificial. It argued that the opposition manufactured a martyr to force the president out of office. It was supported by firsthand experience of the march's bloody conclusion. Witnesses to the event believed that shots were coming from the upper levels of nearby buildings. In the aftermath of the killings, police searched three of these buildings for hidden gunmen and arrested ten suspects. All of them were eventually released. Although a thicket of rumors surrounded these arrests, the police dismissed what they called "the sniper myth" just a few months into their investigation.[51] The story refused to die, in part because of the testimony of Cable News Network

(CNN) correspondent Otto Neustaldt. On April 10, Neustaldt received a phone call telling him that there would be a number of deaths during the demonstration, after which a group of high-ranking military officials would make a statement. Although the CNN correspondent would later distance himself from these statements, most progovernment accounts of April 11 focus on this story as evidence of a premeditated plot.[52]

Edgar Tortoza's Story

Edgar Tortoza and I sat in a café in downtown Caracas overlooking the National Assembly, old newspaper articles spread out in front of us like evidence. "The whole thing was premeditated," he said. "My brother found out something about the newspaper that he was not supposed to know. He wanted to leave." Edgar spoke rapidly and with a strong caraqueño accent, his hands perched atop the blue half-shell of his motorcycle helmet. For more than ten years, he had pushed for a resolution to his brother's death, which he believed was masterminded by Israel Márquez, the former director of Tortoza's own newspaper.[53] Despite his government connections—Edgar was president of the government-backed Association of Victims of April 11 (ASOVIC), and he worked part time for Cilia Flores, one of the most powerful figures in the Chávez government—the case came to a standstill. Edgar and the Tortoza family had few resources at their disposal and he, for one, felt that justice had not been served.[54]

Most of the crime reporters dismissed Edgar's story as political propaganda, but even they admitted that the circumstances surrounding the case were unusual. Hours after Tortoza was killed, the two sons of Israel Márquez along with a third companion, Carlos Aristimuño, were detained as suspects in the murder.[55] All three were carrying concealed weapons (a Walther PPK, a Beretta 9mm, and a Glock 22), and they were in possession of Tortoza's camera. According to the brothers, they were innocent bystanders who were near the head of the march when Tortoza fell. Recognizing the photographer, they contacted their father and rescued the camera at his behest. According to the arresting officer's report, members of the crowd identified the three men as shooters. Gunshot residue tests seemed to confirm that their weapons had not been fired, and so the three were released within twenty-four hours. Nearly four years later, the attorney general's office reopened a case against the arresting officer on charges of tampering with the evidence.[56] According to Edgar, the original residue tests were forged, and they marked the beginning of a cover-up intended to shield the Márquez family and the newspaper.

Following the twists and turns of Edgar's story was like falling into a mystery thriller, complete with missing photos, falsified documents, and a ballistics riddle. It involved everyone including the police, the courts, the public prosecutor's office, and figures inside the Chávez government. At the center of this version was the Márquez family, who plotted the murder and then conspired to cover it up as part of a personal vendetta. Although the story seemed to merge with the larger narrative about April 11 as a "media coup," Edgar maintained that his brother was the victim of a private feud and not a political assassination. In this key respect, his story was at odds with the official versions of what happened on April 11. Rather than associating Tortoza's death with the coup plot, he believed that the circumstances were a diversion that hid a common murder. From Edgar's perspective, unmasking the killer would not unravel the riddle of who was to blame for the violence that precipitated the coup. More striking still, he believed that powerful individuals appointed by the Chávez government were party to the cover-up. Aside from the deceased prosecutor Danilo Anderson (who was investigating Tortoza's death at the time of his own spectacular assassination), Edgar trusted no one, not even his ostensible allies. According to him, powerful "interests" prevented the resolution of the case, interests that implicated actors on both sides of the political divide.

The Photographers' Perspective

Tortoza's brother and his fellow photojournalists faced one another from either side of the chavista/opposition divide. If the former embraced his political position within chavismo, the photographers were associated with the opposition. While the two parties had disparate interpretations about what happened that day, there were surprising resonances between Edgar's story and the one told by the photojournalists. I fully expected that the crime photographers would echo the account given by the crime reporters in which the chavista gunman in the yellow hat killed Tortoza. After all, they worked with the reporters day in and day out, so it would seem natural for them to reach the same conclusion. Much to my surprise, most of the crime photographers explicitly rejected the chavista gunman theory. They remained convinced that Tortoza and the other photographers were targeted by snipers. When I asked who killed Tortoza, they all shrugged their shoulders and said that they did not know and that we would never know. However, they were certain that the shots came from above, although they refused to speculate whether the hidden gunmen were working under the auspices of the government or the opposition. From their perspective, that missed the point entirely.[57]

The point, for the photojournalists, was their own vulnerability. Caught between warring factions, they found themselves the targets of animosity of progovernment supporters and the sacrificial victims of the opposition. As one photographer put it, they were "cannon fodder."[58] Like Edgar, they were suspicious of authorities on both sides of the political divide. If most distanced themselves from the Chávez government, they entertained no illusions about the benevolence of their own employers. Indeed, labor disputes frequently put them at odds with owners and high-ranking directors. Photojournalists and cameramen in Venezuela were poorly remunerated and rarely recognized despite the dangers of their work. They had developed a strong sense of professional solidarity with one another based on shared work experiences and a common socioeconomic background that was different from their employers. The photojournalists were deeply affected by Tortoza's death, and they resented the way that the newspaper deflected financial responsibility. They saw, clearly, that they were the ones taking on all the risks for a cause in which they had little or no stake and from whose success or failure they had little to gain. I interpret their silence about the identity of Tortoza's killer as an indictment of power holders on both sides of the political divide and a tacit acknowledgment that danger came "from above." Their perspective offers us an alternate way of understanding the political dynamic that created two Tortozas, each a reflection of the enemy other.

Taken together, these divergent accounts of Tortoza's death provide a glimpse of the tenuous alliances behind the facade of political polarization. The point is not that multiplicity somehow disproves the division of the country into opposing factions. Rather, it demonstrates that polarization was a powerful political dynamic that ordered disparate social groups into two seemingly coherent political blocs. These factions were always provisional, and a more complete story of the coup would need to consider the social sectors aligned and in conflict for control of the state, not to mention the material conditions governing these relations.

By following the figure of the photojournalist Jorge Tortoza, this chapter demonstrates how the chavista/opposition binary shaped political identities in Caracas. It was not simply what one believed that determines how one was hailed in the Chávez era, but how one was perceived by others. This was hardly a problem for those who openly identified with chavismo or the opposition. However, there were millions of borderline cases in Venezuela, people like Jorge Tortoza whose allegiances were neither obvious nor fixed. For them, the dance of political identity was decidedly more complex.

As it stood, the vast majority of accounts of Tortoza's political identity and the details of his death were also arguments about who bore responsibility for the violence of April 11. They were narratives that created a distinction between friends and enemies, which allowed no space for third parties. When followed to its logical conclusion, this representational practice of sorting the world into opposing camps created a kind of split vision, which, in turn, might explain why, despite their commonalities, the Tortoza family and his fellow photojournalists were estranged from the start, or why a third narrative—of shared responsibility between parties on both sides of the political divide—was rarely acknowledged.

The Photographer's Body

The Tortoza case was just one example of the political logic that divided Caracas into two camps, each a reflection of the other. Just as there was a chavista Tortoza and an opposition Tortoza, nearly every issue of political import in Caracas appeared in split screen. A visitor would quickly notice that the state press and the private press seemed to report from two different worlds. It was not simply that these outlets had different standards by which they defined newsworthiness, but they had different beliefs about what was factual. Dueling narratives about violent crime, health care, urban infrastructure, the impact of social programs, and the state of the national economy reflected two conflicting attempts at constituting reality.

One of the challenges of an ethnographic approach to Caracas in the Chávez era was finding a space from which to understand the phenomenon of political polarization without succumbing to it. What I have argued in this chapter is that, starting at the level of collective identity formation, we find important parallels that linked Chávez's Bolivarian Revolution and the movement against it. Both movements adhered to a populist logic in which they defined themselves in the role of victims in opposition to an external enemy. By pointing to this parallel I am not suggesting that these two movements were identical. There were worlds of difference between chavismo and the opposition, which are reflected in the distinct positions that chavismo and the opposition took up on such issues as the economy, the role of the state, and foreign relations. That said, it is important not to lose sight of the fact that these political identities were nonetheless linked, and that both derived their legitimacy from the claim to represent the sovereign will of the people against the machinations of the enemy other.

Photojournalists like Jorge Tortoza were essential to these populist performances of sovereignty. They mediated the distance between the corporeal bodies of citizens and the imagined body politic, between mortal persons and the immortal "people." The suffering body bridged this divide. If such suffering is indispensable for the functioning of modern sovereignty, it is the photographer-as-journalist who transforms the suffering body into spectacle.[59] This is not simply a mechanical transformation in which bodies necessarily become fodder for a political machine (although this is one possibility). Rather, the spectacle of suffering is a performance through which popular sovereignty is repeatedly asserted, subverted, and reconfigured. In populism, these spectacles of suffering—of crime, punishment, torture, disaster, deprivation, and abject poverty—link the performance of political identities to the figure of the victim.

Populist mobilizations are justified by an idiom that internalizes sacrifice and externalizes guilt. It is through this sacrificial idiom that victims are transformed into martyrs and lines of allegiance are drawn. In Tortoza's case, death made him a candidate for martyrdom for both the opposition and chavismo. His transformation from victim into martyr was incomplete for two reasons: first, it was impossible to resolve his existence in life with a simple political identity upon his death; second, it was never clear who bore ultimate responsibility for his murder. These unsuccessful attempts to appropriate his suffering allow us to glimpse the manner in which populist movements attempt to manifest popular sovereignty. It is through victimhood that "the people" can be, momentarily, conjured.

This yearning for an unmediated expression of sovereign power, in which the people become flesh, is a yearning for an impossible union. The experiences of photojournalists attest to the fraught practice of suturing diffuse, fragmented bodies into a single body politic. Nowhere is this difficulty more evident than in the testimonies of photographers who cover violence.

Take the case of Tortoza's colleague Fernando Sánchez who was haunted by memories of April 11. It was not just the death of a close friend that troubled him but also his own divided loyalties in the aftermath of the shooting. Seeing Tortoza's lifeless body on the ground, Sánchez's first instinct was to marshal help, to lend comfort, to mourn. Yet, amid the trauma and tragedy of Tortoza's suffering, Sánchez was aware of his own predicament. When he returned to the newsroom, he could not arrive empty-handed. To do so would mean tendering his resignation. Thinking back on the incident, he imagined the voice of his old colleague chiding him, "You have to do it. You have to take the photo. If I were in your place, I would do the same." That disembodied voice provided some solace for the traumatic memory of training his camera lens on the body of his dying friend. He referred to it as an act of *desdoblamiento*, which literally means "splitting" or "dividing" and figuratively refers to an out-of-body experience. In that moment, Sánchez imagined himself divided between two bodies, trapped between a body in pain, which desperately called out for his attention, and an imagined body politic that it was his duty to serve.[60]

If populism attempts to unify disparate experiences under a common political banner, ethnography reveals the contingency of these populist articulations. Both chavismo and the opposition were fraught with internal contradictions that the spectacle of suffering effectively covered over. The point is not to condemn populism but to probe the limits of democratic politics. If popular sovereignty is the positive condition of our political present, what happens when that sovereignty is stripped of its liberal garments? At the dawn of Thatcherism in the United Kingdom in the 1980s, Stuart Hall cast the future as a competition between popular-democratic and authoritarian populisms.[61] Whether or not we accept this as an accurate description of Venezuela in the Chávez era, Hall's analysis returns in the form of a question. Is it possible to imagine a popular solidarity that starts with a community of sufferers yet resists the temptation to extract its pound of flesh?

pop. vs. authoritarian populism

SIX

Denouncers

The former minister of communication, Andrés Izarra, smirked. "It's a piece of shit, full of inaccuracies," he said, referring to a study not unlike my own. It took me the better part of a year to track down this interview; I was intrigued to finally meet the man whose fingerprints were on so much of the government's communications strategy. His remarks, though, caught me off guard. "It's like comparing pears and avocados," Izarra continued, shaking his head with disapproval. The researchers had refused to recognize the particularities of the press in Venezuela, treating it instead like a subspecies of North American or Western European journalism. If these two styles of reporting might look similar from a distance, they were in reality quite different. They were pears and avocados. On this point, at least, we agreed.

Research on the press and politics in Latin America has been mired in an alien paradigm for some time now. The starting point for investigation is a liberal-democratic framework that fits awkwardly with the norms and practices of journalists in much of the region. Actually existing democracies deserve better. They deserve to be taken seriously and on their own terms. In this spirit, the following chapter makes a simple proposition. The journalism practiced in Caracas during the Chávez era coalesced around an ethos of truth telling.[1] This ethos was rooted in an agonistic vision of democracy, which distinguished it from the style of journalism ascendant in North America for much of the twentieth century. The upshot of my proposition is that journalists in Caracas followed a distinctive set of professional norms and practices, which were tied to qualitatively different beliefs about the role that the press should play in a democratic polity.[2]

Denuncias provided a window onto this journalistic ethos. My contention is that denuncias are acts of truth telling that constitute the popular will. The press was an effective avenue for denouncing injustice because it appealed directly to the will of the people—a power that was, ostensibly, above the police, the courts, and the law itself.

As an outsider, I found denuncias both familiar and strange: familiar because of their emphasis on revelation as a public good and strange because of their belligerence and their tendency to propagate wildly. It is tempting to imagine denuncias as a Latin American twist on investigative reporting, à la Watergate, but such a comparison would be misleading. A more apt analogue is Émile Zola's "J'accuse." Truth was the central conceit of Zola's thunderous appeal to the president of France. The Dreyfus affair was a crime against French society, and Zola set out to right that wrong by pitting himself against Dreyfus's accusers. "As they have dared, so I shall dare. Dare to tell the truth, as I have pledged to tell it, in full, since the normal channels of justice have failed to do so." Denunciations of crime and corruption in Caracas held out a similarly revolutionary promise to which everyone, even the president, was ultimately accountable.

This chapter situates the practice of denunciation and its concomitant ethos of truth telling within a wider history of popular struggles in the Americas. Specifically, it looks at the rise of denunciation as a journalistic practice in Venezuela during the 1980s and 1990s, a moment of profound crisis in which the private press emerged as Venezuela's most influential political institution. Close attention to the practice of denunciation during this period reveals a relationship between the press and populism that media scholars have largely ignored. Although there is a massive body of literature about this crisis and the rise of Hugo Chávez, little has been written on the role of the press. This elision is surprising. Among Venezuelan journalists, it is widely acknowledged that the private press played a key role in the return of populism and the eventual rise of the Bolivarian Revolution. The antagonism that would later put Chávez and the press on opposite sides of the political divide has effectively concealed their historic entanglement.

Before reaching back into Venezuelan history, however, I want to return to Izarra and one of the more exceptional denuncias that I witnessed during the course of my research alongside the crime reporters. The episode is an example of denunciation at its most militant, and it serves notice that the politics of truth telling revolves around something qualitatively different than publics and their spheres.

The Morgue Photo

About a year after our conversation, the minister smirked again, this time on live television. The setting: a debate on CNN Español. The subject: an hour-long documentary, "Los guardianes de Chávez" (the guardians of Chávez), produced for the Spanish news program *REC reporteros cuatro* and disseminated in Latin America by CNN. Izarra was invited to comment on the documentary opposite criminologist Roberto Briceño-León and veteran police chief Elisio Guzmán. "Los guardianes" clearly touched a nerve. It linked rampant violence in Caracas to militant leftist groups, or so-called collectives, associated with President Chávez. Izarra, himself a former CNN correspondent, was visibly annoyed, and he reproached the channel for promoting "journalistic pornography." Later in the program, when one of the other participants began discussing the homicide rates in Caracas, Izarra laughed derisively, clearly in disagreement with the assessment that Venezuela's capital was the most violent city in the world. It was not a polite exchange. After the segment aired, many caraqueños took umbrage. They accused the ex-minister of laughing about insecurity. Izarra backpedaled. His allies made public shows of support.

The carousel of accusations and counteraccusations about "Los guardianes" and Izarra's response was a good example of the kind of denuncias that audiences expected from politicians and pundits alike. Parliamentary elections were just around the corner. In a month, Venezuelans would go to the polls to vote for the representatives to the National Assembly. Given the context, the whole episode was rather pedestrian and, in all likelihood, it would have been forgotten were it not for the photo.

On August 13, 2010, two days after the CNN debacle, *El Nacional* published its response to Izarra—a graphic, front-page photograph of eleven naked corpses strewn haphazardly about the Caracas city morgue (fig. 6.1). The image was intended to shock. It succeeded. Rarely did anything so lurid appear in the press, much less on the front page of an established broadsheet like *El Nacional*. Upon seeing the cover, I braced for a backlash. There was no public access inside the morgue, and cameras were strictly forbidden.[3] A few years earlier, another newspaper did an exposé accompanied by similar images. Just before the piece ran, one of the authors warned me that the photographs would cause a firestorm. As it turned out, her editor buried the pictures in the middle of the newspaper, and the story passed without incident; however, it underscored their potential volatility.

Twenty-four hours after the photo appeared, the atmosphere around the morgue turned toxic. The national director of the investigative police, Wilmer Flores Trosel, announced that he was pressing charges against the newspaper for violating Venezuela's child protection law.[4] It was under the same law that the national ombudswoman, Gabriela Ramírez, filed an official denuncia. Three days later the Twelfth Tribunal for the Protection

6.1. The morgue photo, front page of *El Nacional*, August 13, 2010.
(Imaging by James Gehrt.)

of Children and Adolescents passed a general restraining order prohibiting all media outlets from publishing "violent, bloody, or grotesque images that in one form or another violate the psychic and moral condition of children and adolescents."[5] El Nacional and another newspaper that reproduced that photograph, Tal Cual, were hit with heavy sanctions and ordered to refrain from publishing "images, information, and publicity of any kind" that could be broadly construed as violent or provocative or that otherwise dealt with death and dying. The wording seemed to suggest that even the most quotidian form of crime reporting was prohibited.

Rather than disappearing, the controversy gained steam. El Nacional used the restraining order as a platform to launch a raft of denuncias against both crime and government censorship. I was sitting with about a dozen reporters from various media outlets at the usual café on the day that the restraining order was announced. Attention fixed on El Nacional's defiant response. The front page of the newspaper screamed, "Publication of images and news about violence prohibited." Just below the headline, in bold red type, "censored" was written across a pair of empty image boxes. One of the crime reporters picked up the newspaper, thumbed to the editorial page, and began reading aloud, approvingly,[6]

> When a government exhausts its capacity to lie and loses its ability to deceive a society, it resorts to violence against the media. People need to be informed and know the truth of what is happening in the country, in the city where they live, and at their places of work. One requirement of modern life is that no one has the right—be it a judge, a minister, or a prosecutor—to arbitrarily impede citizens from accessing information that they want and need.[7]

He read on. The editorial denounced government lies, the violation of press freedom, the enrichment of a corrupt class of bureaucrats, the cynicism of state officials, and the rise of leftist extremism that was transforming Venezuela into a new version of Cuba, South Korea, or Iran. Upon finishing, the reporter looked up and clapped theatrically. "Bravo! Bravo! That is exactly what they need to do." Turning to the journalist beside him, he tapped emphatically on the table. "They've got to keep this up. They can't let this one go." His colleague nodded her head in agreement. "One of the editors was saying that they are thinking about running headlines about insecurity every day until the election."[8] For the next month, El Nacional did exactly this. It ran story after story about crime under a banner decorated with a censorship sign (see fig. 6.2 below).

Almost overnight, the morgue photo morphed into a whole series of political demands that far exceeded the problem of crime in Caracas. More than simply a denunciation of urban violence, news coverage of crime symbolized opposition to the Chávez government broadly construed. The point is not simply that the morgue photograph was "political." Rather, it laid the groundwork for a particular kind of community that was constituted around the shared experience of victimhood, be it at the hands of violent offenders or government censors.

Truth in Journalism

As a journalistic practice, denunciation long predated the Chávez era. The rise of denuncias was tied to the growing power of the press in Latin America during the second half of the twentieth century, especially during the 1980s and 1990s. The phenomenon was not limited to Caracas or even Venezuela. Rather, it was part of a region-wide movement in which Latin American journalists transformed themselves into crusaders against the abuse of state power.[9] Seemingly overnight, the presses of Latin America were flooded with muckraking stories about political malfeasance, economic corruption, and human rights abuses.[10] This was a profound shift. For much of the twentieth century, the mainstream media in Latin America was subservient to ruling elites.[11] Military regimes and entrenched political parties used a combination of coercion and brute force to silence opposition from the mass media. Under these circumstances, it was rare for news outlets to denounce wrongdoing. This pattern of behavior suddenly changed in the 1980s and 1990s with a series of press-driven scandals in Argentina, Brazil, Colombia, Mexico, Paraguay, Peru, and Venezuela. Unlike its "lapdog" predecessors, this new brand of journalism prioritized the discovery and denunciation of such wrongdoings.[12] News outlets adopted a crusading style of reporting, which exposed the sordid underbelly of ruling elites and transformed the press into a formidable political force. Nowhere was the rise of press power more evident than in Caracas, where journalists, scholars, and pundits observed the emergence of what was widely known as *el periodismo de denuncia*—the journalism of denunciation.[13]

The euphoria of democratization that swept across Latin America at the end of the twentieth century led many observers to imagine that the journalism of denunciation presaged a shift toward liberal democracy. Take, for example, the well-known historian and literary critic Angel Rama. In his description of the Argentine reporter Rodolfo Walsh, Rama extols him as the archetypal "denouncer-journalist, who is dedicated only to the truth, who discovers secret plots and brings them to light with the written word, the guardian of honesty, the incorruptible servant of justice, in sum, this descendent of North American liberalism, more mythic than real, in whom certain central cultural values of the past have persisted."[14] Lost in Rama's celebration of the denouncer-journalist is the fact that these ideals of truth telling have been anathema to the North American tradition of reporting since the late nineteenth century.[15] What Rama depicts better fits the Spanish-American tradition of representation described by François-Xavier Guerra or Jesús Martín-Barbero.[16] Historians and literary scholars have explored this tradition at great length, describing its impact on everything from elections to telenovelas; however, its importance is most explicitly spelled out in the body of research on *testimonio* (testimonial writing).

Testimonio helps us understand the journalism of denunciation as a cultural form whose political stakes are linked to a particular representational logic.[17] There have been numerous debates about the formal and historical parameters of testimonio that I will not revisit here.[18] Suffice it to say that during the late 1960s it gained recognition as a distinctive literary genre in which the popular sectors, long silenced, asserted their right to self-representation. George Yúdice has defined testimonial writing as "an authentic narrative, told by a witness who is moved to narrate by the urgency of a situation (e.g. war, oppression, revolution, etc.)." It is not biography per se because the witness is doing more than describing his or her own life story. He or she is performing as a self-conscious agent of *el pueblo* who denounces "a situation of exploitation and oppression."[19] Testimonio is popular culture in that its urgency and authenticity are predicated on its identification with popular struggles. The ideal protagonist of testimonio is both a representative of the popular sectors and a witness to their suffering.

The power of testimonio—what captured the attention of scholars worldwide—was its promise to move people who had been marginalized throughout history to the center of national and international politics.[20] Testimonio represented the hope for a popular democratic movement in which subaltern populations finally claimed their rightful place as citizens. According to John Beverley's famous formulation, testimonio was nothing less than the cultural form taken by popular struggles for political representation in the late twentieth century.[21] Just as the eighteenth-century novel heralded the rise of the European bourgeoisie, testimonio was the literary expression of popular resistance in the Americas.

Scholarly interest in testimonio as an emergent cultural form focused almost exclusively on film and book-length works, yet the alternative press played an equally important role in popular struggles. Like testimonio, the alternative press functioned as a forum for popular resistance in which tropes of witnessing and denunciations of wrongdoing were laden with a palpable sense of political urgency. And like testimonio, it provided a medium through which popular political identities became visible as such. From the standpoint of cultural production, testimonio and alternative journalism emerged from the same historical conjuncture, included many of the same figures, and drew on similar representational strategies.[22]

The practice of denunciation marks a subtle but important departure from the ideal of "objectivity" enshrined in North American journalism. "Truthfulness" is the dominant ideal that is recognized by Venezuelan audiences and journalists alike. While facts are one important element in constructing a truthful account, Latin American journalists do not put their faith in facts alone. Truthfulness means recognizing that facts are situated within a sociopolitical context and that journalism thus is an explicitly political endeavor. These values are implicit in the practice of denunciation, which channels popular outrage over persistent injustice and the hidden wrongdoings of the powerful.[23]

A brief illustration must suffice in place of further elaboration on "objectivity" and "truthfulness" as two regimes of truth.[24] In the Anglo-American tradition, news outlets are frequently accused of bias, but they are almost never accused of lying. Until quite recently, labeling someone a "liar" was almost unthinkable for serious journalistic outlets in the United States.[25] In Venezuela, the charge of bias is superfluous and never made because it is assumed from the start; however, it is quite common to call a news outlet, a journalist, or a politician a "liar" because the measuring stick for journalistic integrity is truthfulness rather than objective distance.

The point is not to elevate one ideal—truthfulness or objectivity—over the other; rather, it is to insist that different regimes of truth produce different outcomes and function according to different logics. Objectivity, as it has come to be understood in the Anglo-American tradition, is tied to ideals of consensus and the public good. These beliefs are encapsulated in Jürgen Habermas's description of the bourgeoisie public sphere, the promises and perils of which are well known.[26] Truthfulness, as it functions in Latin America, is more closely associated with ideals of self-determination and popular sovereignty (i.e., government of the people, by the people, and for the people). It is not the public but *el pueblo* that dominates discourse on the body politic. This is not to say that a powerful belief in the public good is absent in Latin America or that the Anglo-American tradition has abandoned "the people" and popular sovereignty. Nor is it to say that these particular ideological configurations will persist.[27] Both concepts of the people and the public were crucial to the development of modern republics at the dawn of the nineteenth century, and they remain constitutive poles of democratic representation. However, it is fair to say that in Latin America, "the people" and popular sovereignty are the ideals that are most often invoked in political discourse, including the discourse of democracy.

We must situate the journalism of denunciation against a historical and ideological backdrop in which "the people" represents the sine qua non of politics. As a style of reporting, it is concerned with mobilizing popular, democratic resistance to the wrongdoings of the powerful. Journalistic denuncias are not intended to foster deliberation on the part of one or many publics. Rather, they are imagined as an articulation of the popular will. In Venezuela at the end of the twentieth century, taking the side of the people against entrenched interests was a conscious choice on the part of a handful of powerful journalists and one that coincided with the professional obligation to expose the truth. Putting themselves at the service of the popular will, journalists became political protagonists who helped create the conditions for populist mobilization.

The Delinquent Society

History is instructive because it underscores what was at stake in denunciations of rampant crime. Starting in the 1970s and accelerating through the late 1980s into the 1990s, outrage over political and economic corruption dominated the Venezuelan media. Press-fueled denuncias of corruption would eventually help topple the two-party system that had governed the country since 1958. More important for our purposes, these denuncias of corruption created the conditions of possibility for the return of populism. During this epoch a small cadre of denouncer-journalists emerged, whose thoroughgoing critiques of corruption transformed the press into a springboard for populist mobilization.

What animated popular outrage against political corruption was the crisis of the Venezuelan petrostate. For three decades tremendous oil wealth created a golden age of prosperity that insulated Venezuela from the social and economic strife afflicting much of Latin America and the Caribbean. The country's two-party democracy rested atop an oil platform and the explicit promise that oil rents were public patrimony. When that wealth dried up and the political pacts between elites began to unravel, one question reverberated in the collective consciousness: "Where has the money gone?"[28] The government was pressed to explain the sudden failure of Venezuela's fortunes, and accusations of corruption and ineptitude were leveled at the two main political parties, Acción Democrática (AD) and Partido Sociál Cristiano (known as COPEI). Popular opinion held that these two parties were staffed by a coterie of incompetents, liars, and thieves, who had squandered the bounty of successive oil booms.[29]

As the promise of national prosperity soured, it was replaced with a discourse about a corrupt, delinquent society fueled by greed and rotting from the inside out.[30] A crime had been committed against the Venezuelan people, or so the story went, and the press set out to discover "who done it."

Journalists did not create the crisis that engulfed Venezuela, but they certainly channeled popular responses to it. As a result of extensive media coverage, corruption scandals became the most visible explanation for the country's declining fortunes. In one neat package, the corruption hypothesis explained why the project of modernity had failed and who was to blame. This is not to say that corruption was a figment of the journalistic imagination. There is good evidence that fraudulent dealings were on the rise in Venezuela,[31] but it is important to stress that corruption was just one facet of a much larger crisis tied to the perils of Venezuela's rentier economy[32] and fractious, intraparty struggles.[33] Nonetheless, corruption came to symbolize the enormity of Venezuela's political and economic failures. Corruption was the master signifier for a whole host of problems that extended far beyond the misuse of public patrimony. And it was underneath the banner of anti-corruption campaigns that a series of new populist movements became visible for the first time.[34]

No politician was more closely linked to corruption than Carlos Andrés Pérez, the two-time president of Venezuela. His first administration (1974–79) overlapped with a massive oil boom, which flooded the country with foreign currency. By the end of his term, the dream of using petrodollars to build a "Grand Venezuela" had soured, replaced with talk of oil's corrupting influence. Evidence suggests that illicit dealings expanded under the administrations of Luis Herrera Campins (1979–84) and Jaime Lusinchi (1984–89). By the time Pérez took office for the second time (1989–93), corruption scandals were rampant. *The Dictionary of Corruption*, a three-volume compendium dedicated to Venezuelan corruption scandals, describes this period as the frenetic culmination of a creeping social decay in which "all the wrath of the gods is unleashed." During the late 1980s and early 1990s, "administrative disorder grows at a vertiginous speed and magnitude, and denuncias multiply . . . as if there is a pool of corruption cases that appear with certain frequency in the collective conscience only to be forgotten all over again, like wayward phantoms searching for the grave."[35]

The spike in corruption scandals at the end of the 1980s reflected a shift in the practices of mainstream news organizations in Venezuela. It was not that corruption suddenly proliferated but that the press began speaking out against it.[36] For decades mainstream news outlets were complicit in covering up stories of official misconduct. Corruption was a public secret that was widely acknowledged, seldom denounced, and almost never investigated by the media.[37] However, as the crisis of the Venezuelan state deepened, the mechanism of controls that kept the press in check diminished appreciably.[38] By the end of President Lusinchi's term in office, "the media had become a sounding board for anyone who wished to make a denuncia" about official corruption.[39] Journalists took it upon themselves to battle the great sin of Venezuelan society, the criminality gnawing away at the very soul of the moral order. A handful of powerful editors, owners, and journalists pursued accusations of corruption with such single-minded determination that commentators heralded the genesis of a new style of journalism. The expression *el periodismo de denuncia* originated at the close of the 1980s. By 1990 it was sufficiently well established for the National College of Journalists to hold a four-day forum in Caracas called "The Journalism of Denunciation as a Social Good."[40]

Elsewhere, I have detailed the seven-decade career of José Vicente Rangel, one of Venezuela's most famous denouncer-journalists.[41] For much of the twentieth century, Rangel was a powerful voice of opposition to the government—first to the Pérez Jiménez dictatorship and later to the pacted democracy of AD and COPEI. During the crisis of the 1980s and 1990s, he formulated a string of denuncias of corruption and criminality, which he supported with strong documentary evidence. Rangel's most famous denuncia, the case of the *partida secreta* (secret party), revealed that President Carlos Andrés Pérez had illegally diverted 250 million bolivars (more than 17 million US dollars) toward the Nicaraguan presidential elections. Details of the case were first revealed in November 1992 on Rangel's television program, *José Vicente Hoy*. The denuncia led to the president's impeachment in 1993 and an eventual criminal conviction for misappropriation of public funds.

Most histories of this period zero in on 1992 as the year that Hugo Chávez burst onto the political scene as one of the leaders of a failed coup d'état that had strong popular support. This rise of Chávez and the Bolivarian Revolution came to overshadow the role that the press and denouncer-journalists including Rangel played in populist mobilization throughout the 1980s and 1990s. We are left with the image of a charismatic leader who emerged fully formed from popular unrest ready to heroically (or opportunistically) shoulder responsibility in a country where no one was responsible for anything. Yet the stage was set long before the failed 1992 coup d'état. While Chávez and his fellow military officers were secretly plotting revolution, the press was openly questioning the legitimacy of Venezuela's political establishment. Denuncias of corruption channeled frustrated demands into a wave of anti-institutional sentiment. The journalism of denunciation further legitimized opposition to the old system and helped create the conditions of possibility for the rise of new populist projects. I stress the plurality of populisms because chavismo was never a foregone conclusion. It was simply one of several possibilities that emerged out of the crisis. After the fall of Pérez, the vast majority of political candidates were competing to direct the crescendo of popular outrage.

Populism and the Press

If President Chávez and his supporters recognized the power of journalistic denuncias like the morgue photo, it was because a similar campaign of denunciation helped create the conditions of possibility for the Bolivarian Revolution in the first place. The power of denuncias was not limited to the revelation of wrongdoing. Denuncias mattered because they functioned as an articulating practice that, under the right circumstances, created the semblance of the popular will. Here, the work of Ernesto Laclau is indispensable for understanding the latent potential of denuncias.

For years, one puzzle that confounded scholars of populism was its lack of ideological coherence. Rather than representing a single constituency or cause, populism mobilizes heterogeneous, often contradictory demands.[42] What holds together such a coalition? How does a movement at cross-purposes with itself emerge in the first place? Ernesto Laclau has gone furthest in explaining this enigma. According to Laclau, populist movements emerge when a series of heterogeneous demands are discursively joined into a "chain of equivalence." To illustrate this logic, he gives us the example of "a large mass of agrarian migrants who settle in the shantytowns on the outskirts of a developing industrial city," which I quoted in the introduction. This group of settlers has a specific request—to help solve issues of housing. If this request is satisfied, then the matter is resolved. However, if the demand goes unfulfilled, then it begins to articulate with other unsatisfied demands. Over time, a chain of unfulfilled demands can eventually overwhelm the system's ability to absorb them.[43]

Laclau's example demonstrates how otherwise unrelated demands are linked through their shared opposition to the institutional system. How are these demands carried beyond their immediate context? What are the mechanisms through which this logic of equivalence transforms diffuse pockets of discontent into movements with a wide base of support? This is where Louis Althusser's concept of "articulation," itself borrowed from semiotics, becomes essential.[44]

Articulation can be defined as the discursive practice whereby disparate elements are joined into an apparently seamless whole. In this sense it draws on the two senses of the word *articulate*, which means "to link" and "to speak."[45] The concept is particularly useful because it allows us to see the contingent, historically situated circumstances that help determine any particular political formation. Articulation is more than simply a sociostructural fact. In respect to populist movements, articulation is also the practice through which chains of equivalence are formed.[46] In Venezuela and much of Latin America, journalistic denuncias have functioned as an articulating practice through which demands are transformed into the raw material of national popular movements. To state it another way, mass mediated denuncias join otherwise disparate demands for political change through appeals to shared discontent. They are the vehicles through which chains of equivalence take shape.

As an articulating practice, denuncias allow us to examine the activities that give birth to "the people," that all-important subject of populist movements. Like "the public," the will of "the people" is never self-evident; it is a performance of collective identity. Populist movements invariably invoke the righteousness of the people against the transgressions of the powerful. While the former is portrayed as the embodiment of good, the latter is treated as the personification of evil. The creation of an external enemy is crucial to the articulation of populist identities, which I have described in the preceding chapter through the story of Jorge Tortoza. Here, I want to focus on the "linking" and "voicing" effects of denuncias.

The journalism of denunciation articulates popular identities through two simultaneous processes; it *links* disparate social sectors behind a common cause, and it *gives voice* to the discontents of an otherwise mute entity, "the people." Properly speaking, these are part of the same process; however, for purposes of analysis, we can distinguish between a *linking effect* and a *voicing effect*.

THE LINKING EFFECT. Cross-class alliances are a hallmark of populist movements. During the 1980s and 1990s, denuncias of corruption created the terrain on which populist alliances could form between otherwise unaligned sectors of Venezuelan society. It is worth noting that corruption was not the only grievance that people had during this period. It was not even the principal concern among voters. Opinion polls from the height of the crisis show that unemployment and inflation were the primary issues of the day.[47] What such polls elide is the fact that there was no consensus over the necessary steps to improve Venezuela's economic crisis. Neoliberal adjustments roiled the popular sectors, while the middle classes were silently complicit in such policies. What these otherwise disparate sectors had in common was shared outrage over corruption and the seeming impunity of powerful elites. The journalistic crusade against corruption created a common cause that transformed these sectors into a powerful political block.

The linking effect of denuncias was evident in the diverse coalition of journalists that came together behind accusations of corruption. This relatively small group of denouncer-journalists included José Vicente Rangel, Marcel Granier, Rafael Poleo, Alfredo Peña, and Miguel Henrique Otero. These were strange bedfellows. Granier (owner of Radio Caracas Television and host of the show *Primero Plano*) was a champion of neoliberalism. He founded the Roraima Group, which argued that the country's crisis was the result of an omnipotent state and ossified political parties.[48] Rangel (host of *José Vicente Hoy* and a number of newspaper columns) and Poleo (director of the newspaper *El Nuevo País* and the magazine *Zeta*) were, in contrast, outspoken critics of neoliberalism. The former was a man of the left, who went on to become a key figure within chavismo. The later was a long-standing member of Acción Democrática who opposed the party's embrace of privatization and austerity. Otero (owner of *El Nacional*) could best be described as a liberal centrist, and his political allegiances vacillated. He eventually teamed up with Peña (host of a news program on Venevisión and future editor of *El Nacional*) who started his journalistic career as a militant leftist before drifting toward the center. Politically, these denouncer-journalists represented constituencies that had very little in common other than opposition to the status quo.[49]

THE VOICING EFFECT. Populist movements become coherent through claims to represent the unified will of the people. By speaking out against rampant corruption, Venezuelan journalists positioned themselves as the voice of the silent majority. They became the conduit through which popular outrage manifested itself. If the journalism of denunciation was unashamedly partisan, this partisanship was not exclusively tied to any particular party or political faction. Time and again, high-profile journalists justified the campaign against corruption by declaring their allegiance to "the people," "the country," or "the majority of decent citizens." Through denuncias of corruption, journalists transformed themselves into the people's champions, a role often reserved for charismatic leaders. Although much of the writing on populism in Venezuela focuses on the person of Hugo Chávez, the private press was actively fulfilling this role long before his rise to prominence. News outlets such as *El Nacional, El Nuevo País,* and RCTV assumed the position of political vanguard. For a time, the media rivaled and even surpassed the executive, the legislative, and the judiciary branches as the most influential institution of state power in Venezuela. As described by sociologist Tulio Hernández, "The media began to echo the frustrations of the population, becoming more active than ever in the diffusion of denuncias of corruption. The majority of media corporations assumed an open position to all kinds of information, denuncias, or analyses that confronted [the political] leadership, marking the beginning of a battle that pitted the media against the government, the institutions of the state, the political parties, and ultimately the ruling class."[50]

By taking on corruption in the name of the Venezuelan people, the journalism of denunciation augmented the power and prestige of the press. In turn, it was through the press that nascent populist movements became visible as such.

The linking effect and the voicing effect are two aspects of denunciation as an articulating practice, which allows us to see the discursive labor that goes into creating the will of the people. Before "the people" can emerge as the protagonists of popular struggles, it must first be invoked. Denuncias provide the performative scaffolding for such invocations. They are the discursive form through which a multitude of demands are transformed into an expression of the popular will. Like all performances, denuncias do not necessarily achieve their desired outcome—they are not always "felicitous," as J. L. Austin would say.[51] Timing is essential, as is the skill of the performer. Here it is useful to return to the morgue photo, as an example of how denuncias of crime and insecurity intersected with competing invocations of the popular will.

Populist Denuncias

Compared with the denuncias of corruption that gave voice to the popular uprisings of the 1980s and 1990s, the morgue photo was a clumsy, all-too-transparent affair. That transparency is useful because it makes it easy to observe how both the government and the opposition attempted to mobilize Venezuelans in the name of security. Let me begin with the opposition, specifically with the newspaper *El Nacional.*

El Nacional aspired to be the broadsheet of Venezuela's political vanguard. The newspaper regularly waded into the thick of political battles, and its owner Miguel Henrique Otero had a penchant for denunciation. During the crisis of the 1990s, *El Nacional* was a tireless critic of the country's two political parties. Otero's newspaper strongly supported the candidacy of Hugo Chávez before breaking with the charismatic former colonel barely one year into his presidency. For most of the Chávez era, *El Nacional* was a leading voice of the opposition. The morgue photo was consonant with its provocative style of denunciation. In an interview with CNN, Otero explained that "the editorial reasoning behind the photo was to create a shock so that people could in some way react to a situation that the government has done absolutely nothing about."[52]

There was more to the morgue photo than just shock. News coverage of crime at *El Nacional* concentrated almost exclusively on two themes: crime victims and anticrime protests.[53] Ronna Rísquez, the section editor in charge of the crime desk, explained that the newspaper prioritized victimhood over criminality. "We always try to focus on the victims, not the perpetrators. The pieces in which we focus on delinquents or criminal groups are exceptional." When I asked Rísquez the reason for this editorial focus, she took me through a quick thought exercise: "Suppose that in Venezuela there are approximately fifty thousand delinquents. That's a lot, but in a country of twenty-eight million, that's an infinitesimal number. In other words, the majority of us are victims. There are fifty thousand people out there who are affecting more than twenty-seven million. What I am saying is, *we are all victims*" (my emphasis).[54] Crime victimhood provided not only the grounds of a shared experience but also the basis for making a collective demand in Laclau's sense of the term. Giving voice to such demands was what inspired *El Nacional's* coverage of demonstrations against insecurity. Rísquez explained, "We try to underline the spontaneous actions of the communities and of civil society that are demanding security and appealing for their right to life."[55] The point of covering protests was to "awaken public consciousness" so that people could feel empowered to push for an effective response from the government.

These twin themes of crime victimhood and anticrime protests allowed *El Nacional* to field a steady stream of denuncias, which simultaneously linked diverse strata of Venezuelan society vis-à-vis the mutual experience of violent crime and voiced popular discontent with governmental failure. The morgue photo exemplified both facets of this strategy. The naked, brutalized corpses were framed as a metaphor of crime victimhood and as a denuncia of government inaction; the subsequent campaign against the censorship of crime news was couched as a protest in which the newspaper interceded on behalf of the Venezuelan people (fig. 6.2).

6.2. *El Nacional*'s campaign of anticrime, anticensorship denuncias featured eye-catching headlines. (*Top*) Front page for August 19, 2010. The headline reads, "Do you believe that the media is the main reason for the sensation of insecurity?" (*Bottom*) Front page for August 20, 2010. The headline reads, "Official 2009 Figures: Total Homicides 19,113." (Imaging by James Gehrt.)

The government clearly recognized the political threat posed by the morgue photo and denuncias of crime more broadly. Theirs was a bifurcated response. Although the Chávez government openly admitted the extent of the problem, it also denounced media coverage of crime as politically motivated (at best) and as a potential threat to national security (at worst). In this particular instance, *El Nacional* was accused not only of morbid sensationalism but more dangerously of trying to create a "matrix of opinion" that could topple the government. In a book coauthored and coedited with Félix López, the previously mentioned minister, Andrés Izarra, drew together an array of commentaries that likened the episode to the following: a lynching, an act of media terrorism, the assassination of Gaitán, the death of Simón Bolívar's dream of a Gran Colombia, the working of the fifth column in fascist Spain, the murder of Che Guevara, the occupation of Afghanistan by the United States, a psi-ops campaign, fourth-generation warfare, and a form of mass mediated necrophilia. Above and beyond all these media-assisted atrocities, they argued that the morgue photo reenacted the steps leading up to April 11 and the failed coup d'état.[56]

Chávez himself weighed in forcefully on the subject on several occasions, "calling attention to the strategy of defamation and intrigue" and "alerting *el pueblo*" that the media were attempting to sow discord.[57] More than a year later, in an address to the National Assembly, he returned to the subject of the morgue photo:

> There are some media outlets that send journalists to the morgue to see how many cadavers arrive. Some think that we are hiding the truth. No? This is something sick. Counting how many cadavers there are in the morgue. On one occasion they took a terrible, terrible photograph of the morgue. No? Now who is doing this? I am sure that they are not contributing to solving the problem. No. It makes them happy [pause]. I believe, I believe. Pardon me in advance if I am wrong [pause], but I think that those that are hunting deaths, I imagine that they're happy to see how many cadavers there are. The more there are the better it is for them. This is terrible. It is terrible and it's part of the problem.[58]

This was not simply about refuting the opposition. It was about rallying support through denuncias of an ongoing plot. Security was national security, and news of crime was not innocent information but rather a tool of political struggle.

Denuncias begot denuncias and more denuncias. In all this, it was hard to determine who or what was ultimately responsible for the horrific state of the morgue, the violence on the streets, the failure of the police, or the state of political upheaval. Some might point to the whirlpool of accusations that swirled around the morgue photo as evidence that objectivity should take precedence over truth telling or that the journalistic ethos of denunciation quickly gives way to propagandizing. This is not the response that I would expect from the journalists with whom I worked in Caracas or, for that matter, anyone else reporting under situations of extreme urgency. People engaged in the actual day-to-day work of journalism in Caracas tended to draw distinctions between good denuncias and bad ones, sincere denouncers and jaded opportunists, pressing truths and petty squabbles. Like positivism's faith in facts, the certainty of truth gets hazier the closer we approach it. If the work of crime journalists was tied to a general ethos or political logic of truth telling, this was an ethos or logic that grew organically from below, which is to say that each journalist had his or her own beliefs about what constituted honest reporting, and that professional codes of conduct were generated out of practices, such as denunciation, that were essentially contested. The practice of denunciation is the topic to which the next chapter turns.

SEVEN

Radicals and Reformers

Making a denuncia to the press was a common remedy for anyone facing a situation of injustice in Caracas. Take the case of Regina Rojas. On an early morning in March, Rojas took a jeep, then the subway, and then a bus from her home in one of the barrios of Petare to the morgue in Bello Monte. When the crime reporters arrived that morning, they found her waiting patiently, a dark brown folder at her side. Because it was a slow news day, the reporters listened intently even after they realized she was not there on account of a homicide. Details of her case were tucked inside the brown folder. As she talked, out came signed letters of employment, diplomas, identification cards, and a story about how the police dragged her husband and four other members of her family from their living rooms to a prison in the state of Yare. According to Rojas, their wrongful incarceration was the result of a family feud.

For half an hour, Rojas presented her evidence with quiet confidence. The reporters warmed to her immediately. They were convinced that she had a legitimate case. When the interview drew to a close, they gave her the number of a nongovernment organization that worked with families of police violence and promised to publish her side of the story. True to their word, the next day an article appeared in *Últimas Noticias*, Venezuela's largest daily newspaper. "Denuncia: [Police] dragged them from their homes without a warrant; Family is certain that detainees are innocent; Attribute the accusations to act of vengeance within the family." This is why Rojas traveled all the way across the city, a journey that from door to door probably took the better part of three hours. She did not come to see the police or to file a report. She came looking for the crime reporters, denuncia in hand.[1]

Up to this point, I have treated all denuncias as if they were the same, and it is true that all denuncias shared key characteristics. First, they were claims of wrongdoing made in the name of victims. To make a denuncia was to assert victimhood publicly. Second, these claims of wrongdoing were staged before an imagined tribunal of "the people" rather than the police or the courts. Taking a denuncia to the press was sensible because journalists claimed to represent a power that was above even the law. Denunciations made in front of the cameras appealed to the sovereign will of the people and, in so doing, they were more than simply acts of naming and shaming. Even a relatively circumscribed denuncia, like the one just described, tapped into the force of popular opinion. Third, and relatedly, all denuncias carried a latent revolutionary potential. The average supplicant, someone like Regina Rojas, was not looking to instigate a political movement. Nevertheless, government officials could not afford to simply brush off these kinds of requests. A critical mass of unanswered denuncias could potentially galvanize public sentiment around a sense of shared wrongdoing. Thanks, in part, to the power of the press, thousands of little requests quickly added up to very large demands. Fourth, and finally, the denuncias that I observed were intentional actions recognized by both their performers and their audiences. In this last respect, they took the form of what J. L. Austin refers to as "speech acts" or "performative utterances"—statements that, in the proper context, "do" things.[2] What denuncias attempted to do, however, varied.

If denunciation was an expression of a shared professional ethos, there was no consensus among journalists about best practices. What constituted a good denuncia was subject to debate. That point was made clear just a few weeks into my tenure on the crime beat when a journalist pulled me aside. "Follow the interviews closely," he said, nodding toward a small cluster of reporters. "Have you noticed the kinds of questions that they're asking?" I had, in fact, noticed that along with the standard who-what-when-where routine, reporters regularly prodded people to voice their opinions. Questions like "What do you think about insecurity?" or "Do you believe the government's claim that violence is decreasing?" elicited a few types of responses. Some people shrugged and said that violence was everywhere. Other people reacted angrily, saying that the reporters had no right to politicize their personal tragedy. Needless to say, neither of these two responses typically made the news. The reporters were looking for people who used this question as an opportunity to denounce the government, the police, the courts, the gangs, the lack of justice, or the cloud of fear hanging over the city. These denuncias were sometimes tearful, sometimes angry, but always followed closely by the reporters who jumped to film them or to copy them word for word into their notebooks.

Over the course of my research, I came to distinguish two general styles of denunciation: the radical and the reformist. The reporters asking provocative questions about insecurity fell into what we might call the radical camp. Radical denuncias tied a raft of complaints about crime to the failures of the Chávez government. A radical strategy of denunciation made crime victimhood the common ground that united disparate socioeconomic sectors (i.e., elites and the working poor) into an anti-institutional bloc, in much the same way that corruption functioned as the grounds for populist mobilization in an earlier era. In contrast, the journalist who pulled me aside was a reformer. The reformist style of denunciation targeted specific problems and resisted the impulse to make crime victimhood a rallying cry for antigovernment agitation. Reformers pressed for the resolution of particular cases or for institutional changes within the police, the judiciary, and the Ministry of Justice. Whereas reformers were content to work within the system, radicals believed that the only solution was "regime change."

Most crime reporters steered a middle course between these two styles. When they came across a denuncia that scaled up—to the Chávez government, to the police, or to any other manifestation of the state—they gladly followed it. When the chain of equivalence was less clear, they were happy to drop hints but did not attempt to manufacture a scandal. How any given crime reporter handled any given denuncia was determined by a multiplicity of factors, beginning with the reporter's interpretation of best practices, social positioning, political commitments in general, and the political commitments of his or her news outlet. The nuances were infinite. In this respect, every denuncia was a singular event. It would be a mistake, however, to imagine that the significance of any denuncia was limited to the context of its enunciation.

The political potential of any denuncia was tied, simultaneously, to the specific context in which it was enunciated and to the fact that, like an echo, every denuncia exceeded its context. Denuncias referenced other denuncias, as demonstrated by both the morgue photo and the corruption scandals from the previous chapter. This iterative quality meant that even the most moderate "request" could be rearticulated as a more radical "demand." Experienced denouncers were hyperconscious that the articulation of grievances depended on their repetition and that every repetition was also a reframing. What follows is an ethnographic look at the performative politics of denunciation on the crime beat. It describes both the practices that distinguished radicals and reformers as well as the hidden sympathies between them.

The Radical

On a bright Sunday morning, I found myself sitting with a group of crime reporters at the entrance of a barrio overlooking Caracas. The rolling hills and the sounds of church music made us forget, momentarily, the dead boy's body lying at the bottom of a steep footpath (fig. 7.1). Earlier in the day our group had ventured down the hill to take photos and speak with witnesses. There wasn't much in the way of a story. One lone police officer stood guard over a lumpy white shroud. A grandmotherly woman in a floral print gown told us that she heard the dogs barking in the night but only realized what had happened when she came out of her house that morning. Someone else told us that the boy and his family were evangelicals. Camera shutters clicked and the reporters scribbled in their notebooks or typed furiously on their smartphones. We did a few more interviews, snapped some photos, and then climbed back up the long, narrow footpath only to discover that our news trucks were blocked in. The investigative police had arrived. We would have to wait for more than two hours while they conducted their analysis. That was how I found myself sitting beside Hector

7.1. Photojournalists work to document a crime scene at the bottom of a footpath in a barrio. (Photograph by author.)

(a pseudonym) when he and another reporter started talking about the story that they were going to file.[3]

HECTOR: How old are you going to say he was?

REPORTER: Sixteen, seventeen . . .

HECTOR: You can't do that. It screws up everything. Think about LOPNA [Ley Orgánica para la Protección del Niño y Adolescente, or Organic Law for the Protection of Children and Adolescents, which was being used by the Chávez government to stifle crime reporting].

REPORTER: Well . . .

HECTOR: He was eighteen. Write that he was eighteen. What does it matter?

REPORTER: You know my editor's line. I've got to say seventeen.

To forestall a rush to judgment, let me stress that this was an unusual situation. In more than two years of participant observation on the Caracas crime beat, it was the only time that I witnessed a blatant disregard for facts. It was the kind of behavior that conspiracy-minded critics imagine goes on behind the scenes, and yet such behavior was exceedingly rare among beat journalists. I cite this exchange between Hector and one of his fellow reporters because it provides insight into the radical style taken to its extreme. Hector was one of only a handful of avowed partisans on the Caracas crime beat. He frequently used the crime pages as a platform to denounce the Chávez government's mishandling of security. Moves made by the government—including the implementation of the aforementioned LOPNA—were intended to harry journalists like Hector, so it was not surprising that Hector was intent on finding ways around them. In a case like this one, his frustration was understandable. An insignificant detail made the story virtually unreportable. What did it matter if he changed the age? The boy was dead.

Hector had his reasons for posthumously turning a boy into a man. But why try to convince another reporter? And why do it within earshot of an anthropologist? By way of explanation, let me offer another snippet from my field notes.

Early in the day, I am standing with the reporters as they go over the weekend body count. Hector and a few others agree that the tally was 60 (14 on Friday, 22 on Saturday, and 24 on Sunday). Later in the day I comment to another reporter who worked the weekend shift that it must have been a busy couple of days covering 60 murders. She immediately corrects me. "There were 52 murders this weekend, not 60. There were 14 on Friday, 22 on Saturday, and

16 on Sunday. I don't use Hector's numbers. He's pulling them from the hospital morgue and adding them to the total count. I think it's more accurate to wait until they pass through [the central morgue in] Bello Monte." This confirms something that I'd noticed about Hector's figures. They were often much higher than what other reporters were publishing.

Hector, again, had his reasons. He believed that the government was withholding a percentage of homicides from the central morgue in order to artificially reduce the weekend body count. He may have been right. Homicide figures were subject to widespread manipulation, although my own investigations suggest that these figures were just as likely to be overstated as understated.[4] Compiling an alternative homicide count was Hector's countermeasure against what he saw as an ongoing conspiracy, yet it flew in the face of journalistic conventions and the better judgment of his colleagues.

It was as if Hector was shadowboxing the state. He wanted to expose the Chávez government's complicity in the situation of rampant insecurity but found his efforts stymied in subtle and not-so-subtle ways. When this happened, he was prepared to bend the rules. He opined. He jumped to conclusions. He glossed the occasional fact. At his worst, Hector displayed symptoms of Peter Sloterdijk's oft-cited description of cynicism: cynics "know very well what they are doing [is wrong], but still, they are doing it."[5] The point is not to denounce Hector. His defiance of certain professional norms was an outgrowth of the relationship between crime journalists and the Venezuelan government during the later stages of the Chávez era. The radicalism of Hector mirrored the radicalism of the government. They were two sides of the same coin.

The radical style pushed the boundaries of propriety. It was as expansive as it was combative. Radicals made no attempt to draw borders around discrete problems. Quite the opposite: denuncias of crime quickly morphed into denuncias of censorship, corruption, poverty, infrastructural collapse, and a host of other issues. Hector sought to draw connections, to show how a litany of wrongs were linked to one another. When a story or an interview failed to make such linkages explicit, then he did the work himself. Take the following interview. A fellow reporter asked him, on camera, about the murdered relative of an official in the Chávez government. Hector responded:

What can you say? It's terrible what happened to this twenty-five-year-old kid. They killed him. They shot him full of holes for a little, low-cylinder motorcycle. It means that the underworld is taking everyone regardless of what political colors they fly. The underworld does not ask for an identification badge before they attack or kill someone. And unfortunately it is not a priority of our government to confront and combat insecurity for everyone's benefit. Their priority is a long-term political project. Meanwhile the rest of us are paying in blood for the broken dishes of this political project.

Note how Hector's denuncia links a particular tragedy ("this twenty-five-year-old kid") to the larger problem of violent crime ("the underworld is taking everyone") to a denunciation of the Chávez government for refusing to prioritize the battle against insecurity. Note also that his denuncia is made on the behalf of the suffering majority of Venezuelans who "are paying in blood for the broken dishes of this [chavista] political project." We glimpse here another example of how the radical style of denunciation created a chain of equivalences between seemingly heterogeneous elements. We also glimpse its expansiveness. An extended example from my field recordings more fully demonstrates the radical style in action.

"We Eat Each Other Like Meat"

A woman's face frozen midsentence dominated the back cover of the newspaper. Her eyes fixed on the reader. Her lips rounded into an accusing O. Out of an abundance of stories available on that particular day, Hector led with this one. His article spanned half a page, most of it dominated by quotes from the woman whose angry testimony went on for more than twenty minutes. The woman—whom I will call Katerina—arrived at the morgue on Tuesday morning along with two other family members. She came to collect the body of her nephew. More than two dozen crime journalists gathered at the morgue that day. Hector was the first to interview Katerina. She was in the middle of her denuncia when he waved the rest of us over. Katerina was saying, "When they come to kill you they don't say, 'Excuse me sir, are you with the government?' They don't ask that. They didn't ask my nephew. 'Excuse me kid, are you with the government or against the government?' No. 'Excuse me, are you with [the opposition news channel] Globovisión?'[6] No. They don't ask that kind of stuff. All they say is, 'Hey man, take that!' Pow! Pow! Pow!"

The journalists all nodded appreciatively. Katerina was speaking their language. Her argument about the apolitical nature of violent crime was a pointed statement in support of the private press and against the Chávez administration. Yet the testimony was out of order. Except for Hector and another reporter, none of us knew why Katerina was at the morgue or what had provoked her outburst in the first place. Hector tried to get her back to facts of the case and the circumstances surrounding the crime, but the denuncia had already gathered too much momentum.

REPORTER 1: What did the people in the vehicle say?

KATERINA: What?

REPORTER 1: What did the people who shot your nephew say?

KATERINA: Lady, no one said anything, no one heard anything, no one was listening, damn it. No one knows anything. And we don't have enough money to take his body back home to Machiques [a town in the state of Zulia]. Why? Because we don't have the means. Why? Because none of us little people work. Why? Because there is no work! The only people who are employed here are the malandros! Malandros!

[*Lowering her voice*] I am going to tell you something. I am going to put myself through a course with the government in the DISIP [the secret police]. Why? Why would I do such a thing? Because I am going to demand that as a Venezuelan I have my civil rights and that they give me a weapon like the National Guard and the police so that I can defend myself from the malandros.

[*Shouting again*] I need the government to answer me! I need the government to tell me, why they killed my nephew! I need this, do you hear me! I need them to tell me with a sense of shame. Why? Why? When a person is someone who serves humanity? My nephew was not a thief. I need them to answer me and tell me why. Why my nephew? A person who was young, honest, hardworking. Why? When the malandros here do whatever they want. And here there is no government that responds.

[*Turning dramatically toward the television cameras*] But I'll tell you if it is a child of someone in the government who is killed, everybody goes running to help! Everybody goes running! Everybody goes running, saying, "Ay, they killed so-and-so." They defend the government people. Yes, they have the police. Yes, they have the National Guard. Yes they have all kinds of stuff. But us, the poor, we don't have a damned thing. Where is the love that this man [President Chávez] has for us? What love, girl? He was going to do away with hunger. What happened? I want to know this. I'd like this man to tell me when, at what point, are we the poor going to stop starving to death? [He says] there is no hunger in Venezuela? Yes there is! There is no injustice here? Where do you live! What do you eat! There is no poverty? Yes there is! Too much!

HECTOR: Has anyone offered to help you?

KATERINA: [*Pauses momentarily as if shocked by the question*] What? No, nothing. [*Begins shouting again*] Nobody helps anybody here. We eat each other like meat because we don't have the resources to transport the body or for a funeral home or for a damned thing. What has the government done for us? Nothing. They left us locked in a bloodbath this Semana Santa [Holy Week]. One more year of blood in our house! This is the security that we have here? What security do we have here? I wish that this state [television] channel [VTV] would tell the truth, for God's sake. The truth! But they just keep repeating, "Globovisión is a coup plotter, Globovisión is a coup plotter!" The truth must be told. And here for telling the truth you go to jail. What nonsense is this! Here you cannot talk, you cannot have an opinion.

The political tenor of Katerina's denuncia was unmistakable. She was speaking out against the Chávez government from among the ranks of the urban poor, which formed the base of the president's political support. Rather than focusing on the victimization of her nephew, she concentrated on the victimization of an entire class of people, of which both she and her nephew were members. Starting with a specific event, the denuncia spiraled outward to encompass chronic insecurity, unemployment, poverty, and freedom of expression, all of which were laid at the feet of the government. The expansiveness of the denuncia, its tone of outrage, and its accusations of negligence were characteristic of the radical style.

For anyone who followed crime news in Caracas, Katerina's denuncia had a familiar ring. Note her opening statement about the nonpartisan nature of crime and how it echoed the wording of Hector's denuncia ("When they come to kill you they don't say, 'Excuse me sir, are you with the government?'"). This is one of half a dozen tropes that she repeats. These tropes included her accusation that the police protected government officials whereas the poor were left to their own devices ("But I'll tell you, if it is a child of someone in the government who is killed, everybody goes running to help!"); her accusation that the government was more interested in silencing the opposition than dealing with the problem of violent crime ("What security do we have here? I wish that this state [television] channel would tell the truth, for God's sake. The truth! But they just keep repeating, 'Globovisión is a coup plotter, Globovisión is a coup plotter!'"); her accusations that crime was unimpeded ("the malandros here do whatever they want"), that censorship was rampant ("And here for telling the truth you go to jail"), and that poverty continued unabated under Chávez ("I'd like this man to tell me when, at what point, are we the poor going to stop starving to death?").

Such repetitions should come as no surprise. Denuncias are made to be repeated. People who air grievances in front of the press corps expect their accusations to be restaged for the consumption of readers and viewers.

This is the common sense shared by crime journalists, their sources, and their audiences. Such knowledge was implicit in the words of Katerina's testimony, particularly in her references to the Venezuelan press. It was also present in the performance itself, which was exaggerated even for a grieving relative. The demonstrative shouting and the evocative phrasing had her two companions rolling their eyes and stifling embarrassed laughter. Her performance was over the top and everybody knew it.

Eventually, Katerina cracked a smile at her own audacity, and just a few minutes later she was standing with a group of journalists, chatting happily and predicting the future of a pregnant reporter with theatrical flair. Hector approached. "Thank you so much for your words, Katerina," he said, beaming. "It takes courage to say what you did. I wish more people would have the strength to tell the truth like you." The following day he dedicated eight columns above the fold to this episode of truth telling. Katerina's denuncia presented Hector with the performative scaffolding to make an accusation of his own, one that bore her image and his byline.

Staging Denuncias

Crime journalists often described themselves as intermediaries who bridged the testimonies of crime victims and the mass audience for crime stories. Such self-portraits should be recognized as performances of professional identity rather than faithful description of what reporters and photographers did. When it came to the circulation of denuncias, this image could be misleading for several reasons. First, it suggests that it was possible for journalists to reiterate the demands of crime victims without changing their content. There is no such thing as a perfect copy, as readers of Jorge Luis Borges or Jacques Derrida well know. Second, and relatedly, the depiction of journalists as impartial intermediaries minimized the importance of restaging. The denuncias published by crime journalists were not passive quotations. They were modified, framed, and rearticulated through an active engagement with the politics of security, a fact that Hector clearly demonstrated. Third, and perhaps most important, it took for granted the role of reporters and photographers as go-betweens rather than recognizing that the work of mass mediation included the performance of this in-between status.

Crime journalism is an active restaging, and, like all acts of mass mediation, it is performative.[7] Theories of performativity are useful because they provide a robust yet flexible perspective on how discursive practices shape social facts.[8] Turning toward the performative reveals a dynamic field of relationships in which the ethical and political stakes of denunciation are neither fixed nor clearly defined. Such a perspective is in keeping with the radical contingency of politics in the Chávez era. Its precarious balance of alliances and hostilities is precisely what made denuncias powerful.

Ordinary language philosophers would recognize denuncias as archetypal speech acts or performative utterances. According to J. L. Austin, speech acts are utterances whose purpose is not to describe the world but to act on it. Examples include a ship's christening (e.g., "I christen this ship the *Queen Elizabeth*"), a wedding vow (e.g., "I do"), or a wager (e.g., "I bet you a dollar it will rain").[9] Denuncias operate in a similar manner. Rather than christening or vowing or betting, they accuse. Austin argues that the success or failure of a performative, its "felicity" or "infelicity," must be gauged in relation to the circumstances of the utterance, what he calls the "total speech situation." From this perspective, the impact of a denuncia depends primarily on its context.[10]

This contextual approach to denuncias seems intuitive. It underpins much of my own analysis because it highlights the ways in which denuncias were inflected by racial, ethnic, socioeconomic, sexual, gendered, and geographic categories as well as the political polarization of the Chávez era. Take the preceding example. Katerina's performance was structured by her position within a discursive field that judged guilt and innocence along prejudicial lines. She was clearly from the barrios and, moreover, she was clearly Colombian, a fact that did her few favors. Worse still, her nephew did not fit the profile of the innocent victim (sano). Murdered in the middle of the night in a notoriously dangerous sector of the city, his background and his whereabouts already made him suspect in the eyes of both the journalists and their audiences. In a country where homophobia was the norm, the facts of his personal life—he lived alone, had no children, and worked in an HIV clinic—made him an unsympathetic victim. We could end things there. Indeed, the first time I attempted to explain this scene, I concluded that the forcefulness of Katerina's denuncia was an attempt to reframe her nephew's death in terms of the chavista/opposition binary. This interpretation is worth bearing in mind, but it leaves open certain questions and forecloses others.

A narrow understanding of context creates the illusion of singularity and the perception that denuncias, like fingerprints, are the unique property of unique persons.[11] And yet Hector echoed Katerina, who in turn echoed Hector. Such circular ventriloquism was not happenstance. Successful denuncias are predicated on their ability to reference other denuncias. They have a mimetic quality. Their performative power, their ability "to do things," depends on their iterability.[12] Denuncias are like rituals: through repetition they enact a form of collective subjectivity.[13]

The relationship between performativity and subject formation is associated with the work of several scholars. My interpretation hews most closely to approaches pioneered by queer studies, especially the work of Judith Butler, who shows how performances of identity are grounded in the repetition of certain postures, conventions, habits, and practices. In Butler's account, subjects are recursively constructed through discourse in a way that is creative without being autonomous. Every performative is simultaneously singular and predetermined. This double articulation reveals routine processes of "subjectification" that shape persons, most famously in relation to learned categories of gender, sex, and sexuality.[14] Much of Butler's early work describes the processes that mold individual subjects, but performativity is equally useful for thinking about the production of collective ones, as Michael Warner has demonstrated in his writings on publics.[15] A public, like a people, is an imagined community, the materiality of which is grounded in ritualized or performative practices such as denunciation. Every denuncia is an act of faith that hails this collective subject anew. The seventeenth-century theologian and polymath Blaise Pascal made a similar point about the performativity of prayer and its relationship to the divine. "Pascal says more or less: kneel down, move your lips in prayer, and you will believe."[16]

Performativity, understood as a recursive process of subject formation, is an essential feature of all denuncias. Moreover, it demystifies the role that media play in populist movements. By way of explanation, let me return to that not-so-hypothetical barrio on the outskirts of Caracas suggested by Laclau. Rather than a problem of housing, a problem of street crime arises. The residents of the barrio request intervention by the state. Perhaps they go to the police. And perhaps, as is often the case, the police not only fail to resolve the problem but also turn out to be complicit in it. Frustration mounts. Residents recognize that other requests have gone unanswered. There are problems of housing, of food, of waste collection, of water supply, and so on. The problem goes from a specific issue (violent crime) in a specific place (the not-so-hypothetical shantytown on the outskirts of Caracas) to a general demand.

Media play a crucial role in this move from the specific to the general. Instead of going to the police, our crime victims go to the press. They make a denuncia to a group of journalists. Those journalists rearticulate the denuncia with the help of their editors. The next day, tens of thousands of residents in all parts of the city read it or watch it or hear it. A few days later, several of these residents are victims of similar crimes. Perhaps they, too, approach journalists with the intention of making a denuncia; or perhaps they go to the police; or maybe they just speak with friends and family. These "new" denuncias reiterate elements of denuncias already absorbed. They repeat certain frames, figures, and facts. They omit others.

We are dealing with a process of articulation or aggregation that operates via repetition.[17] Every denuncia is a new and specific staging, but it is also part of a longer performative chain. The ability to call on that chain makes denuncias potentially explosive. Journalists are the persons most responsible for maintaining the linkages and managing their excess—which is not to say that they have superhuman control over discourse or that they magically constitute reality. Journalists are not kings or clerics or judges. Their illocutionary utterances may provoke shame, but they rarely determine the outcome of history. The aggregation of such utterances over time, however, is forceful. Every denuncia carries a perlocutionary force that reaches toward the future by drawing on the past. Walter Benjamin's angel of history comes to mind.[18] Instead of a seraph, however, the ontopolitical actor is a collective subject—the people.[19]

Through practices like denunciation, crime journalists enacted the will of the people. They invoked popular sovereignty as an accusing force. It was not simply individual victims who were hurt by crime but Venezuelan society as a whole. Each and every denuncia rearticulated this collective injury. The subject that emerged from this performative chain of denunciations was a wounded subject determined negatively by whom or what it opposed.[20]

By following denuncias we glimpse the discursive architecture that connects the popular will to the politics of security. What I am describing is by no means unique to Venezuela. A similar argument could be made about how denunciations of crime function when channeled via mass media in other parts of the world. What made crime reporting in Caracas exceptional was the sheer quantity of overlapping antagonisms at work. In addition to the complex sano/malandro binary—with its intersecting hierarchies of race, class, gender, and sexuality—denuncias were also positioned vis-à-vis the chavista/opposition divide. Because of these competing registers of inequality, the performance of popular sovereignty was transparently political. For that very reason, persons whose accusations were normally marginalized by the press (i.e., the poor, the racially and ethnically marked) suddenly attracted the media spotlight. The opposition was eager to find cracks in the chavista coalition, and these tensions were most powerfully present around the issue of security. Which brings us back to context, albeit a context that emerges dynamically and in concert with the denuncias themselves.

The Reformer

Reflecting on popular protest in the barrios of Caracas, Alejandro Velasco has distinguished two kinds of demonstration: those staged before the state (*ante-estado*) and those staged against it (*anti-estado*).[21] Hector's denuncias fell into the second camp. He set himself against chavismo and used denuncias to recruit the widest possible constituency. Others adopted a more sympathetic position. Reform-minded journalists framed their denuncias as appeals to the state. Their primary objective was moving government officials to action.

Eligio Rojas was one of the best examples of a reformer on the crime beat. Among the reporters he was something of a rarity. For starters, Eligio was not a native caraqueño. He hailed from a rural province known for its cattle and expansive grasslands. He moved to Caracas in the 1980s to attend the Central University of Venezuela (Universidad Central de Venezuela, or UCV) and brought with him a repository of folksy sayings. He also knew the barrios intimately. During his student years Eligio lived in Antimano and Petare before moving to an apartment in the middle-class section of El Valle. Last and most important, he was one of a handful of journalists on the crime beat who supported President Chávez. Surprisingly, this did not diminish his popularity with his peers.

My first day working with Eligio was Saturday, February 16, 2008. There were four of us in total, including Carlos (the driver) and Frisneda (the photographer). For most of the morning we followed the pack, starting off at the morgue and continuing to the scene of a failed bombing linked to the Frente Venceremos affair described in chapter 2. After an interview with a homeless man who witnessed the explosion, the rest of the reporters headed off to cover a fatal traffic accident across town. Eligio broke with the pack to follow another story. He directed us to a funeral home where witnesses to a double homicide were attending a wake.

The story was a classic example of a denuncia. It appeared in the morning edition of *Últimas Noticias* under the provocative headline "CICPC [investigative police] Accused of Executing Two Men; Witnesses Saw Them Detained." According to eyewitnesses, Félix López and Rafael Matute were rounded up at a police checkpoint on Wednesday afternoon for no apparent reason. Thursday morning their lifeless bodies were discovered in a nearby park. A relative of López denounced the arrests, describing marks of violence on the bodies, which suggested that the men were tortured and then executed. More important, in his denuncia he named the branch police station where the victims were taken after their arrest. That meant strong circumstantial evidence pointed to the involvement of a small circle of officers.

All of this added up to a serious allegation, and Eligio wondered aloud why the other crime reporters chose the traffic accident over the double homicide. Since the case involved several credible denuncias against the police, he assumed it would generate more attention. Although the reporters at *Últimas Noticias* covered the story for the next two weeks, it went almost unmentioned by the other major news outlets.

The execution of López and Matute emblemized the kind of denuncias routinely published by *Últimas Noticias*. No reporter personified this style like Eligio. He relished investigative work, particularly on cases that other reporters consider "too small" to warrant attention. Eligio frequently took up stories on behalf of people who could not defend themselves, particularly the working poor and the popular classes. When following these stories, he was not simply reporting the facts but also hoping to influence their resolutions. For Eligio, good journalism had "the power to uncover these small injustices that are kept quiet, that nobody will listen to because the bureaucracy here is terrible."[22] More important, a good journalist was prepared to intervene on behalf of his subjects. Eligio explained, "Here the justice system is elitist. I mean, here there is no possibility that they are going to investigate a case and so the case will remain. The mother of the dead boy doesn't have money to pay for a lawyer to handle the case and so it remains unsolved. I think of this every day when I am writing. Why do I think about this? Because most of the information that we write is a denuncia against this elitist system of justice, this system to which, unfortunately, the poor have no access."[23]

During our time together, Eligio investigated dozens of denuncias. There were accusations against a group of Metropolitan Police officers extorting protection money, an investigation of government-sponsored death squads in his home state of Guárico, and reports about misconduct on the part of an ex-judge in a key criminal case, to name just a few. Every visit to *Últimas Noticias* occasioned a review of some new piece of evidence: handwritten letters from ex-police officers, old transcripts of court cases, financial records, interviews with government officials, press releases, homicide statistics, or eyewitness testimonies. He shared it all enthusiastically along with rumors, gossip, and updates about the latest threats his reporting had provoked.

Impressed by his dogged pursuit of denuncias, I remarked to another crime reporter that I admired Eligio's reporting. It was the end of another long political season and the journalist seemed irritated by my comment. "Sure, Eligio is a real pest when he has found something damaging on the opposition, but he clams up when it is something that makes Chávez look bad." The reply struck me as telling, although not in a way that is immediately obvious.

All of my interviews with Eligio and my field notes, which span the better part of three years, indicated that despite his political loyalties, the vast majority of denuncias that he investigated were potentially damaging to the Chávez government. He told me, repeatedly, that as a reporter his passion was "to reveal what the state wanted to keep hidden" regardless of who was in charge.[24] What explains his colleague's remark that Eligio was biased in favor of the Chávez administration?

Despite his commitment to denunciation, Eligio rarely, if ever, linked these failings directly to President Chávez. Even his broadest denuncias were provocations in favor of reform. This was in keeping with the style of *Últimas Noticias*; however, it made him suspect in the eyes of peers who believed that the entire system was corrupt. For Eligio, denunciation was a tool that could be used to improve the police, the courts, and the functioning of government, whereas his more radical colleagues believed that nothing short of a revolution would bring about change.

––––––––––––––

My introduction to Eligio was courtesy of Wilmer Poleo, the section editor for crime at *Últimas Noticias*. A tanned, active man in his midforties, Wilmer supervised four full-time reporters, a pair of photographers, and a dozen part-time correspondents who reported from outside Caracas. Our first meeting was characteristically efficient. On a balmy December afternoon just a few weeks before Christmas, my research assistant and I squeezed into the sliver of space between the desk and the door of his office. I came with questions about why a newspaper known for its studied neutrality toward the Chávez administration had adopted an openly critical stance on violent crime. I expected an evasive answer, but Wilmer was direct. "My style is to emphasize insecurity at any cost," he said, punctuating the point with a sharp drag on his cigarette. "In one way or another we must manage to break through the barrier [of silence] so that for once the government acknowledges that what is happening is true." He proudly pointed to his weekly column, "Police Code," which came out every Monday. That day's edition was titled "Bloody Extra Inning." Poleo explained:

> I called it that because President Chávez—who has never spoken about the theme of insecurity—talked about it in one of his [recent] speeches. He said something about how he was convinced that insecurity is a problem that does

not have a solution and that the police are not going to solve the problem of insecurity but rather *el pueblo* must organize against it. He is saying that we are going to solve the problem of insecurity with communal councils [that don't exist]. That gave me the sense that we're going a bloody extra inning, because he is not going to do anything to stop delinquency. . . . We're supposed to sit here waiting until the [communal councils] form, which could take years![25]

This critical assessment of the Chávez government and its security policies echoed the judgments of most of the crime journalists. It was widely known that Wilmer supported the Chávez administration. That only lent his position greater force because Wilmer's columns often struck a defiant pose despite his political sympathies. He regularly published denuncias of the government, of the police, of known gangs and alleged criminals. Informed by an entire team of reporters, "Police Code" provided a glimpse of the rumors, opinions, and accusations that crime reporters carried with them but which rarely saw the light of day.

Generally, Wilmer's denuncias were accompanied by concrete suggestions about how to remedy the problem: more police in a particular zone, better lighting on the streets, sweeping reforms of the judiciary, better conditions in the prisons, and the like. This reformist style, part denuncia and part recommendation, exemplified the tone of crime news at *Últimas Noticias*, which explicitly attempted to influence the government in the name of its readers.

Over the course of my fieldwork, I observed numerous instances of this style in action. The most outstanding example was the "Insufferable Insecurity" campaign, a monthlong series that ran from September to October 2008. The first installment was announced with great fanfare on the front page of the newspaper on September 17. "Insecurity Must Be Halted," read the headline in big, bold letters. "ÚN [*Últimas Noticias*] Initiates a Campaign to Reduce Criminality." By way of introduction, the newspaper's director, Eleazar Díaz Rangel, explained the motivation for the series. "Months ago, insecurity became the country's number one problem," he wrote. "Yet, the efforts of the government have not been successful. How many security ministers have passed through office? How many plans have been announced? With meager results."[26] In the face of political inertia, the newspaper seized the initiative to create a platform for action. For the next five weeks, *Últimas Noticias* featured daily installments of the series. The first major article concerned a stalled project for sweeping police reforms (CONAREPOL), which was initiated in January 2007 and then abandoned. Thereafter, the campaign focused on expert interviews with leading criminologists, ex-police officials, legal scholars, and human rights activists. Some of these experts, such as the sociologist Roberto Briceño-León or the former judge Mónica Fernández, had ties to the opposition; others, including Luis Gerardo Gabaldón and Soraya el Achkar, worked with the Chávez government. Each was asked a similar question: "If you had the power to make changes, what kinds of changes would you make?" Rather than simply denouncing the government or the police or the judicial system, they were pushed to propose concrete solutions.

Starting in its second week, the Insufferable Insecurity campaign solicited denuncias from readers. A selection of these emails formed a separate column of material that corroborated the expert testimonies. The vast majority of these denuncias came from Caracas. Each described a specific locale (e.g., "Apartment Blocks 3 & 4 in Lomas de Urdaneta, Catia" or "the third street in Las Mayas, Coche") so that they functioned as fragmentary maps of the city and its dangers. There were shoot-outs between gangs in the east; crooked cops in the west; prostitution in the center city; pickpockets among the street vendors lining the boulevards; drug dealers operating out of the poor, hilltop settlements; auto thieves casing the middle-class zones. Using these denuncias as evidence, the newspaper made an appeal for reforms directly to the Chávez government, specifically the minister of interior and justice, Tarek El Aissami. The editors were careful to frame the denuncias as petitions from the ranks of the president's political base rather than hostile attacks. Nonetheless, they contained an implicit threat. If the government ignored these denuncias and the efforts of *Últimas Noticias*, it would be ignoring its core political constituency, for which there were consequences. In a column titled "The Voice of the People," Wilmer reveals as much:

> Hopefully, the Ministry of Interior [and Justice] has designated a team that can at least verify the certainty of these denuncias. We are not dealing with the incessant denuncias of experts, nor are they part of a campaign by sectors of the opposition. They are the urgent expositions of the people themselves, of the man on the street, of those who live in the working-class districts and who feel that they have been abandoned by the state. These are the true experts, because they have to live—or survive—with this problem, which has been denounced time and again. The other option would be [for the ministry] to ignore the voice of the people, to turn a deaf ear to this desperate clamor, which reverberates all the way to the top.[27]

When we met in Wilmer's office to discuss the progress of the campaign, he was visibly pleased. He told me that the new minister had responded positively to the newspaper's efforts, agreeing that it was time to evaluate the problem of violence. More important, the minister promised to convene a council of experts dedicated to the subject. Wilmer was looking forward to concluding the Insufferable Insecurity campaign on a high note. "In a few weeks," he explained, "we are going to systemize our findings and have a breakfast with the minister in which we will present our work."[28] This had been the plan from the beginning: to use journalistic resources to put pressure on the government in a way that, the journalists hoped, would yield results. Such tactics were common at *Últimas Noticias*. Wilmer described similar campaigns around the problems of garbage and automobile traffic in Caracas. These projects aimed to influence rather than inflame. In contrast with the radical style, the denuncias published in *Últimas Noticias* did not try to mobilize popular outrage against the government to oust it. Rather, they used the simmering threat to spur officials to action.

The Victim's Voice

In their article "Dismembering and Remembering the Nation," Fernando Coronil and Julie Skurski draw attention to the constitutive role of violence in the formation and representation of the nation.[29] According to Coronil and Skurski, the Venezuelan state is linked to *el pueblo* through a populist discourse that is violently inscribed on the bodies of the subaltern. This discourse, rooted in Venezuela's colonial history, alternately casts *el pueblo* as an innocent victim in need of assistance or as a violent, irrational mass that must be subdued. Nowhere is this Janus-faced figure of *el pueblo* more present than in crime news, with its tropes of innocence and savagery, civility and barbarism, lawfulness and disorder.

Not unlike populist leaders, crime journalists imagined themselves as the intermediaries who spoke in the name of *el pueblo*.[30] Reporters including Hector, Eligio, and Wilmer used denuncias to intervene publicly on behalf of those who could not help themselves. They consciously adopted the pose of social advocates working for the benefit of victims and the greater good.

One of my first conversations about crime journalism was with a young reporter who worked for the television station RCTV. His job, he said, was to help make violence visible to the police and to government officials. "We are the mouthpieces of this insecurity that exists," he told me. "We are the ones who transcribe this reality that otherwise might never reach those in power."[31] Another, more veteran, reporter explained it somewhat differently. In her mind, the fundamental purpose of crime journalism was to broadcast the suffering of victims and their families to the general public: "As a crime reporter, you denounce. You transform yourself into the person who speaks for the dead."[32] What stood out in both of these statements and many others was their emphasis on the role of the reporter as the metaphorical voice of victims.

Since everyone in Caracas was a crime victim or a potential crime victim, this constituency could be imagined expansively so that it extended beyond the morgue, beyond even the city, to encompass the nation in its entirety. The crime victim as a symbol routinely jumped scale. My contention is that denuncias were the practice through which victimhood-as-citizenship is formed (and performed) as a symbol of the nation. It was through a totalizing narrative in which everyone was a victim or a potential victim that journalistic denuncias acted as the discursive building blocks of populist movements. If there was a resemblance between crime journalists and populist leaders, it was because they employed a similar representational logic and envisioned themselves playing a similar role.

Through their mediation of victims' denuncias, crime journalists made visible the demands so crucial to the birth of populist movements. It was thanks, in part, to the work of reporters that crime victimhood became a platform for political mobilization in Caracas. By linking specific grievances to the figure of the victim, crime journalists provided evidence for the claim that urban violence had spiraled out of control and that far-reaching reform or radical change was necessary. A regular consumer of crime news encountered scores of denuncias every week. It is not hard to imagine how depictions of grieving relatives, heinous crimes, and impotent officials all fed a sense of moral outrage. Journalists were acutely aware of this political potential. As one reporter explained, "For me the fundamental role of the crime beat is the denuncia. In a city like Caracas you cannot stand by and allow there to be thirty, forty, up to fifty deaths every weekend. I mean, the purpose is that you have to make it better. Each story is—I don't want to say an excuse—but rather a link [eslabón] that allows you to make denuncias every day, so that you can show this is a macrolevel project."[33]

What is remarkable about this statement is that the reporter verbalized the implicit knowledge shared by journalists, their sources, and their audiences. Journalistic denuncias self-consciously fused the suffering of specific victims with larger narratives about violence, el pueblo, and the nation's tortured body.

In this sense, denuncias reverse the classic example of interpellation described by Louis Althusser. Whereas Althusser's state hails the subject through the intermediary of a police officer, denuncias are an example in which subjects hail the state through the intermediary of the press. Just as there are consequences for a citizen who does not respond to the police officer, the state cannot afford to be unresponsive when confronted with a raft of denuncias. Governments and state officials that are unresponsive to demands voiced in the name of *el pueblo* find themselves the target of popular protests, riots, and even revolutions.[34]

Crime journalists like Eligio and Hector performed a kind of inadvertent good-cop, bad-cop routine, alternately cajoling and compelling the Chávez government. What these otherwise unaligned actors shared was a commitment to channeling the voice of victims as the voice of the Venezuelan people. Crime victimhood converged diverse constituencies around a series of common grievances. It functioned as a point of inflection, a kind of charismatic signifier that drew together otherwise dissimilar experiences of violence. This dynamic was similar in certain respects to the posthumous martyrdom of Jorge Tortoza. What distinguished crime victims from political martyrs was their ability to bridge the chavista/opposition divide—which is not to say that crime victimhood was politically neutral but that it forged popular consciousness around a different set of antagonisms.

EIGHT

The Subject of Wrongs

We were standing beside the bombed-out rubble of what was once a police station on the outskirts of Caracas (fig. 8.1). "What media are you with?" the woman asked me with a mixture of wariness and curiosity. She had her groceries in hand. I had my notebook. My first and only news assignment for the *San Francisco Chronicle* brought a fellow freelancer and me to this barrio in La Dolorita, a district on the city's eastern edge. The two of us were writing a story on crime in Venezuela, and the police station captured our attention. Days earlier, members of the community had burned it down to protest a lack of security in the zone. This spectacular act of defiance was precipitated by the murder of a young man from the neighborhood. He was gunned down on the doorstep of the police station. As usual, the police were nowhere to be found. The press, too, would have ignored the murder except for the protest and its aftermath. Burning down a police station was extraordinary even by Venezuelan standards. We wanted to know what had driven people to such lengths. What did residents have to say about crime, insecurity, the police, and the upcoming elections? What could we learn about their political allegiances? Did this attack on the police station suggest that segments of the popular sector were shifting away from chavismo over the problem of insecurity?

Before I could ask any of these questions, my interviewee had questions of her own. "What's your editorial line?" she wanted to know. "Are you with the opposition?" Like everyone else in Caracas, she knew that crime journalism was acutely political. Not surprisingly, her responses were polite but brief.[1]

If speaking to the press could be seen as an act of political allegiance, there was something strangely nonpartisan about burning down an empty police station. Opinion held that police in Caracas were worse than ineffective: they

8.1. Burned-out police station in La Dolorita. It was burned down by members of the community who were outraged over the shooting death of a young man from the neighborhood. (Photograph by Lurdes R. Basolí.)

were part of the problem. Both the opposition and the Chávez government concurred on this point. Indeed, the Ministry of Interior and Justice estimated that more than 20 percent of all violent crime in the country was committed by off-duty police officers.[2] As an act of protest, burning down a police station was open to interpretation. It was clearly a demand, but was it a demand staged before the government or a demand directed against it? That was the question at stake, not just in the protest but also in the way that it was framed by the press. Protests, like denuncias, were ritualized moments in which the fictive voice of the people was embodied in the actions of specific persons. Sometimes protests were tied to discrete communities with bounded requests, as in direct-action protests or the reform-minded denuncias described in the previous chapter. Sometimes they were tied to revolutionary demands that challenged the very authority of the state, as in radical denuncias or what Charles Tilly describes as "representational protests." Either way, their legitimacy depended on claims made in the name of "the people."[3]

This chapter concerns the relationships between democracy, citizenship, and the politics of security in Venezuela. Increasingly, "citizen security" and "democratic security" have become buzzwords among policy makers throughout the Americas.[4] Scholars have drawn attention to how this emerging discourse of citizen security nests crime control within a regime of rights, in a way that can potentially undermine democratic values.[5] This paradox of citizen security—in which rights undo democracy—is symptomatic of a more general impasse that confronts scholars, activists, and policy makers.[6] My objective is not to resolve this impasse but to propose a shift of perspective that casts the problem in a somewhat different light.

Rather than beginning, as is customary, with the citizen as bearer of rights, populism performs an interesting inversion in which the citizen appears, first and foremost, as the subject of wrongs.[7] Seen from this perspective, it is the force of injustice that provides the impetus for democratic subjectivity—which is neither to reject rights as irrelevant nor to dismiss yearnings for enfranchisement. Rather, it is to assert that before struggles for enfranchisement take on wider significance, they are usually grounded in grievances both real and imagined. Those who feel wronged, in one way or another, are those who most passionately pursue political demands.[8]

What snaps into focus when we view democratic subjectivity through the lens of wrongs is the ways in which victims and victimhood mediate the body politic. As symbolic figures, victims fuse specific wrongs into common political demands, thereby enabling collective action. Crime victims are a case in point. Time and again I was struck by the centrality of crime victims as a channel for political subjectivity. The shock of crime jolted people into action. It produced an effect akin to what Émile Durkheim called "collective effervescence."[9] Beginning with wrongs allows us to analyze how these expressions of solidarity coalesced around certain victims and how these victims became the symbolic scaffolding of the popular will.

Plan Secure Caracas

Although no one was arrested or otherwise punished for burning down the police station in La Dolorita, the community's actions entreated an official response. It came in the form of a police delegation. The following day, the commissioner for the Metropolitan Police made an appearance in La Dolorita. He arrived with a pack of journalists and a list of promises. He promised that the police would capture the killer, that 250 security officers would be stationed in the district, and that the armed forces would build a new police station with the help of the community. All of these promises were made under the aegis of the new security program, Plan Caracas Segura, or Plan Secure Caracas.[10]

Plan Secure Caracas was launched to great fanfare eight months before the episode in La Dolorita. It was just one of a string of security initiatives that dated back to President Hugo Chávez's first term in office.[11] Most of these initiatives were national in scope. Secure Caracas was the first to focus exclusively on the capital city. Aside from the name, however, not much distinguished it from earlier efforts. Like the initiatives that preceded it, Secure Caracas promoted a multiagency response that flooded the streets with officers from the National Guard, the Metropolitan Police, the investigative police, and various municipal and state agencies. Heavily armed men on motorcycles set up checkpoints, swarmed through barrios, and conducted coordinated tactical operations in four of the city's poorest districts: Petare, El Valle, Catia, and San Juan. Everywhere they went, they went en masse, drawing the attention of onlookers and news cameras alike.

The official launch of Plan Secure Caracas took place on a bright Friday morning in an otherwise nondescript parking lot. We arrived to find nearly five hundred officers standing at attention in neat, diagonal rows. In front of them a small clique of high-level functionaries from the National Guard and at least six police agencies milled about. Everyone was packing heat, wearing bulletproof vests, sporting badges, and generally making a display of ass-kicking force.[12]

The half-dozen reporters who showed up for the press conference seemed supremely uninterested. When I asked one journalist, a friend, about Plan Secure Caracas, she replied that it was just another show and not a substantial effort at reform. Gatherings like these were old news. A second reporter was even more dismissive:

> Useless. These are sensationalist plans, plans that they keep repeating. It began with Jesse Chacón when he was in the Ministry of Interior and Justice [2004–7]. He applied this Plan for Citizen Security in high points of the city—for example, in Petare. What does it do? It concentrates a large police force in these zones. So you bring police from the west to the east, you concentrate them there, you make a show of force, you show no tolerance, and you round up some kids who are consuming alcohol or drugs in public. You are not investigating the presence of armed gangs, and [the plan] is only going to be carried out over the weekends. You are going to set up a tent instead of a permanent police station. What we are talking about is a festival of management that is being set in motion.[13]

If Plan Secure Caracas was just *farandula,* or "show,"[14] as the crime reporters liked to say, it was a show that went on for the next two years. The Ministry of Interior and Justice continued to promote it despite another administrative turnover. During this period, there was no shortage of press conferences that trumpeted success. Frequently, this success was exaggerated. In response, the private press regularly published interviews with experts, victims, and ordinary citizens, all of whom declared the government's security efforts an abysmal failure. However, it was clear that Plan Secure Caracas was never intended to lower crime rates. While government officials and journalists argued about its efficacy, neither party was under the illusion that it would actually diminish crime. Like most contemporary policing strategies, Plan Secure Caracas had another objective. Its purpose was to demobilize protests, denuncias, and other demands that were staged in the name of *el pueblo*.[15]

Constituent Moments

There are at least two ways that we can interpret Plan Secure Caracas. The first is consonant with a Foucauldian approach. It reads the plan as an expression of liberal governance whereby the security of a population replaces the freedom of the people.[16] Such an analysis would foreground the use of spectacle in the service of state power. It would emphasize, as I have, Plan Secure Caracas as a technique of demobilization. The second interpretation seems to run counter to the first. It reads demands for security and the restriction of freedoms as the grounds on which the people are staged in the first place. Such an analysis would foreground popular sovereignty's constituent power in shaping the modern nation-state.[17] It would emphasize how demands for security create the foundation of an imagined community.

These two interpretations of Plan Secure Caracas do not cancel each other out. They represent two sides of a contradiction that propels the politics of security. Denuncias and anticrime protests allow us to understand the second half of this equation, the relationship between securitization and the popular will.

The burned-down police station was just one example of how this will was mediated thanks, in part, to the work of journalists like my colleague and me. We went to La Dolorita searching for someone to channel the grievances of "the community" and the popular sectors more broadly. It did not take long to find a willing representative. A gentleman named Nelson Villareal explained that residents were angry about a string of recent killings in the sector and the ineffectiveness of the police. Although pleased by the response of Plan Secure Caracas, he issued a warning: "We don't want this to be a 15-day love affair. If after 15 days there are no longer police there, we will rise up again."[18] Note the "we" in his statement. My colleague and I certainly did. That collective "we" transformed a specific action into a representation of shared sentiment, a forceful expression of constituent power. This is the kind of performative utterance on which crime journalism depends. Likewise revolutions.

Our article framed the events in La Dolorita as an expression of popular unrest that pointed to a breakup within chavismo. That framing elided something important, however. As a manifestation of constituent power, the protest in La Dolorita was also faithful to the legacy of the Bolivarian Revolution, which grew out of popular uprisings not unlike this one. Burning down a police station recalled an earlier episode when the demands of the urban poor coalesced in open revolt. This begins to explain why an act that would normally be seen as an assault on the state did not meet overt reprisal. The protest presented itself as an expression of the very constituent power that ousted the old regime and helped sweep Hugo Chávez into office.

Few moments shaped the Bolivarian Revolution like the events of February 27 to March 3, 1989.[19] What came to be known as the Caracazo was precipitated by skyrocketing poverty and decades of failed promises. Protests broke out in urban centers across Venezuela after President Carlos Andrés Pérez announced a shock adjustment to the price of oil. The most intense outbursts concentrated in Caracas. They were brutally put down. Today, the Caracazo is remembered as the world's first major uprising against neoliberalism and the bloodiest single offensive against civilians in contemporary Latin American history.

For a young Hugo Chávez, the Caracazo represented the constituent moment in which the Bolivarian Revolution was born because it revealed an irreparable rift between the will of the people and those entrusted with governing it. He consistently referred back to this moment as a betrayal of the popular will. Turning the military against one's own people was unjustifiable, and it represented a turning point for himself and other soldiers. Take the following excerpt from a 2004 interview:

In the 20th century, Venezuela became a country rich with oil and resources of every description, but it was also full of poverty—a rich country full of poor people. We were soldiers in an army that was directly descended from Bolívar's United Liberation Army of South America. We had been told since we were kids, or child soldiers, that we were heirs to Bolívar's glory. But soon we realized they were using us to massacre our own people who were in the streets demanding justice and protesting against the "electro-shock" therapy of the International Monetary Fund (IMF). That is when the "Caracazo" massacre occurred and Bolívar's curse fell upon us. Bolívar had once said,

"Damned is the soldier who uses his weapon against his own people." After the Caracazo I said to my comrades, "We have been cursed and we must exorcise that curse from our consciences." Three years later we rose up in the February 4 rebellion, and the curse was lifted.[20]

The Caracazo as popular rebellion framed the way in which the Bolivarian Revolution understood barrio-based protests. They were expressions of *el pueblo's* constituent power rather than assaults on the state. In this respect, the protest in La Dolorita echoed an earlier era of urban revolts. There were, however, key differences between these moments of popular insurgency—namely, the wrongs in question. The primary demands put forward in 1989 were for economic justice. The Caracazo was about lack of food, rampant poverty, rising gas prices, and a corrupt political class. In contrast, the primary demand put forward by residents in La Dolorita was for security. Burning down a police station was one way to protest unchecked violence, petty crime, police inaction, and the all-too-absent presence of the state. One subject of wrongs was a hungry, impoverished people brutally repressed; the other was an abject crime victim callously abandoned. If the popular will is mediated by wrongs, then we are dealing with two highly contrasting versions of "the people," and it is safe to say the popular consciousness that emerged out of the Caracazo during the early 1990s was qualitatively different than the popular consciousness that emerged out of anticrime protests during the middle of the first decade of the twenty-first century.

Much of the scholarship on protest reproduces what E. P. Thompson famously called the "spasmodic view of popular history."[21] Too often we concentrate on individual protests as moments of rupture, rather than considering how they combine with other expressions of discontent to form a whole that is greater than the sum of its parts. I want to propose approaching protests much like denuncias—as an articulating practice through which the popular will is made manifest. When protests are considered as an articulating practice, a few things snap into focus. First, it gives us a better perspective on the internal heterogeneity of popular protests—that is, the competing demands that make up any kind of protest movement. Second, thinking about protest as an articulating practice allows us to understand how protests seem to spread contagiously, how they go from being "moments" to "movements."[22] Third, and important for my purposes, it suggests why media coverage is critical to their success. Chains of protests combined with similar expressions of discontent are powerful manifestations of a revolutionary will.

Anticrime Protests

Crime journalists in Caracas spent a significant portion of their energies covering anticrime protests. During my time on the crime beat, I observed scores of blockades, marches, and demonstrations against crime. Transportation unions, whose members were vulnerable to violence and accustomed to collective action, organized many of these protests. Neighborhood associations and student organizations were behind others. In most instances, a homicide was the catalyst and the central actors were relatives or friends of the murder victim.[23] These victims were, in turn, linked to a larger landscape of political struggle.

Many of the people who joined anticrime protests were veterans of the struggle against the Chávez government. In this sense, the protests were a continuation of the opposition's earlier mobilizations, including the failed coup d'état described in chapter 4 (2002), the ensuing oil strike that paralyzed the national economy (2002–3), and the presidential recall referendum (2004). They differed, however, in at least one respect. Anticrime protests were ostensibly apolitical. Demonstrators could credibly argue that crime affected people across the political spectrum, and therefore they could also claim that the protests were a spontaneous expression of the general will. This was a powerful claim.

The first major wave of anticrime protests erupted in early 2006, when tens of thousands took to the streets following a cluster of high-profile homicides. The most impactful of these was undoubtedly the Faddoul case. On February 23, 2006, the Faddoul brothers—John (seventeen years old), Kevin (thirteen), and Jason (twelve)—and their chauffeur, Miguel Rivas, were stopped on their way to school at a police checkpoint and abducted by unidentified kidnappers. Six weeks later their dead bodies were found in a field outside the city. Forensics reports indicated that they were tortured and executed. Overnight, their deaths became the object of widespread mourning. Mass protests followed, concentrated in the wealthy enclaves of eastern Caracas. These protests were fueled by wall-to-wall media coverage, which in turn ratcheted up pressure on the Chávez government. By early April the situation was so dire that the minister of information and communication threatened at least two television stations, RCTV and Globovisión, with charges of incitement.

The Faddoul case was unusual from a journalistic standpoint. Families of kidnapping victims rarely go to the media, but the Faddouls called a press conference in early March, while the boys and Rivas were still in captivity. All of the major news outlets in Caracas ran the story. They circulated photos of the three brothers along with short articles about the kidnapping and possible links to the Metropolitan Police. When this first round of media attention began to fade, the family and their friends organized demonstrations begging for the release of the boys. Photographs of people wearing T-shirts and carrying banners with slogans like "Free the Faddoul Brothers" and "No to Kidnapping!" accompanied the articles and helped move the story into the public eye.

The mother of the three boys, Gladys Diab de Faddoul, became the focal point of media attention after she penned an open letter to the kidnappers that channeled both her suffering and her Christian faith. "Dear kidnappers," it began. "You cannot imagine the enormous damage done to a family by a kidnapping and, hence, to a society as beautiful as Venezuela. In the name of God and thousands of mothers in the world I want to tell you: I forgive you." Diab went on to beg *misericordia* (mercy or loving-kindness) for the captives. She renounced hatred toward the kidnappers and even thanked them for her suffering, through which she had come closer to her family, her friends, and the divine. Such expressions of piety did not match what was expected of a crime victim. Instead of prostrating herself before the state, Diab turned to Roman Catholic theology. Her sentiments were not fully intelligible within the dominant, secular idiom. As the mother of three kidnapped schoolboys, she was expected to beg for their lives, to rail against injustice, or to pour forth her inconsolable sadness. She was not expected to calmly accept the possibility of their death. Many of the crime journalists portrayed her as a mother driven mad by grief.

The case had all the elements of a serial melodrama that played out in the public eye.[24] Its conclusion came in April when the four bodies were found facedown in a clearing about forty miles south of Caracas. Overnight, the story morphed from back-page reading material to full-blown national tragedy. Public mourning over the deaths quickly turned to antigovernment protests, and the protests threatened to blossom into much more. For three days the murder of the Faddoul brothers and Miguel Rivas was at the center of a media storm. Newspapers went cover to cover with the story. It dominated the front page, the politics page, the obituaries, the op-eds, and the crime pages. Every facet of the story was analyzed, including the media coverage itself.

Caracas was perched on the brink of a popular uprising. The protests might have spiraled out of control were it not for Diab, who gave two live interviews on national television. During the first she spoke of her suffering and her wishes for the future. The death of her sons was not an end but rather "the beginning of a Venezuela that all of us want. We want a Venezuela that is united, without distinctions according to creed, race, social or political position."[25] Some interpreted this statement as a rallying cry against the Chávez government and an incitement for more protest. However, the following day Diab gave a second interview with the same television station in which she rejected the politicization of the case. She spoke highly of President Chávez and his humanity in her time of grief. "I do not want my pain to be used towards political ends," Diab said. "I do not need to start a rebellion or political front against anyone. That does not interest me. My interest is simply to humanize, to think, and to know that there exists a God above all of this. . . . To those persons who want to use my words for political ends, I ask you, I beg you to respect my pain, because my pain is the pain of millions of people the world over."[26]

The case of the Faddoul brothers and Miguel Rivas came to symbolize the betrayal of innocent citizens by the very authorities sworn to protect them. Consequently it called into question not only the legitimacy of the police and the justice system but also the entire political structure, especially the administration of President Chávez. For his first six years in power, Chávez had been all but silent on the subject of violent crime. The Faddoul case marked a turning point. Polling data show that it was at this precise moment, April 2006, that "insecurity" overtook unemployment as the number one voter concern in Venezuela.[27] A raft of security initiatives followed.

For the Chávez government, operations like Plan Secure Caracas were driven by the need to defuse protests against crime. For the opposition, this same backlash presented an opportunity to merge the discontent of the middle class and elites with that of the popular sectors. For both camps the affective force that poured into the streets—the expressions of grief, outrage, and resentment—was something that had to be alternately managed or mobilized.

Charismatic Signifiers

Crime victims have a charismatic quality. This was especially true of the Faddoul case, the aftermath of which was characterized by a mixture of pathos and outrage. We are familiar with crime victims as objects of collective grief. Denuncias and protests show that they are also the focal point for collective grievances. It was this combination of grief and grievance that made the murder of the Faddoul brothers and Miguel Rivas powerfully symbolic. The sacredness of mourning shielded the mother, Gladys Diab, from excessive scrutiny and lent her testimonies added weight. Journalists gravitated toward the case because it came to symbolize a larger condition of injustice. It was in this capacity, as subjects of wrong, that crime victims such as the Faddouls fulfilled a symbolic function that was not unlike charisma.

As a term of social scientific analysis, *charisma* has a checkered career beginning with Max Weber's writings on religious and political authority. The concept is most commonly associated with the personal magnetism or superhuman agency of an individual leader. If this association is at least partially supported by Weber's work, the German sociologist explicitly links charismatic authority to the presence of a charismatic community so that it is unclear which takes primacy, the leader or the led.[28] More often than not, this equivocation between charisma as a property of the person or as a characteristic of a social movement is reproduced uncritically. As a result, the term lacks precision. The problem is so intractable that some scholars have advocated abandoning the concept of charisma altogether—a position to which I am not unsympathetic. And yet the specter of charisma persists, even flourishes, despite its lack of conceptual coherence.

Here I would like to propose that charisma's incoherence may actually account for its success and, moreover, that it lends itself to thinking through the antimonies of democratic citizenship.[29] Martin Riesebrodt traces this incoherence back to Weber's original formulation of the concept, which was inspired—at least in part—by anthropological debates about mana around the turn of the twentieth century.[30] This derivation is tremendously suggestive. As Claude Lévi-Strauss famously argued, mana is not so much an analytical category as it is a function of thought itself. More specifically, it is a function of symbolic or magical thinking. According to Lévi-Strauss, the value of such terms as *mana* and *charisma* is that they fill the gap between signifier and signified, langue and parole. They are what he calls "floating signifiers," whose value is derived from the simultaneous discontinuity (of the parts) and unity (of the whole) that is internal to symbolic thinking. The power of such floating or "empty" signifiers is their plasticity, their openness, and their availability to a range of meanings.[31]

It is essential to note that the empty signifier takes the place of charismatic leadership in Ernesto Laclau's theory of populism.[32] This revision matters because it places the paradox of popular sovereignty *before* its charismatic resolution. Populist movements do not originate with any single person or symbol. They coalesce around them. Moreover, charisma is not limited to persons, much less leaders. It is also a quality of things (a fact to which anthropology attests). Those persons, things, and symbols that bridge democracy's internal incoherence are what we might call *charismatic signifiers*. Not only are these signifiers empty, but their emptiness is what "magically" resolves the contradictions of democracy.

More often than not, we eschew the magical thinking internal to democracy, which is rooted in the principle of popular sovereignty. Government of the people, by the people, for the people is only possible if we agree to make the leap between embodied experience and collective representation. Rather than recognizing the disjunctive and discontinuous fabric of democratic politics, normative approaches attempt to contain it within a regime of rules, regulations, and pseudoscience. As a result, populism is usually treated as an aberration. Such a perspective conveniently overlooks the fact that populism is an enactment of popular sovereignty, and that popular sovereignty is the ontopolitical ground on which democracy is imaginable in the first place. Appeals to democracy are appeals to the "demos." One might argue that other forms of government are preferable—for example, polyarchy or anarchy—but minus the rule of the people, they are not *democracy*. If populism is dangerous, it is not because it is inherently authoritarian. Populism is dangerous because it is democracy in action. The promise and peril of populism is no more and no less than the promise and peril of democracy. In fact, populist movements might be better characterized as a species of "democratic revival," a term that forces us to recognize democracy's charismatic dimensions.[33]

Both of Venezuela's democratic revivals, the Bolivarian Revolution and the opposition, were predicated on a series of deeply felt wrongs. As I explained in chapter 4, certain types of victims took on the role of charismatic signifiers whose function was to mediate the distance between those discrete bodies that constitute a body politic. The Bolivarian Revolution was propelled by the disjuncture between the promise of fantastic oil wealth and persistent socioeconomic disparities. Its emblematic citizen-victims were the poor and the racially marked. Hugo Chávez came to embody their suffering. Like chavismo, the opposition was propelled by a sense of injustice and wrongdoing, albeit one that was more inchoate. Aside from its opposition to the governments of Hugo Chávez and Nicolás Maduro, this populist revival failed to coalesce around a unifying grievance. For much of the Chávez era, the opposition was a movement in search of its own charismatic signifier. Which brings us back to the figure of the crime victim.

Who Is the Subject of Wrongs?

If crime victims have a charismatic quality, then it is not tied to the extraordinary qualities of the person but to the symbolic operation of their death. The figure of the crime victim was well suited to the polarized landscape of Venezuelan politics because the experience of violent crime cut across party lines. Crime victimhood was routinely depicted as an experience that united citizens. However, in death, as in life, not all citizens were equal. The discourse on crime in Venezuela alternately elided or emphasized these inequalities. Like citizenship, the politics of victimhood was shaped by a constitutive tension between inclusion and exclusion. The very practices that created a community of suffering also distinguished categories of sufferers.[34]

This fundamental inequality was on display in the memorialization of the Faddoul brothers and the suffering of their mother, Gladys Diab de Faddoul. The boys were pictures of innocence. The two youngest were little more than children, beloved by their peers and devoted to Venezuela. The eldest was a devoted brother on the cusp of adulthood. Their driver, Miguel Rivas, was an honest employee and a hardworking father. It would be difficult to fabricate four crime victims who better matched the profile of the sano. The same was true of the mother. Gladys Diab was a devout Christian and a dutiful wife from a well-to-do background. In this sense, then, the suffering of the Faddouls was simultaneously marked and unmarked: marked in that they represented an elite social stratum; unmarked in that through their suffering this social stratum came to stand as a symbol of the nation as a whole.

Perhaps the best illustration of how crime victimhood mediated unequal demands in the name of national unity was the grassroots campaign Projecto Esperanza, or Project Hope. In November 2011, a group of photographers and student activists collaborated on a photomural project that featured images and testimonies of fifty-four mothers of homicide victims. The inspiration for the project was an international campaign by the French street artist "JR" who rose to prominence thanks to his work in the banlieues of Paris and the favelas of Rio de Janeiro. The first phase of Project Hope hewed closely to the guidelines set out by JR's *Inside Out: The People's Art Project*.[35] Volunteers plastered massive, six-by-eight-foot portraits of the mothers in various locations throughout Caracas. Each portrait was accompanied by a short testimony on the Project Hope website. The project's aim was "to promote respect for life in Venezuela through art." Simple enough.[36]

During the second phase of the campaign, Project Hope modified its visual strategy. Under the slogan "Put Yourself in Her Place" (*Ponte en su lugar*), they invited celebrities and activists to pose with mask-size portraits of the mothers. The original black-and-white pictures were halved along their vertical axes. People then held the portraits in front of their own faces in a visually explicit merger of the identities. Perhaps the most arresting image from the campaign was a photograph of one Maria Elena Delgado—a mother who lost all three of her children—surrounded by people wearing her image. The photo recalls the famous frontispiece of Thomas Hobbes's *Leviathan*.[37] Instead of the king, however, the figurative head of the body politic is the suffering crime victim.

The charisma of crime victimhood could be likened to a mask. Project Hope makes this simile explicit. It also provides a visual record of the racial and economic contradictions that the crime-victim-as-mask attempts to resolve. A quick look at images from the campaign reveals that most of the crime victims are disadvantaged minorities. Most of the people wearing their images are not. This is a pattern. Homicide victims are overwhelmingly poor, young men of color, and yet on the road to collective subjectivity, the figure of the crime victim undergoes a kind of whitewashing.

Project Hope's depiction of the crime-victim-as-mask demonstrates the simultaneous plasticity and concreteness that is essential to the success of any charismatic signifier. On the one hand, it shows us the discursive underpinnings of crime victimhood. It is a reminder that collective identities are constructed and that they are always internally heterogeneous. On the other hand, it also reminds us that every telling is a doing. Identities are produced through embodied experiences and material practices. Think of this as a pragmatic modification of Philip Abrams's famous thesis from "Notes on the Difficulty of Studying the State."[38] Rather than a mask that obscures political practice, we might understand masking or masquerade as one of the fundamental elements of any state-making project. As a result, the properly materialist response is not to fetishize the fetish (the mask or the charismatic signifier) but to study how it is brought to life.

The Primacy of Wrongs

During the second half of the Chávez era, the sting of violent death crystallized the popular will around demands for security.[39] Crime victimhood allowed the opposition to find common ground with constituencies inside chavismo. In the process, protests, denuncias, and other manifestations of popular discontent became platforms for antigovernment mobilization. Was this opportunism? Perhaps. Populist leaders are often accused of manipulating tragedy in their quest for personal power. Absent a leader, the media or some hidden cabal is discovered. President Chávez and his supporters frequently accused the private press and the opposition of exploiting crime for political gain. This may have been true, but such accusations also minimized the experience of crime itself.

Populist movements draw on injuries that are simultaneously real and imagined. There is nothing immaterial about the shock of a homicide, a kidnapping, or an assault. Millions of Venezuelans empathized with the Faddouls and other crime victims because they had suffered, or could imagine themselves suffering, similar tragedies. To accuse crime journalists of manufacturing a crisis ignores the very grounds on which political subjectivity is constituted in the first place. It ignores the lived experience of wounds, of injury, of injustice—in short, a multitude of wrongs.

Emphasizing the primacy of wrongs is a modest attempt to reorient how critical scholars approach the problem of crime. This is as much a methodological point as a theoretical one. Beginning with wrongs allows us to study democratic subjectivity from the ground up.[40] It allows us to observe the practices through which individual grievances are articulated into a semblance of the popular will. Consider, for example, the relationship between that burned-down police station in La Dolorita and Plan Secure Caracas. From a micropolitical perspective, it illustrates how the grievances of crime victims were linked to a proliferation of political practices. Attacking an empty police station could be added to a list of tactics that included denuncias, protests, demonstrations, vigils, blockades, the formation of victims' movements, vigilantism, the lynching of suspected criminals, and journalistic exposés against crime. From a macropolitical perspective, the attack on the police station was a manifestation of popular discontent that the Chávez government could ill afford to ignore. Plan Secure Caracas was an attempt to address that discontent, and it helped initiate a punitive turn within the Bolivarian Revolution.

When the micro and the macro are put in dialogue, we begin to see the outlines of a phenomenon that I call *the will to security*. What I have in mind is a particular articulation of the popular will that coalesces around demands for protection, punishment, and social order. Like any expression of popular sovereignty, the will to security emerges as a kind of spectral presence from a chain of performative provocations (e.g., burning down an empty police station) that depend, in part, on practices of mass mediation. Although the press is instrumental to such practices, that does not mean reporters, activists, or demagogues can create the will to security sui generis. They must articulate a multitude of grievances, injuries, and demands, all of which reflect the lived experience of violent crime and its aftermath.

Starting with wrongs gives us an outlook on the politics of crime that avoids essentialism without minimizing the conditions of life and death in cities like Caracas. If, as Marx once wrote, social consciousness is inextricably bound up with social being, then the social fact of crime is something that scholars and activists cannot afford to ignore.[41] Violent crime was a material condition that produced the will to security in Caracas and Venezuela more broadly. It is not enough to simply denounce its politicization. The will to security must be confronted more directly, if for no other reason than because the wrongs in question have everything to do with the rights that are subsequently demanded.

The Will to Security

August 2014. Two lines of graffiti scrawled along a busy thoroughfare in eastern Caracas: *HAZ PATRIA. MATA UN MALANDRO.* ("Be patriotic. Kill a malandro.") Those two lines—glimpsed through a bus window—exemplify an especially virulent version of the will to security. The phrase *haz patria* was a sardonic twist on the populist nationalism of chavismo, and it frequently appeared in antigovernment humor. *Mata un malandro* modified and darkened the joke. Kill a thug. Or kill someone who looked like a thug, someone deviant, racially marked, from the popular sectors. The statement had a terrifying simplicity, but it was hard to ascertain the intent. Was it a call to arms? Dark comedy? Another denuncia?

Be a patriot. Kill a thug. Everything in this book could be hung on the hook of those two lines; they expose how crime and other forms of victimhood came to justify an oppressive solidarity against a particular category of persons. Yet there was more to those words than just another case of structural violence against minorities and the poor. They also communicated a kind of simmering fury that transformed the politics of security from the inside out. It is vitally important that we pay attention to why that fury emerged and how it was channeled. The future depends on it, and not just in Venezuela.

The global resurgence of populism raises a number of questions, none more urgent than these two: Can we distinguish left-wing from right-wing populism? Should we? My response is a provisional yes. Two general tendencies have emerged under late capitalism. As John Judis explains, left-wing populism is dyadic. It champions "the people against an elite or an establishment" in a "vertical politics of the bottom and middle against the top." Right-wing populism, in contrast, is triadic. It champions "the people against an elite that they accuse of coddling a third group, which can consist of, for instance, immigrants, Islamists, or African American militants."[1] Schematically, we could say that left-wing populism merges the grievances of the subaltern into the body politic, whereas right-wing populism identifies the subaltern as a threat to the body politic that must be purged.[2]

Like any other object of populist mobilization, demands for security have no necessary political valence. Progressives, liberals, centrists, and some leftists have used them to promote new forms of social, economic, and environmental justice. Think "social security," "food security," campaigns against global warming, or attempts to protect vulnerable populations from environmental risks. That being said, it is right-wing populism that has made the will to security its calling card. In the name of security, right-wing populism transforms the popular will into something brutish and bloodthirsty, something that subsumes the rule of law to an unapologetically murderous order.

Kill a thug. Jail a thug. Beat a thug. Lynch a thug. Build a wall to prevent thugs from overrunning the country. The pattern should be familiar by now. Since the 1970s, calls for law and order have propelled a series of revolutions that paired "the invisible hand" of the market with the "iron fist" of the penal state.[3] We often forget the populist appeal of neoliberalism, but we can certainly observe its effects, which were especially pronounced in the domain of criminal justice.[4] For most of the twentieth century, the dominant paradigm of criminal justice in the United States and Western Europe focused on rehabilitation. Practitioners believed that it was possible to reform even the most violent offenders. That correctional consensus endured for almost a century. Then, quite suddenly, it vanished. In its place emerged a punitive paradigm that promised to be tough on crime and even tougher on criminals.[5]

We are just beginning to grasp the extent to which "punitive populism" or "the punitive turn" reshaped democracies around the world.[6] In the United States, its history is tied to Richard Nixon, Ronald Reagan, the war on drugs, the "broken windows" theory of crime control, and the rise of mass incarceration. In Great Britain, it involved Margaret Thatcher, street crime, and John Major's slogan "prison works." In Latin America, the punitive paradigm emerged in concert with the set of economic policies known as the Washington Consensus, the internationalization of the war on drugs, growing fears about street gangs, and a tough-on-crime approach known as *mano dura* ("hard hand"). Everywhere this punitive turn has been as draconian as it has been ineffective at curbing crime. That was never the purpose.[7]

Scholars have paid close attention to the shifting economic, ideological, and technocratic aspects of neoliberalism, yet in spite of the volume of literature, its political success remains something of a mystery. Why would masses of people support cuts in social spending, the upward redistribution of wealth, and the rapid expansion of the carceral apparatus? The popular appeal of crime control holds some of the answers. British cultural studies recognized the relationship between the promise of security and the rise of right-wing populism during the 1970s. Here I have in mind the work of Stuart Hall, Tony Jefferson, John Clarke, and Brian Roberts in their now classic study *Policing the Crisis: Mugging, the State, and Law and Order*. Through interviews with journalists and content analysis of crime news, Hall and his colleagues showed how the press produced a racially inflected panic around the subject of "mugging" (a new term at that time). Mugging was important because it explained the discursive practices through which poor, black youth came to bear the brunt of social censure. More important, it allowed them to demonstrate how the state was being transformed from the bottom up through demands for "law and order" that were fueled by racial and economic animus. In this respect, *Policing the Crisis* was prescient, and it reads like a historical record of right-wing populism's rise.[8]

Popular culture has been instrumental to the emergence and continued success of punitive populism. It is the terrain on which consent is manufactured and dissent is mobilized. Crime stories construct the figure of the criminal Other, and they create the discursive architecture of a victimized collective subject. "We the victims" becomes synonymous with "We the people." The condition of victimhood, in turn, justifies an entire range of practices that might be unthinkable were it not for injured subjectivities. As Émile Durkheim observed, the symbolic practices of retributive justice—punishment in its most vengeful form—play an essential role in the formation of what he called the "collective consciousness."[9] Where Durkheim was mistaken was his assumption that punitive justice was a feature of small-scale societies that could be relegated to a "primitive" past. Advanced democracies also have their sacrificial objects, their wounded subjects, and their moments of collective effervescence.[10]

Over the course of my fieldwork in Venezuela, I observed a series of gradual transformations that added up to a sea change in the politics of security (see chapter 1). The most dramatic was the death of Hugo Chávez and the transition to the presidency of Nicolás Maduro. Chávez was the face of the Bolivarian Revolution for nearly fifteen years. When he died in March 2013, no one was well positioned to assume the mantle of national leadership. Maduro, a former union leader who served almost seven years as minister of foreign affairs (2006–13), was elevated to the vice presidency in October 2012 and hurriedly tapped as Chávez's successor. In April 2013, he won a closely contested presidential election against opposition candidate Henrique Capriles Radonski. Maduro's reward was a situation in which plummeting oil prices presaged Venezuela's greatest economic crisis in living memory. This crisis, coupled with two other factors, accelerated an already perceptible shift in the politics of security. First, Maduro could not replicate Chávez's charisma, which had effectively plastered over the cracks within the Bolivarian Revolution.[11] Second, and perhaps more important, he lacked Chávez's personal and professional ties to the armed forces. As a result, Maduro was far less capable of resisting demands for punitive action from within his base.

Although it is important not to overstate the differences between chavismo and "madurismo," there was an unmistakable rightward shift in the presidential discourse on crime and punishment.[12] This shift became apparent nine months after Chávez's death when another national symbol, the Venezuelan actress and former beauty queen Mónica Spear, and her ex-husband, Thomas Berry, were murdered along a strip of highway in the state of Carabobo. The couple was enjoying the New Year's holiday with their five-year-old daughter, who survived despite a gunshot wound to the leg. The murders inspired a wave of demonstrations, editorials, and televised homages calling for more and greater security. It recalled the Faddoul case described in chapter 8: another charismatic victim, another wave of popular mobilizations.

Mónica Spear was not just any beauty queen turned actress. She was a former Miss Venezuela, which in a country obsessed with beauty pageants made her akin to royalty.[13] At the time of her death, Spear had reached the apex of her stardom thanks to leading roles in a number of internationally popular telenovelas. She played the exquisite protagonist of *La mujer perfecta* (*The Perfect Woman*, 2011), the dutiful heroine of *Flor salvaje* (*Wildflower*, 2012), and the tormented lead of *Pasión prohibida* (*Forbidden Passion*, 2013). All of this celebrity made Spear a success story and a symbol of national pride despite the fact that she lived in the United States and held dual citizenship. News coverage of her death made this symbolism explicit. "Mónica was in love with Venezuela," her father was quoted as saying to CNN. "What happened should never happen to anyone else in this beautiful country. We must work together to make the country safe. We must disarm the people. We must make it so we can go out at night, like we did before."[14]

No sooner had news of Spear's murder broken than President Maduro and his administration were hurrying to contain the fallout. That morning, the president made a lengthy statement to reporters from the state television channel. Maduro acknowledged the murders as a national tragedy, one that united all Venezuelans. He discussed details of the crime, announced plans for a new security initiative, and asked that the case not be used for political ends. Most notably, though, Maduro passionately promised to respond with an "iron hand" (*mano de hierro*). This pronouncement underlined a shift in the government's anticrime discourse. While President Chávez explicitly rejected the language of punitive populism, his successor took up the gospel of law and order. This shift was propelled, at least in part, by nearly a decade of political pressure.[15]

Political tension receded for a few weeks, only to flare up again when a series of volatile student protests racked the country in February 2014. Youth armed with Molotov cocktails took to the street, first in the border town of San Cristobal and later in major urban areas including Caracas. Insecurity was one of the primary grievances of the student protesters. They held up the Spear and Berry murders as emblematic of a larger problem and identified it as a driving force behind the protests. Ironically, success on this front also spelled defeat. No sooner did the Maduro government take up the gauntlet of security than it was directed against the opposition. The same *mano de hierro* ("iron hand") that the president promised to use against the killers of Mónica Spear was, just weeks later, applied to opposition protesters.

Less than a year after the death of President Hugo Chávez, the killing of Mónica Spear and the ensuing student protests marked a moment of change in the politics of security in Venezuela. Chávez came to power in large part on the strength of promises made to the urban poor. Among the most radical of his promises was his commitment to finding a nonrepressive solution to crime. Chávez initially followed through on this promise, but over time his resolve softened. By the beginning of his second term in office, Chávez and the opposition began to find common ground on the subject of crime.[16] That said, the former president never embraced the language of *mano dura*.[17] On this he was consistent unto the end.

President Maduro's promise to pursue and punish crime severely was a significant outward shift in the Bolivarian Revolution. The evidence of this shift was everywhere, but nothing emblemized it better than Operation Free the People (known by the abbreviation of its name in Spanish as OLP), a security initiative launched in July 2015.[18] Under the auspices of crime control, police and military officers conducted sweeps of the barrios. These were the very tactics that Hugo Chávez previously denounced—and with good reason. In its first six months, the OLP was responsible for upward of two hundred deaths and more than fourteen thousand arrests.[19] These new "security" measures—which grew out of the "broken windows" school of crime control—were as draconian as they were ineffective.[20] There was little evidence to suggest that these measures actually curbed crime in Caracas. Like Plan Secure Caracas (described in chapter 8), Operation Free the People projected the spectacle of order. What differentiated OLP from previous security initiatives was that it explicitly valorized the use of deadly force against the popular sectors.[21]

The thing that set the Maduro era apart from the Chávez era was not the existence of police and paramilitary death squads but their legitimation. This is not a trivial detail. The protections in place for vulnerable populations are thin and porous under the best of circumstances. When the will of the people is used to justify a killing machine, those protections vanish; there is no recourse to law, rights, or high-minded ideals of justice. All that is left is the hope of revolution, which in the Venezuelan context is not likely to ameliorate the suffering of the popular sectors. Meanwhile, people keep dying.

What happened to the Bolivarian Revolution? Initially, the Chávez administration attempted to resist the draw of punitive populism. It addressed the crime problem by seeking out experts who emphasized social justice and human rights. Most of their proposed reforms, while excellent in spirit, lacked the financial and institutional backing that they needed to succeed. They also lacked political support. As my colleagues Rebecca Hanson and David Smilde point out, police reforms initiated by the Chávez government were not particularly popular with its political base. The opposition was actually more receptive to the spirit of these reforms, but it was also dead set on resisting anything implemented by the Chávez government.[22] During the period covered by this ethnography (2007–14), many of the president's most ardent supporters joined a chorus of voices demanding tougher police, more prisons, and harsher punishments. Pressure mounted with every killing, and crime journalists played a key role in mobilizing that pressure.

Despite the importance of crime news in shaping the politics of security, the transformation of the Bolivarian Revolution and its security policies cannot be laid at the feet of the media. It is true that many news outlets were aligned against the Chávez government; it is true that they used crime and crime victimhood as instruments for popular mobilization; and it is true that this coverage reproduced existing structures of racial and economic domination. However, blaming "the media" for initiatives like Operation Free the People would be a bridge too far. None of the journalists or editors that I worked with endorsed such policies. To the contrary, they recognized that the use of deadly force by police and the military was an integral part of the problem. More important, to put the blame on crime journalists would absolve the Chávez and Maduro governments of responsibility for implementing the very strategies that the Bolivarian Revolution had once denounced.

It is at this level of analysis that the left/right distinction becomes something of an impediment because it makes populism seem more stable and less slippery than it really is. Populist movements are internally heterogeneous. Maintaining a populist coalition is difficult, especially after that coalition comes to power. New demands emerge. New problems arise. New threats are identified. Populist movements evolve—sometimes quite rapidly—to address shifting political conditions. If we assign a political valence to any given populist movement, it is important to stress that such valences are always provisional because populist movements change over time.

Violent crime coupled with demands for security transformed the terrain of popular struggles in Venezuela in a way that resembled what Antonio Gramsci called a "war of position."[23] The more crime, the more demands to address it; the more these demands circulated, the more pressure they exerted. The will to security was not the product of a right-wing conspiracy. It was the all-too-predictable result of grassroots activism mobilized in the name of crime victims in a context in which institutional reform had failed. Similar scenarios have played out in the United States and Western Europe. Self-styled moderates have repeatedly embraced punitive populism—with its thinly veiled racism, classism, xenophobia, homophobia, and Islamophobia—as a necessary evil. When President Maduro took up the gauntlet of security, he was merely parroting a strategy that had worked so well for the Bill Clintons and Tony Blairs of the world.

What happened to the Caracas crime beat? Instead of an iron fist, journalists found themselves at the mercy of a not-so-invisible hand. When I arrived in Venezuela, the press brimmed with crime stories, but by the summer of 2014 the flood of news had slowed to a trickle. The crime pages had shrunk in some cases to a quarter of their previous size. The number of journalists covering the beat shrank as well. More important, the tone of news coverage changed. It became muted. The pursuit of denuncias dwindled. Everything was diminished except for the steady flow of families in and out of the morgue.

This stifling of crime journalism was the culmination of policies that dated back to the Chávez era. The government initially responded to negative news about crime by questioning the motives of crime reporters and cutting their ties to official sources. Neither tactic proved effective in stemming the flow of denuncias; if anything, it encouraged them. Starting in 2007, the Chávez government targeted media outlets directly. The first such case was the revocation of broadcasting concessions for Venezuela's largest television station, Radio Caracas Television (RCTV). A similar strategy was leveraged against radio stations such as Circuito Nacional Belfort (CNB). In addition to its control over broadcasting concessions, the Chávez government applied economic pressure to opposition news outlets. It levied heavy fines against television stations including Globovisión and placed barriers on the procurement of the materials for newspapers including *El Nacional*. All of these penalizing actions had the effect of creating a more docile if nonetheless still critical press corps.

The Maduro administration took economic pressure to a whole new level. In the span of fifteen months, three of the four most important private news outlets in Caracas were sold to owners more amenable to the government. Globovisión, the twenty-four-hour news station, changed hands in April 2013. *El Universal*, the country's oldest and best-known conservative broadsheet, was sold in July 2014. Both of these transactions were shrouded in secrecy, both resulted in a clear change of editorial line, and both altered the dynamic of news reporting. However, the development with the most far-reaching consequences was the sale of news conglomerate Cadena Capriles, which included *Últimas Noticias*, the newspaper with the highest circulation numbers in Venezuela.

More than any other news outlet during the Chávez era, *Últimas Noticias* had mobilized denuncias as an instrument of political reform. The sale of the newspaper in October 2013 effectively curbed this practice from the inside out. Journalists who have since left the newspaper described a dramatic shift in its day-to-day operations.[24] Previously, decisions on content were made by the newspaper's editorial staff and its director, Eleazar Díaz Rangel. Under the new management, the editors were largely stripped of their decision-making power. Stories that painted the government in a negative light were buried and replaced with headlines praising the accomplishments of the Maduro administration. Journalists who refused to comply were forced out. Those who stayed on faced a systematic campaign of intimidation.

The crime desk of *Últimas Noticias* was one of the first to draw the scrutiny of the new management. Shortly after the paper was sold, the new president director—Héctor Dávila, a member of the governing party—called a meeting with the crime reporters. They were publishing too many stories about death, he told them. Going forward, the bulk of crime news would be consolidated into one brief article per day. Opposite that the newspaper would run a story celebrating the efficacy of the police or the armed forces. This would restore "balance," Dávila claimed. However, the real bombshell was his stance on anonymous sources. Crime reporters were to stop using them. Without the ability to cite unnamed sources, it became far more difficult for journalists to publish denuncias or to do any kind of investigative reporting. That was the intended effect, and it worked. Thereafter, the use of denuncias by crime journalists at *Últimas Noticias* diminished appreciably.

These changes to the crime section of *Últimas Noticias* were a microcosm of changes that swept the field of crime reporting. For most of my time on the Caracas crime beat, things were relatively stable. The people, routines, and style of reporting that I observed in 2007 remained largely unaltered until 2014, at which point everything changed. A wave of crime journalists retired, changed jobs, or moved abroad. Those who remained no longer congregated at the old street corner, la matica. They rarely visited crime scenes. They curtailed the use of denuncias. To add insult to injury, the Ministry of Justice put a chain-link fence around the parking lot of the morgue to keep reporters out. The journalists protested via social media under the hashtag "The fence does not prevent crime" (#LaCercaNoEvitaCrimenes). True. But it certainly prevented crime reporting.

More than 180,000 people have died violent deaths since I began this project in 2007. That's approximately one out of every 200 Venezuelans. The scope is overwhelming. During my time on the Caracas crime beat, I witnessed thousands of people waiting outside the morgue; I listened to hundreds of tragic stories; I attended scores of crime scenes; and I saw more than my share of corpses. At the outset of the project, I wondered, "Is it really that bad?" It took only a few weeks to dispel any doubt. Yes, the situation really is that bad. It is also unexceptional. Since the 1970s, similar problems have confronted scores of cities the world over. Baltimore. Cape Town. Detroit. Guatemala City. Juarez. Kingston. Medellín. Moscow. São Paulo. San Salvador. Saint Louis. Tegucigalpa. Washington, DC. Like the crises of capitalism that hopscotch around the globe, the crises of urban violence are constantly in motion. They are part of a larger phenomenon linked to rapid urbanization, a sharp upturn in socioeconomic inequality, the extraction of rents, and the transformation of labor and kinship under late capitalism.

The Chávez and Maduro governments have been quick to point out these structural factors, but structural explanations of violence leave much to be desired by those who suffer its sting. That was certainly the case in Caracas. Most of the people that I met wanted solutions, not explanations. Justifiably. Here I am at a loss. Like the journalists that I studied, the tools at my disposal are better equipped for denouncing injustice than rectifying it. What I can offer—and what this book supports—is a parting observation about political positioning.

My time on the Caracas crime beat convinced me that critical scholars must rethink our received wisdom about the politics of security. I have drawn a parallel between the rightward drift of the Bolivarian Revolution and the history of right-wing populism because what transpired in Venezuela fits a general pattern. Democratic projects for social and economic equality have been undermined repeatedly by unmet demands for security. Sometimes these demands are little more than a moral panic whipped up against the poor, the foreign, the queer, the racially marked, or the religiously different. That does not mean that they can be summarily dismissed. In Venezuela, the problem of crime was acutely felt by every sector of the population and yet the Chávez government's response was insufficient to the task of ameliorating it. For years the president offered little more than abstract critiques of capitalism and denunciations of the opposition. In retrospect, it would have been wise to take demands for security more seriously both as representative of injustice and for their latent political force. The failure to do so eventually unraveled one of the Bolivarian Revolution's most forward-looking positions.

Apparatuses of security (e.g., laws, police, courts, prisons) are historically contingent. They emerge out of a series of socioeconomic conditions inherited from the past, but that does not mean their form or content is etched in stone. Like the will to security, the provisioning of protection, punishment, and social order is open to different political articulations. We need to continue denouncing right-wing and conservative projects of security, but it is even more vital to begin imagining what a left art of security might entail.[25] Such a project was largely abandoned in the 1970s and 1980s by scholars disillusioned with the Soviet Union. What they bequeathed us is a critique of states and sovereignty that repeats itself without advancing viable alternatives.[26]

Nothing is more central to the operation of the state than the monopoly of legitimate force.[27] To cede security is to cede the state. It does not melt into air or wither away. It passes to other actors. More often than not, the law and apparatuses of security operate as tools of socioeconomic exploitation, but—as Walter Benjamin reminds us—history is not a game of chess played against structural forces destined to win every time.[28] It is an all too human struggle, albeit an uneven one. If leftists cannot respond to demands for justice and security, others will.

Since I have invoked Benjamin's theses on history, they may as well be quoted. "In every era the attempt must be made anew to wrest tradition away from a conformism that is about to overpower it."[29] Critiques of the state that once had genuine historical urgency threaten to succumb to such conformism. The time has come for critical scholars to stop vilifying popular sovereignty and begin thinking about how it might be channeled toward progressive ends. Engaging populism offers such an opportunity. We do so when we level denuncias against powerful institutions such as the police, the courts, or the prisons, and when we expose malign actors in the press or on social media. But denunciation is not enough. Critics of the contemporary security state must also be prepared to respond to popular demands for protection when they arise. If we learn anything from the Bolivarian Revolution's undoing, it might be this: the articulation of wrongs is in vain if it is not coupled with concrete plans for how to set things right. Otherwise, the revolutionary promise of populism can devolve into a vengeful spiral of violence.

INTRODUCTION

1. "Gabriel" is a pseudonym. This account draws on my field notes and field recordings from spring 2010. I have left out the precise date for purposes of anonymity. Hereafter, I cite such materials using an abbreviated format that includes my initials and the date of the event. Unless otherwise noted, all translations are my own.

2. The most recent year for which the Venezuelan government released official statistics that hint at the number of homicides in Caracas is 2015. For that year, the Ministerio Público reported 2,355 violent deaths in Distrito Capital and 3,837 in Miranda state (one-third of the population of Miranda lives within Greater Caracas); see Ministerio Público, *Informe anual de gestión 2016* (Caracas: Ministerio Público, 2017), https://observatoriodeviolencia.org.ve/wp-content/uploads/2017/08/MP_InformeAnualGesti%C3%B3n_2016-1.pdf. This report is consistent with what I observed during my fieldwork (2007–14), when between 200 and 300 victims of violent death passed through the morgue every month. In a bad month the number could range upward of 500. In 2015, New York City recorded a total of 352 cases of "murders and non-legal manslaughters" (New York City Police Department, "Historical New York City Crime Data," accessed 06.15.18, https://www1.nyc.gov/site/nypd/stats/crime-statistics/historical.page).

3. This point will be discussed further in chapter 1. Unlike many cities in the region, Caracas's crime problem was not initially tied to organized crime, narcotrafficking, or paramilitary violence. Instead, it originated in changes to the fabric of the city that undermined institutional structures and informal ties of trust that had held crime in check.

4. In its annual survey, the Mexican nongovernmental organization Seguridad, Justicia, y Paz (SJP) ranked Caracas as the most violent city in the world for 2015 and 2016 and the second most violent city in the world for 2017. There are some observers who have critiqued SJP's methods and motives, but there is no denying that homicide rates in Venezuela's capital city are inordinately high.

5. "Chávez era" is a historical marker that I use for the sake of clarity. Although Hugo Chávez became the most visible incarnation of the popular movement that brought him to power, he was neither its originator nor its sole representative.

6. When I began research, *chavista* was a term largely used by the opposition. It became a self-referential term after a series of debates among intellectuals within the Bolivarian

Revolution in 2009 on the question of "chavismo sin Chávez." See Daniel Hellinger, "Chávez and the Intellectuals," *NACLA Report on the Americas* 45, no. 4 (2012): 51–52.

7. I arrived in Caracas for preliminary research in January 2006. The bulk of my fieldwork was conducted in two stints. The first was a two-year period from August 2007 to July 2009. The second was a six-month period from December 2011 to May 2012. In addition to preliminary fieldwork in January 2006 and July–August 2006, I made half a dozen short (three-to-six-week) research trips in spring 2010, summer 2010, summer 2011, summer 2013, summer 2014, and winter 2015. Participant observation was augmented by (1) more than one hundred interviews with key figures in the press, the field of security, activists, and politicians; (2) a series of thirty-six interviews and three focus groups with readers or viewers of crime news; (3) four weeks of interviews and participant observation alongside kiosk vendors in Caracas; (4) eight life histories of crime journalists; and (5) archival research at *El Nacional, Diario 2001,* Universidad Central de Venezuela, and Biblioteca Nacional.

8. Chapter 1 will provide further information on the transformation of the Chávez government's security policies.

9. The political ferment of the Chávez era is captured by a trio of edited volumes: Steve Ellner and Daniel Hellinger, *Venezuelan Politics in the Chávez Era: Class, Polarization, and Conflict* (Boulder, CO: Lynne Rienner, 2003); Steve Ellner and Miguel Tinker Salas, *Venezuela: Hugo Chávez and the Decline of an "Exceptional Democracy"* (Lanham, MD: Rowman and Littlefield, 2007); David Smilde and Daniel Hellinger, *Venezuela's Bolivarian Democracy: Participation, Politics, and Culture under Chávez* (Durham, NC: Duke University Press, 2011).

10. Javier Corrales underlines the extent of political polarization in his essay "In Search of a Theory of Polarization: Lessons from Venezuela, 1999–2005," *ERLACS: European Review of Latin American and Caribbean Studies,* no. 79 (10.15.05): 105–18. My own analysis points away from regime type and toward the dynamic of populism. Kirk Hawkins makes a similar point in *Venezuela's Chavismo and Populism in Comparative Perspective* (New York: Cambridge University Press, 2010). On the persistence of polarization following the death of Hugo Chávez, see Amy Cooper, Robert Samet, and Naomi Schiller, "Protests and Polarization in Venezuela after Chávez," *Cultural Anthropology,* 02.05.15, https://culanth.org/fieldsights/630-protests-and-polarization-in-venezuela-after-chavez.

11. RS 06.13.08.

12. Felicita Blanco, "Noticia," *El Carabobeño,* 06.15.08.

13. RS 06.15.08.

14. RS 06.15.08.

15. Gustavo Rodríguez, "Protestaron en la morgue el asesino de un conductor," *El Universal,* 06.16.08.

16. Rodríguez, "Protestaron en la morgue."

17. In Latin America during the late twentieth and early twenty-first centuries, denuncias were associated with publicity. This is not universally the case. Under nondemocratic regimes, denunciation is a covert affair. See Sheila Fitzpatrick and Robert Gellately, eds., *Accusatory Practices: Denunciation in Modern European History, 1789–1989* (Chicago: University of Chicago Press, 1997).

18. As a political practice, denunciation rose to prominence during the second half of the twentieth century thanks to human rights activists mobilizing against state terror. See Iain Guest, *Behind the Disappearances: Argentina's Dirty War against Human*

Rights and the United Nations (Philadelphia: University of Pennsylvania Press, 1990); Winifred Tate, *Counting the Dead: The Culture and Politics of Human Rights Activism in Colombia* (Berkeley: University of California Press, 2007). As an explicitly legal instrument, denuncias were introduced into Venezuelan jurisprudence thanks to the 1903 Code of Criminal Procedure (*Código de enjuiciamiento criminal de los Estados Unidos de Venezuela*). The Venezuelan law was a direct translation of the 1865 Italian Code of Criminal Procedure (*Codice di procedura penale*), which in turn was inspired by the Napoleonic Code of 1808. Thanks to my colleague Leo Zaibert for helping me untangle this historical puzzle. On the origins of the Venezuelan law see Humberto Bello Lozano, *Historia de las fuentes e instituciones jurídicas venezolanas* (Caracas: Librería La Lógica, 1985); on the Italian, see Giulio Illuminati, "The Frustrated Turn to Adversarial Procedure in Italy," *Washington University Global Studies Law Review* 4, no. 3 (2005): 567–81.

19. Paul Fournier, *Les officialités au moyen age* (Paris: E. Plon et cie, 1880); Helmut Coing, "English Equity and the 'Denunciatio Evangelica' of the Canon Law," *Law Quarterly Review* 71 (1955): 223–41.

20. Felipe Guaman Poma de Ayala, *The First New Chronicle and Good Government: On the History of the World and the Incas up to 1615* (Austin: University of Texas Press, 2010); Bartolomé de Las Casas, *Brevísima relación de la destrucción de las Indias*, ed. José Miguel Martínez Torrejón (Barcelona: Galaxia Gutenberg, 2009).

21. See Colin Lucas, "The Theory and Practice of Denunciation in the French Revolution," *Journal of Modern History* 68, no. 4 (1996): 768–85; and Jacques Guilhaumou, "Fragments of a Discourse of Denunciation (1789–1794)," in *The French Revolution and the Creation of Modern Political Culture*, vol. 4, *The Terror*, ed. Keith Michael Baker (Oxford: Pergamon, 1994), 139–56. For a take on denunciation in contemporary France, see Luc Boltanski, *Love and Justice as Competences: Three Essays on the Sociology of Action*, trans. Catherine Porter (Cambridge: Polity Press, 2012).

22. The transformation of denuncias from instrument of royal prerogative to tool of popular justice reveals the shifting locus of sovereign power in Latin America. During the late eighteenth and early nineteenth centuries, popular sovereignty became the dominant ideology of state power in the Americas. The wars of independence ushered in a transition from the sovereignty of kings to the sovereignty of the people. This transition had radical implications for the capture, consolidation, and exercise of state power. Nonetheless, key elements of the ancien régime carried over into the new republics. The means of production remained in the hands of elite landowners, and the racial categories of settler-colonialism continued to structure the exercise of power. Popular sovereignty's radical implications for subaltern groups only begin to manifest themselves at the turn of the twentieth century. On this point, David Nugent's history of popular sovereignty in Peru is instructive: David Nugent, "Democracy Otherwise: Struggles over Popular Rule in the Northern Peruvian Andes," in *Democracy: Anthropological Approaches*, ed. Julia Paley (Santa Fe, NM: School for Advanced Research Press, 2008), 21–62.

23. See Francisco Panizza, "Introduction: Populism and the Mirror of Democracy," in *Populism and the Mirror of Democracy* (New York: Verso, 2005), 3.

24. Including Gino Germani, Torcuato di Tella, Francisco Weffort.

25. Ernesto Laclau, *On Populist Reason* (New York: Verso, 2005); Ernesto Laclau and Chantal Mouffe, *Hegemony and Socialist Strategy: Towards a Radical Democratic Politics* (New York: Verso, 1985).

26. This is a schematic gloss on a vast body of scholarship. For a recent overview of the work on populism in Latin America and the United States, see Richie Savage, *Populist Discourse in Venezuela and the United States* (Cham, Switzerland: Springer, 2018).

27. Gino Germani, *Authoritarianism, Fascism, and National Populism* (New Brunswick, NJ: Transaction Publishers, 1978); Torcuato di Tella, "Populism and Reform in Latin America," in *Obstacles to Change in Latin America*, ed. Claudio Veliz (London: Oxford University Press, 1965), 47–72; Francisco Weffort, "State and Mass in Brazil," *Studies in Comparative International Development* 2, no. 12 (1966): 187–96; Ernesto Laclau, *Politics and Ideology in Marxist Theory: Capitalism, Fascism, Populism* (New York: Verso, 1979); and Ernesto Laclau, *On Populist Reason.*

28. Kurt Weyland, "Clarifying a Contested Concept: Populism in the Study of Latin American Politics," *Comparative Politics* 34, no. 1 (2001): 1–22.

29. The first generation of scholars who wrote on populism in Latin America self-consciously eschewed charismatic leadership for both empirical and political reasons. Empirically, charismatic leadership tells us very little about why populist movements emerge. A study of populism in the United States that focused exclusively on Donald Trump would overlook the seemingly obvious fact that right-wing populist mobilization was well under way long before Trump declared his presidential bid. The same could be said for the relationship between Bernie Sanders and popular mobilization on the left. Politically, beginning with charismatic leadership allows scholars to dismiss populism as "irrational" or otherwise undemocratic. Defense of the status quo is much easier if analysis begins with a cult of charisma rather than the grievances of ordinary people.

30. This point should not be confused with what Francisco Panizza calls the clichéd lament about populism's supposed lack of clarity or doubtful utility. While populism may be a "contested concept," Panizza is right to assert that there is "an analytical core around which there is a significant degree of academic consensus" ("Introduction: Populism and the Mirror of Democracy," 1).

31. Claude Lévi-Strauss, *Totemism*, trans. Rodney Needham (Boston: Beacon Press, 1971).

32. For this insight, Ernesto Laclau credits Peter Worsley's essay "The Concept of Populism," in *Populism: Its Meaning and National Characteristics*, ed. Ghita Ionescu and Ernest Gellner (London: Macmillan, 1969). Worsley, in turn, credits Edward Shils's book *The Torment of Secrecy: The Background and Consequences of American Security Policy* (Glencoe, IL: Free Press, 1956).

33. Popular sovereignty rests on an even deeper principle of self-determination or constituent power, which is both collective and singular.

34. The importance of discourse or language is a point of consensus among most scholars of populism. Michael Kazin, for example, defines *populism* as "a language whose speakers conceive of ordinary people as a noble assemblage not bounded narrowly by class, view their elite opponents as self-serving and undemocratic, and seek to mobilize the former against the latter." Michael Kazin, *The Populist Persuasion: An American History* (Ithaca, NY: Cornell University Press, 2017), 1.

35. Laura Grattan, *Populism's Power: Radical Grassroots Democracy in America* (New York: Oxford University Press, 2016).

36. See Laclau, *On Populist Reason*; and Ernesto Laclau, "Populism: What's in a Name?" in Panizza, *Populism and the Mirror of Democracy*, 32–49. The qualities that make Laclau's theories useful also make him controversial in many circles. Along with Chantal Mouffe, Laclau unearthed the armature beneath such collective identities as "the people" and "the working class." The project that the two scholars outlined in

Hegemony and Socialist Strategy was a response to the failings of orthodox Marxism. Although I have deep misgivings about their attempts to replace class struggle with popular struggle, Laclau's description of populism—set forth in *Politics and Ideology in Marxist Theory* and refined in *On Populist Reason*—is rigorous, empirically sound, and well suited to Venezuela. Despite its acknowledged importance, his work is often misunderstood by those who reduce it to a theory of discourse. It is true that Laclau was interested in the discursive underpinning of populist identities. However, he stressed discourse as a socially situated *practice*. Laclau himself is to blame for confusion on another front. His interest in populism is connected to a project that is both descriptive and normative. In Laclau's attempts to claim populism for leftist struggles, he self-consciously engages in what Gayatri Spivak calls "strategic essentialism." Uncareful readers frequently confuse Laclau's normative stances (on "democracy," "the political," or "the working class") with his descriptive account of subject formation. On strategic essentialism, see Gayatri Spivak, "Subaltern Studies: Deconstructing Historiography," in *Selected Subaltern Studies* (Oxford: Oxford University Press, 1988).

37. "Chains of equivalence" is one of Ernesto Laclau and Chantal Mouffe's most important contributions to the study of politics. See Laclau and Mouffe, *Hegemony and Socialist Strategy*.

38. Claude Lévi-Strauss, *Introduction to the Work of Marcel Mauss*, trans. Felicity Baker (London: Routledge, 1987).

39. Laclau, *On Populist Reason*, 73.

40. See Carl Schmitt, *The Crisis of Parliamentary Democracy* (Cambridge, MA: MIT Press, 1988); Ernst Kantorowicz, *The King's Two Bodies* (Princeton, NJ: Princeton University Press, 1957).

41. Kantorowicz's argument is based on his study of English kingship, but there is strong evidence that a similar fiction existed in the Spanish empire; see, for example, Alban Forcione, *Majesty and Humanity: Kings and Their Doubles in the Political Drama of the Spanish Golden Age* (New Haven, CT: Yale University Press, 2009). Anthropological work on kingship and sovereignty suggests that key elements of this problem, while not universal, are certainly widespread. See Marshall Sahlins and David Graeber, *On Kings* (Chicago: HAU, 2017).

42. Thomas Hobbes, *Leviathan* (London: Penguin Classics, 1982).

43. Sheldon Wolin, "The People's Two Bodies," *Democracy* 1, no. 1 (1981): 9–24; Claude Lefort, "Permanence of the Theologico-Political," in *Democracy and Political Theory* (Cambridge: Polity Press, 1991); Edmund S. Morgan, *Inventing the People: The Rise of Popular Sovereignty in England and America* (New York: W. W. Norton, 1989); Eric Santner, *The Royal Remains: The People's Two Bodies and the Endgames of Sovereignty* (Chicago: University of Chicago Press, 2012).

44. My earlier comments notwithstanding, we are still missing an account of how popular sovereignty emerged and evolved differently in different contexts. Thanks to historians such as François-Xavier Guerra, we know that the history of self-rule in Spanish America was different than in France, Haiti, or the United States. Rather than beginning with an insurgency against the Spanish crown, the wars of independence began with a crisis of abdication. See François-Xavier Guerra, "The Implosion of the Spanish Empire," in *The Collective and the Public in Latin America*, ed. Luis Roniger and Tamar Herzog (Eastbourne, UK: Sussex Academic Press, 2000). That means that popular sovereignty (and, by extension, populism) would have its own particular genealogy in Venezuela and Latin America more generally. Rafael Sánchez has begun to

excavate this genealogy in *Dancing Jacobins: A Venezuelan Genealogy of Latin American Populism* (New York: Fordham University Press, 2016).

45. None of which are mutually exclusive.

46. This approach looks closely at who owns media outlets and how economic interests influence what is put into circulation, as in Edward S. Herman and Noam Chomsky, *Manufacturing Consent: The Political Economy of the Mass Media* (New York: Pantheon, 2002).

47. Here I have in mind the work of scholars like Norbert Weiner and Marshall McLuhan. See Norbert Weiner, *The Human Use of Human Beings* (Boston: Da Capo Press, 1988); Marshall McLuhan, *Understanding Media: The Extensions of Man* (New York: MIT Press, 1984).

48. To insist that collective identities such as "the people" and "the popular" are the outcome of representative practices does not mean reproducing essentialist distinctions between essence and appearance or nature and culture. It means directing attention toward political praxis as it operates in and through popular culture. See Antonio Gramsci, *Selections from the Prison Notebooks* (New York: International Publishers, 1971); Stuart Hall, "Notes on Deconstructing 'the Popular,'" in *People's History and Socialist Theory*, ed. Raphael Samuel (London: Routledge and Kegan Paul, 1981); Enrique Dussel, *Twenty Theses on Politics*, trans. George Ciccariello-Maher (Durham, NC: Duke University Press, 2008). On mediation, see Jesús Martín-Barbero, *Communication, Culture and Hegemony: From the Media to Mediations* (London: SAGE, 1993). For a trenchant critique of the term mediation, see Raymond Williams, *Marxism and Literature* (Oxford: Oxford University Press, 1977).

49. I use "the people" and "the popular" interchangeably in a way that is consistent with the origins and definition of these two terms.

50. On the importance of the popular to media and politics in Latin America, see Martín-Barbero, *Communication, Culture and Hegemony*.

51. This argument closely follows the analysis by Stuart Hall in "Notes on Deconstructing 'the Popular.'" My understanding of the popular and popular culture is also indebted to Jesús Martín-Barbero, E. P. Thompson, Raymond Williams, and Antonio Gramsci.

52. Since the wars of independence, *el pueblo* has been the privileged subject of Venezuelan and Spanish-American politics. Like "the people," *el pueblo* refers to both the nation as a unified whole and to "the common people" as the most authentic representatives of that whole. In addition to having explicit socioeconomic connotations, the synecdochic logic whereby a part of the nation comes to represent the whole has an explicitly territorial dimension in Latin America, where *pueblo* also refers to a town or village. These pueblos, along with the popular classes, are the imagined locus of national identity. On the meanings of *pueblo* in Latin America, see the excellent overview by Paul Eiss, *In the Name of El Pueblo: Place, Community, and the Politics of History in Yucatán* (Durham, NC: Duke University Press, 2010), 1–16.

53. That being said, neither class identity nor geography exhausts the possibilities of who or what can claim to represent *el pueblo*. Venezuelan elites have used *el pueblo* to justify various nation-building projects. What Julie Skurski calls the double discourse of national identity in Venezuela imagines a "tutelary" relationship between elites and the popular classes that is "at once inclusionary and exclusionary, horizontal and hierarchical." See Julie Skurski, "The Leader and the 'People': Representing the Nation in Postcolonial Venezuela" (PhD diss., University of Chicago, 1993), 18.

54. In 2018, 81 percent of Latin America was urbanized, trailing only North America and by only one percentage point. United Nations Department of Economic and

Social Affairs, "2018 Revision of World Urbanization Prospects," 05.16.18, https://www.un.org/development/desa/publications/2018-revision-of-world-urbanization-prospects.html.

55. In "Notes on Deconstructing 'the Popular,'" Hall writes, "Popular culture is one of the sites where the struggle for and against a culture of the powerful is engaged. It is also the stakes to be won or lost in that struggle" (239). Hall's analysis reinforces work by scholars of Latin America who have long recognized the importance of popular culture to processes of state formation. See Martín-Barbero, *Communication, Culture and Hegemony*; Gilbert Joseph and Daniel Nugent, eds., *Everyday Forms of State Formation: Revolution and the Negotiation of Rule in Modern Mexico* (Durham, NC: Duke University Press, 1994); Dussel, *Twenty Theses on Politics*.

56. This idea will be explored further in chapter 7.

57. Germán Rey, *El cuerpo del delito: Representación y narrativas mediáticas de la (in)seguridad ciudadana* (Bogotá: Centro de Competencia en Comunicación para América Latina, 2005).

58. What I refer to as the crime beat was known among journalists as *la fuente de sucesos*, literally "the source of events." Here "source," or *fuente*, is the term generally used for different journalistic assignments, such as sports, politics, and crime. The closest English equivalent is "beat." Thanks to Fernando Armstrong, Hannah Appel, and Austin Zeiderman.

59. The most famous example is Freud's concept of stimulus shield, which was taken up and developed by Walter Benjamin. See Sigmund Freud, *Beyond the Pleasure Principle*, ed. James Strachey (New York: W. W. Norton, 1990); Walter Benjamin, "The Work of Art in the Age of Mechanical Reproduction," in *Illuminations* (New York: Schocken Books, 1969). Susan Buck-Morss spells out the connections in her essay "Aesthetics and Anaesthetics: Walter Benjamin's Artwork Essay Reconsidered," *October* 62 (1992): 3–41. See also Wolfgang Schivelbusch, *The Railway Journey: The Industrialization of Time and Space in the Nineteenth Century* (Berkeley: University of California Press, 2014).

60. "Affect management" is a term borrowed from William Mazzarella's article "'Very Bombay': Contending with the Global in an Indian Advertising Agency," *Cultural Anthropology* 18, no. 1 (2003): 33–71. My take on affect is very much in line with what Mazzarella sets out in his essay "Affect: What Is It Good For?" in *Enchantments of Modernity*, ed. Saurabh Dube (New York: Routledge, 2009), 291–309. While I am sympathetic toward certain elements of what is sometimes called "the affective turn" and its application within anthropology, the emphasis of this monograph is on the mediation of violence rather than its experiential immediacy.

61. For an overview, see Sylvia Yanagisako, *Producing Culture and Capital: Family Firms in Italy* (Princeton, NJ: Princeton University Press, 2002).

62. This affective quality also leads to the common albeit incorrect assumption that the popular classes are the main audiences for crime news. In Caracas, crime was the most consumed news genre for both elite broadsheets and popular tabloids.

63. News coverage of crime is often criticized because it violates the sacred space of death for cheap thrills. It is also accused of doing exactly the opposite—anesthetizing audiences by creating distance between the victim and the witness. Both critiques carry an element of truth, but it would be more accurate to say that crime news jumps back and forth between distance and intimacy, and that this rapid oscillation is what makes it powerful. Michael Taussig describes a similar pattern in *Shamanism, Colonialism, and the Wild Man: A Study in Terror and Healing* (Chicago: University of Chicago Press, 1991).

64. José Roberto Duque, *Guerra nuestra: Crónicas de desamparo* (Caracas: Editorial Memorias de Altagracia, 1999), 5–7.

65. These justifications notwithstanding, José Roberto Duque and his colleagues were fully aware of what Michael Taussig calls the "epistemic murk" surrounding narratives of violence. As Duque asserts, "We are sensationalists because the material that we work with—our daily reality—is sensational. What would someone nicer, more bearable do? Work a different beat. Or better yet, make it so in this country there were fewer police who killed for sport, fewer all-powerful lawyers, fewer untouchable politicians, less suffering. But as long as things continue to be as they are, my writing will only provoke ulcers, rings under the eyes, and a desire to react with a touch of fear, a touch of rage, a touch of laugher or a need to urinate" (*Guerra nuestra*, 7). Note here the playful irony and the recognition that narratives of violence have a ludic element.

66. William James, *Pragmatism and Other Writings*, ed. Giles Gunn (New York: Penguin Classics, 2000); Donna Haraway, "Situated Knowledges: The Science Question in Feminism and the Privilege of Partial Perspective," *Feminist Studies* 14, no. 3 (1988): 575–99.

67. RS 10.18.08. I was struck by the parallel between this reporter's statement and Walter Benjamin's famous comments on what happens when the state of emergency becomes the norm. Walter Benjamin, "Theses on the Philosophy of History," in *Illuminations* (New York: Schocken Books, 1969). See also Carl Schmitt, *Political Theology* (Chicago: University of Chicago Press, 1985).

68. For a similar approach to deconstructing the will, see Tomas Matza and Kevin Lewis O'Neill, "Introduction: Politically Unwilling," *Social Text* 32, no. 3 (2014): 1–10.

CHAPTER ONE

1. RS 08.04.14. These figures are from a 2014 census and were presented at a meeting between residents of La Torre de David and Minister Ernesto Villegas.

2. Alfredo Brillembourg and Hubert Klumpner, eds., *Torre David: Informal Vertical Communities* (Zurich: Lars Muller Publishers, 2012); Alejandro Velasco, *Barrio Rising: Urban Popular Politics and the Making of Modern Venezuela* (Oakland: University of California Press, 2015); Lisa Blackmore, "El Helicoide and La Torre de David as Phantom Pavilions," *Bulletin of Latin American Research* 36, no. 2 (2016): 206–22.

3. RS 02.16.08.

4. Jon Lee Anderson, "Slumlord," *New Yorker*, 01.28.13.

5. Brillembourg and Klumpner, *Torre David*, 26.

6. Luis Buitrago Segura, *Caracas la horrible* (Caracas: Editorial Ateneo de Caracas, 1980).

7. Sylvio Waisbord observes that debates about press freedom are also debates about political legitimacy. Everyone defends press freedom—military juntas and armed guerrillas, media moguls and grassroots media activists, neocolonial powers and national liberation movements. Too often the debates devolve into declarations of patriotic faith, so that press freedom is reduced to "what we defend and what our enemies oppose." Sylvio Waisbord, *Watchdog Journalism in South America* (New York: Columbia University Press, 2000), 3.

8. Some scholars emphasize the lack of media production in Venezuela from the 1980s forward. It was true that Venezuela's profile as an *exporter* of media content such as telenovelas, film, art, fashion, and music lagged behind the likes of Argentina, Brazil, Colombia, Cuba, and Mexico. That said, the domestic market for news content was extraordinary. In terms of the audience and sheer quantity of news journalism, Venezuela likely outstripped most of the Western Hemisphere.

9. RS 12.22.08. This figure comes from my interview with the head of distribution of a major Caracas newspaper.

10. Anne Nelson, "No Gloom Here: In Latin America, Newspapers Boom," Media Shift, 05.11.11, http://mediashift.org/2011/05/no-gloom-here-in-latin-america-news papers-boom131/.

11. Andrés Cañizález and Jairo Lugo-Ocando, "The Media in Venezuela," in *The Media in Latin America*, ed. Jairo Lugo-Ocando (New York: Open University Press, 2008), 192.

12. For data on internet see World Bank, "Individuals Using the Internet (% of Population)," accessed 09.23.18, https://data.worldbank.org/indicator/IT.NET.USER.ZS ?locations=VE&year=2011. For data on cell phone penetration see World Bank, "Mobile Cellular Subscriptions (per 100 People)," accessed 09.23.18, https://data.world bank.org/indicator/IT.CEL.SETS.P2?locations=VE&view=map&year=2011. Internet usage continued on an upward trajectory from 2012 to 2017, but cell phone penetration dropped precipitously in 2015. On Twitter usage in Venezuela, see Uri Friedman, "Why Venezuela's Revolution Will Be Tweeted," *Atlantic*, 02.19.14, https://www .theatlantic.com/international/archive/2014/02/why-venezuelas-revolution-will -be-tweeted/283904/.

13. Andrés Cañizález, *Los medios de comunicación social*, Curso de formación sociopolitica 26 (Caracas: Centro Gumilla, 1991); Cañizález and Lugo-Ocando, "Media in Venezuela."

14. The vast majority were family firms, and none of them were publicly held corporations. There were at least ten major ownership groups and very little overlap between print and broadcast properties.

15. This is not counting the scores of radio stations acquired by the government in 1994 after a massive bank bailout. See Jairo Lugo-Ocando and Juan Romero, "From Friends to Foes," *Sincronía* 4 (2003), http://sincronia.cucsh.udg.mx/lugoromero.htm.

16. Marcelino Bisbal, ed., *Hegemonía y control comunicacional* (Caracas: Editorial Alfa, 2009).

17. In 2007 there were 229 officially registered community radio stations and 36 community television stations across Venezuela. Because community newspapers did not require licensing, it was more difficult to estimate their numbers. In my interview with the general director of Alternative and Community Media at the Ministry for Communication and Information (Ministerio del Poder Popular para la Comunicación e Información, or MINCI for short) in January 2008, he estimated that there were more than 100 nationwide. One year later, the head of MINCI, Andrés Izarra, counted nearly 600 total alternative/community media outlets, as reported by Raisa Urribarrí, "De comunitarios a gobunitarios: Los medios alternativos en tiempos de revolución," in Bisbal, *Hegemonía y control comunicacional*.

18. Many of the community media activists—groups including Catia TVe and ANMCLA— traced their roots back to the economic and political crisis of the late 1980s and early 1990s. See Sujatha Fernandes, *Who Can Stop the Drums? Urban Social Movements in Chávez's Venezuela* (Durham, NC: Duke University Press, 2010); Naomi Schiller, *Channeling the State: Community Media and Popular Politics in Venezuela* (Durham, NC: Duke University Press, 2018). An even longer history of alternative media in Venezuela dates back to the 1960s, when intellectuals and activists such as Antonio Pasquali tried to rethink the use and abuse of media on a global scale. See Pasquali, *Comunicación y cultura de masas* (Caracas: Monte Ávila Editores, 1960). This work played an important role in the creation of the influential MacBride report released by the

United Nations Educational, Scientific, and Cultural Organization (UNESCO), and it helped make Venezuela a key location for experiments with alternative media.

19. Fernandes, *Who Can Stop the Drums?*; Schiller, *Channeling the State.*

20. "Journalistic field" refers to Pierre Bourdieu's formulation of a field as a social setting governed by relations of force between actors who are differentially situated. See Pierre Bourdieu, "The Political Field, the Social Science Field, and the Journalistic Field," in *Bourdieu and the Journalistic Field*, ed. Rodney Benson and Erik Neveu (Cambridge: Polity Press, 2005).

21. RS 05.21.08. This emergence of two distinct "tracks" was underscored in my interviews with the communications faculty at the new Universidad Bolivariana de Venezuela (UBV) in Caracas. This new institution aimed to democratize access to higher education, and it was closely associated with chavismo. Students earning degrees from the UBV were much more likely to be employed by agencies connected to the Chávez government than to the private press. For an ethnographic perspective on the UBV's experiment in higher education, see Mariya Ivancheva, "The Bolivarian University of Venezuela," *Learning and Teaching* 6, no. 1 (2013): 3–25.

22. As the former minister of information and communication Andrés Izarra explained in an interview with *El Nacional* published on January 8, 2007.

23. Television stations (6): VTV, TVes, Vive TV, ANTV, Ávila TV, Telesur. Radio Circuits (3): RNV, YVKE, Radio del Sur. Newspapers (2.5): *Correo del Orinoco, Ciudad Caracas,* and *Diario Vea* (privately owned, but almost entirely funded by the national government). News Agencies (1): ABN.

24. Figures are drawn from Mark Weisbrot and Tara Ruttenberg, "Television in Venezuela: Who Dominates the Media?" *MR Online,* 12.13.10. Their data come from AGB Panamericana de Venezuela Medición S.A., a local affiliate of Nielsen Media Research International. In the article they show that the audience share for private broadcast television fell from approximately 80 percent in 2000 to just over 60 percent in 2010. At the same time, the audience share for state television and paid private television increased. State television had an audience share of just over 2 percent in 2000, and in 2010 it was approaching 6 percent of the national viewing audience. For brief periods during 2007, 2008, and 2009, the audience share for state television peaked at 8.5 percent, mostly during periods of political contestation. During this same period, private paid television (cable and satellite) doubled its audience share from around 17 percent in 2000 to nearly 33 percent in 2010. Looking at the figures, there is no doubt that the revocation of RCTV's broadcasting license had the effect of migrating a large portion of the Venezuelan audience to paid private television.

25. Lugo-Ocando and Romero, "From Friends to Foes."

26. For corroborating evidence, see Rebecca Hanson and David Smilde, "Who Is Responsible and What Should Be Done? Public Opinion on Crime and Citizen Security Reform in Venezuela," paper presented at conference "The Paradox of Violence in Venezuela," Tulane University, New Orleans, October 29–31, 2015. A similar attitude toward crime and punishment is described by George Ciccariello-Maher in *We Created Chávez: A People's History of the Venezuelan Revolution* (Durham, NC: Duke University Press, 2013), 77–78. On the surprising continuities that link the Bolivarian Revolution to the modernist vision of the Marcos Pérez Jiménez dictatorship, see Aaron Kappeler, "From Reactionary Modernization to Endogenous Development: The Revolution in Hydroelectricity in Venezuela," *Dialectical Anthropology* 41 (2017): 241–62.

27. See PROVEA's 2009 and 2011 synopses. PROVEA, "Derecho a la seguridad ciudadana," *Situación de los derechos humanos en Venezuela: Informe Anual Octubre*

2008–Septiembre 2009 (Caracas: PROVEA, 2009); PROVEA, "Derecho a la seguridad ciudadana," *Situación de los derechos humanos en Venezuela: Informe Anual Octubre 2010–Septiembre 2011* (Caracas: PROVEA, 2011).

28. Alcaldía de Chacao, "Plan 180: Propuesta para la justicia y la seguridad en Venezuela" (Caracas: Editorial BC Veneuniverso C.A., 2007).

29. *López Mendoza v. Venezuela*, Case 12.668 Inter-Am. Ct. H. R. (September 1, 2011).

30. Leopoldo López, "Un territorio seguro," *El Nacional*, 11.12.11.

31. Verónica Zubillaga, "The February Protests and the Unequal Experience of Violence," *Cultural Anthropology* (blog), 02.05.15, https://culanth.org/fieldsights/637 -the-february-protests-and-the-unequal-experience-of-violence.

32. As Luis Duno-Gottberg demonstrates, the attempt to link President Chávez with criminality was a long-standing element of opposition discourse that had explicit racial and class connotations. See Luis Duno-Gottberg, "The Color of Mobs: Racial Politics, Ethnopopulism and Representation in Venezuela in the Chávez Era," in Smilde and Hellinger, *Venezuela's Bolivarian Democracy*, 271–97. López confronted the government for failing to provide security, but more radical elements criminalized the president and his followers.

33. A. Blanco Muñoz, *Habla el comandante* (Caracas: Catedra Pio Tamayo, 1998), 626; quoted in Andrés Antillano, "Seguridad y política en la Venezuela bolivariana: La seguridad en el debate político venezolano entre 1998–2009," *Espacio abierto* 21, no. 4 (2012), 708.

34. This paragraph draws on Andrés Antillano's essay "Seguridad y política en la Venezuela bolivariana." Two contradictions were evident in the president's stance on crime. First, it was painfully obvious that the problem of violent crime had not subsided despite efforts to fight the social, economic, and political exclusion of the popular classes. Second, policing in Caracas became brutally repressive despite the president's repudiation of *mano dura* policies. Although the new constitution included a number of progressive laws guaranteeing civil, political, and human rights, police practices went in the opposite direction.

35. I divide the politics of security under Chávez and later Maduro into three periods: the early years of hopeful idealism in which the government largely ignored crime and focused on economic justice (1998–2005); a period of intense political maneuvering in which the government pursued a mixture of progressive and heavy-handed policies (2006–12); and the eventual embrace of a hard-line position on crime that targeted the popular sectors in a way that was sharply at odds with Chávez's original vision (2013). Thanks to David Smilde for asking me to clarify this point.

36. Further discussion of this series of crimes appears in chapter 8.

37. See Rebecca Hanson, "Civilian Policing, Socialist Revolution, and Violent Pluralism in Venezuela" (PhD diss., University of Georgia, 2017).

38. "Broken windows" refers to the policing philosophy of George Kelling and James Q. Wilson, which emphasizes perception management over the actual reduction of crime.

39. The difference is not epiphenomenal. Perception management is at the heart of punitive populism, and especially the "broken windows" model of policing.

40. For a summary of factors contributing to violent crime in Venezuela, see David Smilde, "Crime and Revolution in Venezuela," *NACLA Report on the Americas* 49, no. 3 (2017): 303–8; and Verónica Zubillaga, "Menos desigualdad, más violencia: La paradoja de Caracas," *Nueva sociedad* 243 (2013): 104–18.

41. This is a description of violent crime in *Caracas*. Most scholars emphasize the fact that the *national* homicide rate climbed precipitously under the Chávez administration,

but this was not the case for Venezuela's capital city, where the high rate of violent crime was the continuation of a preexisting trend. Before violent crime became a national crisis, it was first an urban problem. For corroborating evidence, see Josbelk González Mejías and Dorothy Kronick, "Measuring Lethal Violence in Venezuela" (working paper, Center for Inter-American Policy and Research, Tulane University, New Orleans, last modified April 13, 2008).

42. The sudden spike in crime that transpired in the 1980s and early 1990s was unprecedented and signaled a change in the material conditions of urban violence in Caracas. However, as Rebecca Jarman and others have shown, urban crime was already a political preoccupation for caraqueños in the 1960s when the criminalization of poverty went hand in hand with the brutal suppression of political dissidents. See Tosca Hernández, *La ideologización del delito y de la pena* (Caracas: UCV, 1997); Emilio Gómez Grillo, *La historia fea de Caracas y otras historias criminológicas* (Caracas: Academia Nacional de la Historia, 1982); Velasco, *Barrio Rising*; Rebecca Jarman, "Representing the Barrios: Culture and Politics in the Venezuelan City 1958–2008" (PhD diss., Cambridge University, 2016). Calculating the homicide rate for cities is notoriously difficult, and this is especially true for Caracas. See Robert Samet, "Getting a Handle on Homicide Rates in Caracas," *Venezuelan Politics and Human Rights* (blog), 08.17.12, http://venezuelablog.tumblr.com/search/samet?og=1. To make matters worse, the Venezuelan government stopped granting direct access to homicide statistics, and researchers have had to cobble together information from alternative sources. See González Mejías and Kronick, "Measuring Lethal Violence in Venezuela."

43. Alejandro Portes and Bryan Roberts, "The Free-Market City: Latin American Urbanization in the Years of the Neoliberal Experiment," *Studies in Comparative International Development* 40, no. 1 (2005): 43–82.

44. Evelina Dagnino, "Citizenship: A Perverse Confluence," *Development in Practice* 17, no. 4/5 (2007): 549–56.

45. Such inequalities were already present in Caracas, but the reforms of the 1980s and 1990s exacerbated the situation. See María-Pilar García Guadilla, "Crisis, actores sociales y geografía urbana: Segregación urbana y castas socio-ecologicas," working paper, Universidad Simon Bolívar, 1993, http://observatoriogeograficoamerica latina.org.mx/egal4/Geografiasocioeconomica/Geografiaurbana/13.pdf; Cecilia Cariola, Miguel Lacabana, and F. J. Velasco, *Impacto socio-ambiental del ajuste estructural: Mercado de trabajo, pobreza y medio ambiente urbano* (Caracas: Cendes, 1999). What is often overlooked in narratives about Venezuela in the late twentieth century is that popular demands for the deepening of democracy were entangled with neoliberal visions of privatization and decentralized control. These two projects intersected and overlapped so that revolutionaries and technocrats found themselves strange bedfellows. To describe the transformation of Caracas as simply the result of "neoliberalism" is dangerously naive. Ideals of grassroots democracy were also influential.

46. Roberto Briceño-León offers a slightly different interpretation of the relationship between violence and the crisis of the petrostate in his essay "Violence in Venezuela: Oil Rent and Political Crisis," *Ciência y saúde coletiva* 11, no. 2 (2006): 315–25.

47. Venezuela and Iran were the two countries that took the lead in establishing OPEC. The other three founding members were Iraq, Kuwait, and Saudi Arabia. At the time of Hugo Chávez's death, Venezuela was believed to have the world's largest reserves of oil thanks to a combination of rising costs and new extraction techniques.

48. Between 1987 and 1992—a span of just five years—poverty levels in Venezuela jumped from 37 percent to 66.5 percent. By 1992 nearly 28 percent of Venezuelans were in a situation of "critical" poverty. See Julia Buxton, *The Failure of Political Reform in Venezuela* (Farnham, UK: Ashgate, 2001).

49. The official death toll was 277, but most experts believe the actual figure was well into the thousands.

50. On the significance of the Caracazo, see Margarita López Maya, "The Venezuelan *Caracazo* of 1989: Popular Protest and Institutional Weakness," *Journal of Latin American Studies* 35, no. 1 (2003): 117–37; Fernando Coronil and Julie Skurski, "Dismembering and Remembering the Nation: The Semantics of Political Violence in Venezuela," *Comparative Studies in Society and History* 33, no. 2 (1991): 288–337.

51. "Venezuelan exceptionalism" refers to the belief prevalent among social scientists and foreign policy analysts of the 1960s, 1970s, and 1980s that the country was unlike its neighbors in Latin America. Democracy, prosperity, peace, and progress set Venezuela apart. The United States actively promoted Venezuelan exceptionalism, using Venezuela as an example for the region and as an important counterweight to the influence of the Cuban Revolution. See Steve Ellner, "Recent Venezuelan Political Studies: A Return to Third World Realities," *Latin American Research Review* 32, no. 2 (1997): 201–18.

52. Briceño-León, "Violence in Venezuela," 321, Ana María Sanjuán, "Democracy, Citizenship, and Violence in Venezuela," in *Citizens of Fear: Urban Violence in Latin America*, ed. Susana Rotker (New Brunswick, NJ: Rutgers University Press, 2002), 91; Susana Rotker, "We Are the Others," in Rotker, *Citizens of Fear*, 224–39.

53. This analysis is consonant with ethnographic studies that link spikes in urban crime to the sociospatial fragmentation of neoliberalism, most notably Teresa Caldeira's study of São Paulo, *City of Walls: Crime, Segregation, and Citizenship in São Paulo* (Berkeley: University of California Press, 2000).

54. Luís Gabaldón and Andrés Antillano, *La policía venezolana: Desarrollo institucional y perspectivas de reforma al inicio del tercer milenio*, vols. 1–3 (Caracas: Conarepol, 2007).

55. As both David Smilde and Verónica Zubillaga point out, the diminution of socioeconomic inequality during the Chávez era did not bring about a drop in homicide rates in Caracas. See Smilde, "Crime and Revolution in Venezuela"; and Zubillaga, "Menos desigualdad, más violencia." At a national level, decreasing rates of inequality coincided with a precipitous increase in crime rates. Political polarization explains only part of this puzzle. Three contributing factors were the rise of narcotrafficking, struggles to monopolize illegal markets, and patterns of rent-seeking behavior associated with oil revenue.

56. Figure 1.2 shows two different estimates of the annual number of homicides. The first measure is based on homicide data collected by the forensic police (CICPC). The second is based on records of violent death kept by the Ministry of Health. For a discussion of the difference between these two measures and on the overall trends in homicide/violent death rates in Venezuela, see in Mejías and Kronick, "Measuring Lethal Violence in Venezuela." Data on homicide and violent death rates courtesy of Dorothy Kronick.

57. So while the homicide rates for the city of Caracas remained relatively stable, the homicide rates for Venezuela increased during the Chávez era.

58. PROVEA, "Derecho a la seguridad ciudadana," *Situación de los derechos humanos en Venezuela: Informe Anual Octubre 2006–Septiembre 2007* (Caracas: PROVEA, 2007).

59. PROVEA, "Derecho a la seguridad ciudadana," *Situación de los derechos humanos en Venezuela: Informe Anual Octubre 2009–Septiembre 2010* (Caracas: PROVEA, 2010).

60. See Ministerio Público, *Informe anual de gestión 2016*. According to my conversation with a knowledgeable source, there is some question as to the accuracy of the ministry's figures and whether it confused the category "homicides" with "violent deaths."

61. See Claire McEvoy and Gergely Hideg, *Global Violent Deaths, 2017* (Geneva: Small Arms Survey, 2018). The intentional homicide rate for South America was provided via email communication with Small Arms Survey and Gergely Hideg on 03.19.18.

62. United Nations Office on Drugs and Crime (UNODC), Jean-Luc Lemahieu, and Angela Me, *Global Study on Homicide* (Vienna: UNODC, 2013); McEvoy and Hideg, *Global Violent Deaths, 2017*.

63. In an effort to maintain the Bolivarian Revolution's grip on power, Chávez's successor, Nicolás Maduro, made security a primary focus. I turn to this new security state in chapter 9. Here at the outset it is important to sound a note of caution. The zeal with which the opposition denounced Chávez and later Maduro tends to obscure the fact that many of the very actors struggling against "dictatorship" forged the chains of their own oppression by linking security to "regime change."

CHAPTER TWO

1. Caracas is divided into five municipalities. The westernmost, Libertador, is the constitutionally designated Capital District, while the four eastern municipalities—Baruta, Chacao, El Hatillo, and Sucre—are part of Miranda state. For my purposes, "Caracas" refers to all five municipalities.

2. The neighborhood name corresponds with the date January 23. On the history of revolutionary struggles in 23 de Enero, see Ciccariello-Maher, *We Created Chávez*; and Velasco, *Barrio Rising*.

3. RS 03.15.08.

4. Henri Lefebvre, *The Production of Space* (Cambridge, MA: Wiley-Blackwell, 1992).

5. Urban planner Kevin Lynch in the mid-twentieth century introduced the concept of cognitive mapping in *The Image of the City* (Cambridge, MA: MIT Press, 1960), and it has been usefully adapted to the humanities and social sciences—see, for example, Frederic Jameson, "Cognitive Mapping," in *Marxism and the Interpretation of Culture*, ed. Cary Nelson and Lawrence Grossberg (Chicago: University of Illinois Press, 1988), 347–57. More recently, Daniel Hallin and Charles Briggs have developed the idea of communicative cartography, which is perhaps better suited to reading social geography. See Daniel Hallin and Charles Briggs, "Biocommunicability: The Neoliberal Subject and Its Contradictions in News Coverage of Health Issues," *Social Text* 25 (2007): 43–66.

6. CICPC stood for "Cuerpo de Investigaciones Científicas, Penales y Criminalísticas." This was the police force responsible for forensic work. For purposes of clarity, I sometimes refer to them as the "forensic" or "investigative" police. Previously, this same police force was known as the National Judicial Police (Cuerpo Técnico de Policía Judicial, or PTJ for short), and many of the journalists still referred to it by this name.

7. RS 06.20.09.

8. On February 21, 2008, Santa Bárbara Airlines Flight 518 crashed in the Venezuelan Andes just moments after takeoff. All forty-six passengers and crew died in what was one of the worst airline crashes in Venezuelan history.

9. The name Frente Venceremos, which roughly translates as "Victorious Front," referenced a slogan of chavismo that was borrowed from the Cuban Revolution: ¡Patria o muerte, venceremos! (Homeland or death—we will be victorious!)

10. RS 11.16.07.

11. In her profile of an earlier generation of crime reporters in Caracas, Damarys Márquez Balza documents the homosocial bonds of male friendship between police and journalists. See Damarys Márquez Balza, El reportero de sucesos (Caracas: Ediciones Joel, 1983).

12. On the close relationship between crime journalists and police see Richard Ericson, Patricia Baranek, and Janet Chan, Representing Order: Crime, Law, and Justice in the News Media (Toronto: University of Toronto Press, 1991); Mark Fishman, Manufacturing the News (Austin: University of Texas Press, 1988); Ieva Jusionyte, Savage Frontier: Making News and Security on the Argentine Border (Oakland: University of California Press, 2015); Rey, El cuerpo del delito.

13. In my conversations with the crime journalists, they emphasized that the closing of the CICPC press offices radically transformed the dynamic of the Caracas crime beat. Archival research fleshed out the story. The closing of the CICPC press office was precipitated by an unauthorized press conference with a dissident colonel in the National Guard, Manuel Carpio Manrique. Carpio had previously called for the ouster of president Hugo Chávez. This particular press conference centered on his denuncias about an illicit arms smuggling ring that was importing weapons with the help of government officials. This denuncia received wide coverage in the press, and it provoked an immediate reaction from the government. The same day, the director of the CICPC, Marcos Chávez, closed the press offices. He also did his best to cut off official and unofficial communication with journalists through any channel other than himself. This was an extraordinary response on the part of the CICPC head, and it is important to understand the broader political context. Carpio's accusations and Marcos Chávez's response took place during the sixth week of a general strike that attempted to shut down oil production in Venezuela and force President Hugo Chávez out of office. The strike was openly supported by many of the private newspapers and television stations in Caracas, which ran ads urging citizens to take to the streets. The country seemed on the verge of civil war. It was only under these extraordinary circumstances that the director of the CICPC had the wherewithal to sever official ties between crime journalists and the investigative police.

14. RS 01.31.09.

15. On the hierarchy that sets news texts above news images, see Zeynep Gürsel, "U.S. Newsworld: The Rule of Text and Everyday Practices of Editing the World," in The Anthropology of News and Journalism, ed. Elizabeth Bird (Bloomington: Indiana University Press, 2009), 35–53.

16. Mark Pedelty's War Stories: The Culture of Foreign Correspondents (New York: Routledge, 1995) documents a similar dynamic among journalists in El Salvador.

17. RS 01.01.08.

18. Márquez Balza, El reportero de sucesos.

19. The gang was named "Los Capriceros" after the street on which they were known to operate—Calle Capri in Pinto Salinas.

20. RS 12.26.08.

21. RS 02.25.08.

22. The term *pack journalism* originally described coverage of US presidential campaigns. Timothy Crouse, *The Boys on the Bus* (New York: Random House Trade Paperbacks, 2003); Hunter S. Thompson, *Fear and Loathing on the Campaign Trail '72* (New York: Simon and Schuster, 2012).

CHAPTER THREE

1. On the relationship between crime news and scale, see Jusionyte, *Savage Frontier*.
2. Charles Briggs, "Mediating Infanticide: Theorizing Relations between Narrative and Violence," *Cultural Anthropology* 22, no. 3 (2007): 315–56.
3. María Alejandra Monagas, "Dos muertos dejó tiroteo en una fiesta en Mariches," *Últimas Noticias*, 02.26.08.
4. Gustavo Rodríguez, "Apagaron la luz en una fiesta y asesinaron a dos jóvenes," *El Universal*, 02.26.08.
5. Thabata Molina, "Mataron a dos personas en una fiesta," *El Nacional*, 02.26.08.
6. Janice Perlman, *The Myth of Marginality: Urban Poverty and Politics in Rio de Janeiro* (Berkeley: University of California Press, 1980).
7. Alfred Brillembourg, Kristin Feireiss, and Hubert Klumpner, eds., *Informal City: Caracas Case* (New York: Prestel Publishing, 2005).
8. Gustavo Rodríguez, "En El Valle el hampa azota a los vecinos y policías por igual," *El Universal*, 02.26.08.
9. Ciccariello-Maher, *We Created Chávez*; Velasco, *Barrio Rising*.
10. The alternate exaltation and denigration of *el pueblo* is not unique to contemporary Venezuela. It is a pattern that recurs throughout Latin American history. As numerous scholars have noted, the term *el pueblo* has at least three meanings that overlap and contradict each other. *El pueblo* can refer to the nation as a whole; it can refer to a territorial entity, not unlike a village; and it can refer to the popular sectors, made up of the poor and working-class persons. For an overview of the significance of *el pueblo* in Latin American history and politics, see Paul Eiss, *In the Name of El Pueblo*.
11. Daniel Goldstein's reflections on the phantom state and its absent presence in the barrios of Cochabamba, Bolivia, was relevant to certain (although not all) of the barrios in Caracas. See Daniel Goldstein, *Outlawed: Between Security and Rights in a Bolivian City* (Durham, NC: Duke University Press, 2012).
12. D'yahana Morales, "El Gobierno tiene pillados a todos los ponebombas," *Últimas Noticias*, 02.26.08.
13. Gustavo Rodríguez, "Era ex disip muerto en explosion," *El Universal*, 02.26.08.
14. Thabata Molina, "Identificados autores de colocación de explosivos en Caracas," *El Nacional*, 02.26.08.
15. The Frente Venceremos affair led investigators to El 23 de Enero. The man who died placing the explosive in front of Fedecameras was identified as Héctor Amado Serrano Abreu, a longtime resident and community leader. According to news reports filed the following day, most of the members of the mysterious group resided in El 23 or Propatria. See Sandra Guerrero's *El Nacional* article from February 27, 2008, "Funcionarios de la PM y Policaracas implicados en explosiones." These revelations led to a series of police operations in the zone, which were met with strenuous resistance. The ensuing struggle between factions within chavismo eventually enlisted the private press. A group of normally reclusive collectives staged a series of small but forceful demonstrations. See the April 4, 2008, coverage of demonstration staged in El 23 by *El Nacional*, "Armed strike in El 23 de Enero: Leaders of 30 collectives protest forcible entries in search of a police officer accused of placing explosive."

The participants described their action as a "popular and revolutionary strike against police repression and persecution." See Sandra Guerrero, "Tomaron el 23 de Enero," *El Nacional*, 04.04.08.

16. David González, "La urbe de los sucesos," *Comunicación* 142 (2008): 23.

17. Charles Tilly, "Spaces of Contention," *Mobilization: An International Quarterly* 5, no. 2 (2000): 135–59; William Sewell, "Space in Contentious Politics," in *Spaces of Contention: Spatialities and Social Movements*, ed. Walter Nichols, Byron Miller, and Justin Beaumont (London: Ashgate, 2013).

18. Tilly, "Spaces of Contention."

19. Allan Silver, "The Demand for Order in Civil Society," in *The Police: Six Sociological Essays*, ed. David J. Bordua (New York: Wiley, 1967), 1–24.

20. In 1992 Chris Hale counted some two hundred works dedicated to the topic. Less than a decade later, that number had jumped to more than eight hundred articles, books, and monographs. Add to this the massive amount of financial and social scientific capital that goes into the victimization surveys that are used by governments and police departments worldwide, and it becomes clear that we are dealing with a cottage industry. See Chris Hale, "Fear of Crime: A Review of the Literature," *International Review of Victimology* 4, no. 2 (1996): 79–150; Jason Ditton and Stephen Farrall, eds., *The Fear of Crime* (Burlington, VT: Routledge, 2000); Murray Lee, *Inventing Fear of Crime* (London: Routledge, 2013).

21. It seems curious that a phenomenon as complex as reactions to crime has been reduced to a single emotional register, even though ethnographers have long recognized that violence engenders a wide and shifting range of responses. See E. Valentine Daniel, *Charred Lullabies* (Princeton, NJ: Princeton University Press, 1996); Allen Feldman, *Formations of Violence: The Narrative of the Body and Political Terror in Northern Ireland* (Chicago: University of Chicago Press, 1991); Nancy Scheper-Hughes, *Death without Weeping: The Violence of Everyday Life in Brazil* (Berkeley: University of California Press, 1993); Taussig, *Shamanism, Colonialism, and the Wild Man*. Fear of crime is not unlike what Bruno Latour calls a "black box." In the social sciences and the humanities, it often functions as a kind of technopolitical shorthand that links the affective force of violence—the immediate experience of pain, suffering, and death—to the ways in which persons and groups respond to it. The black box of fear sits squarely atop the problem of mediation. It magically resolves the thorny, often torturous process of coming into language. Bruno Latour, *Science in Action: How to Follow Scientists and Engineers through Society* (Cambridge, MA: Harvard University Press, 1987).

22. E. P. Thompson, *Customs in Common: Studies in Traditional Popular Culture* (New York: New Press, 1993).

23. Caldeira, *City of Walls*, 21–34.

24. Caldeira, *City of Walls*, 21–34.

CHAPTER FOUR

1. RS 10.10.08.

2. The word comes from the Portuguese term *malandragem*, and it likely made its way to Venezuela from Brazil. Jarman, "Representing the Barrios"; Yolanda Salas, "Imaginaries and Narratives of Prison Violence," in Rotker, *Citizens of Fear*, 207–23.

3. The malandro is a complex figure—part hero, part villain—that is both celebrated and feared. See Yves Pedrazzini and Magaly Sánchez, *Malandros, bandas, y niños de la calle* (Valencia, Venezuela: Vadell Hermanos Editores, 1992); Francisco Ferrándiz,

"The Body as Wound: Possession, Malandros, and Everyday Violence in Venezuela," *Critique of Anthropology* 24, no. 2 (2004): 107–33; Jarman, "Representing the Barrios."

4. Mary Douglas, *Purity and Danger* (New York: Routledge Classics, 2002).

5. RS 04.20.09.

6. According to a 2009 victimization survey conducted by Venezuela's National Statistics Institute, 81 percent of homicide victims were men, 84 percent were from the popular sectors ("strato IV and V"), and 83 percent were between the ages of fifteen and forty-four. See PROVEA, "Derecho a la seguridad ciudadana," 2010.

7. This feminization of innocence has deep historical roots, as Skurski points out in "The Leader and the 'People,'" 18. Elif Babül describes a similar dynamic in Turkey: Elif Babül, "The Paradox of Protection: Human Rights, the Masculinist State, and the Moral Economy of Gratitude in Turkey," *American Ethnologist* 42, no. 1 (2015): 116–30.

8. The gendered dimension of crime reporting demands further study. During my research, crime reporters treated violence against women in a different manner than they treated homicides. Most of the news outlets ran regular features on the topics of sexual and domestic violence, which were intended to raise awareness. Such features were usually couched in general terms and channeled the work of advocacy groups. It was less common for specific cases to be reported in the press, for a number of reasons, including concern for the safety of victims and the reluctance of victims to go to the press.

9. On the inequalities built into Venezuela's "racial democracy," see Winthrop Wright, *Café con leche: Race, Class, and National Image in Venezuela* (Austin: University of Texas Press, 1993). On its performance, see David Guss, *The Festive State: Race, Ethnicity, and Nationalism as Cultural Performance* (Berkeley: University of California Press, 2000). For a discussion of racial politics in the Chávez era, see Louis Duno-Gottberg, "'The Color of Mobs.'"

10. RS 02.24.09.

11. Reporting on "los colectivos" was the exception that proved the rule. The colectivos were associated with a long history of leftist struggle in Venezuela and they represented a quasi-mythical faction within chavismo. Within the 23 de Enero neighborhood, they exercised a very strong police function. For a sympathetic history of the colectivos, see Ciccariello-Maher, *We Created Chávez*. As Ciccariello-Maher points out, news reporting on the colectivos usually cast them as a species of political malandros: George Ciccariello-Maher, "Collective Panic in Venezuela," *Jacobin*, 06.18.14, https://www.jacobinmag.com/2014/06/collective-panic-in-venezuela/.

12. Carrie Rentschler identifies a similar dynamic in *Second Wounds: Victims' Rights and the Media in the U.S.* (Durham, NC: Duke University Press, 2011).

13. The first installation in the series "Rostros de la violencia"—"Portraits [or Face] of Violence"—appeared in *El Nacional* on December 1, 2008.

14. See Jo Fisher, *Mothers of the Disappeared* (Boston: South End Press, 1999); Lynn Stephen, "Women's Rights Are Human Rights: The Merging of Feminine and Feminist Interests among El Salvador's Mothers of the Disappeared (CO-MADRES)," *American Ethnologist* 22, no. 4 (1995): 807–27. On the groundswell of Latin American social movements during this period see Sonia Alvarez, Evelyn Dagnino, and Arturo Escobar, eds., *Cultures of Politics, Politics of Cultures: Re-Visioning Latin American Social Movements* (Boulder, CO: Westview Press, 1998).

15. This is an example of what Bourdieu calls "habitus," that which "goes without saying because it comes without saying." Pierre Bourdieu, *Outline of a Theory of Practice*

(New York: Cambridge University Press, 1977), 167. Bourdieu in turn borrowed from Marcel Mauss, "Techniques of the Body," *Economy and Society* 2, no. 1 (1973): 70–88.

16. Thabata Molina, "'Pido que agarren a los que mataron a mi hijo,'" *El Nacional*, 06.20.09.

17. I use "gay" as a placeholder here. I did not have the opportunity to interview García, and so I do not know how he identified himself.

18. RS 06.29.08. For the reporter to describe García's outing as a denuncia was peculiar and telling. Eve Kosofsky Sedgwick's observations about the "epistemology of the closet" are too relevant to pass unremarked. The "outing" central to denuncias was strongly structured by the homo/hetero binary that Sedgwick describes. Eve Kosofsky Sedgwick, *Epistemology of the Closet* (Berkeley: University of California Press, 1990).

19. RS 06.16.08.

20. RS 06.17.08.

21. *La Hojilla*, 06.16.08. Informativovenez, "Mario Silva: Asesinato de Javier Garcia no es por inseguridad," YouTube, posted 06.17.08, video, 7:13, https://www.youtube.com/watch?v=XtPxuVxrMW4. For a critique of heteronormativity and homophobia within chavismo, see María Teresa Vera-Rojas, "En nombre del amor: Políticas de la sexualidad en el proyecto socialista bolivariano," *Cuadernos de literatura* 18, no. 36 (2014): 58–85.

22. RS 06.15.08.

23. *La Hojilla*, 06.16.08.

24. RS 06.22.08.

25. See Naomi Schiller, "Reckoning with Press Freedom: Community Media, Liberalism, and the Processual State in Caracas, Venezuela," *American Ethnologist* 40, no. 3 (2013): 540–54; Andrés Cañizález, "Medios y pluralismo en Venezuela," *Chasqui* 98 (2007): 4–9.

26. This list is intentionally gendered to underscore the fact that young men represented the overwhelming majority of the homicide victims in Caracas.

CHAPTER FIVE

1. *Escuálido* is a derogatory term used by Hugo Chávez to describe persons associated with the opposition. It connotes "squalor" as well as weakness or frailty.

2. RS 03.16.08.

3. Hawkins, *Venezuela's Chavismo*.

4. One important exception was the 2012 presidential campaign of Henrique Capriles Radonski. In this campaign, the opposition candidate intentionally distanced himself from populist rhetoric.

5. This description is based on a combination of archival research and interviews: RS 03.16.08; RS 03.01.09; RS 03.11.09; RS 03.12.09; RS 02.23.09; RS 08.04.10.

6. RS 03.25.10.

7. RS 03.01.09.

8. "La figura de hoy: Jorge Tortoza," *Diario 2001*, 06.27.02; "Homenaje a un mártir," *Diario 2001*, 06.28.03.

9. This account of the coup draws on archival research in *El Nacional* and *Diario 2001* along with a number of secondary sources. See Luis Britto García, *Venezuela: Investigación de unos medios por encima de toda sospecha* (Caracas: Colección Análisis, 2004); Sandra La Fuente and Carlos Meza, *El acertijo de abril: Relato periodístico de la breve caída de Hugo Chávez* (Caracas: Ediciones Cyngular, 2004); Brian Nelson,

The Silence and the Scorpion: The Coup against Chávez and the Making of Modern Venezuela (New York: Nation Books, 2009); Gregory Wilpert, "The 47-Hour Coup That Changed Everything," *Venezuelanalysis* (blog), 04.13.07, https://venezuelanalysis.com/analysis/2336.

10. Amy Cooper reveals another dimension of the relationship between bodies and politics in Venezuela through the encounters between doctors and patients. See Amy Cooper, "The Doctor's Political Body: Doctor–Patient Interactions and Sociopolitical Belonging in Venezuelan State Clinics," *American Ethnologist* 42, no. 3 (August 2015): 459–74.

11. Luis Duno-Gottberg, "Social Images of Anti-Apocalypse: Bikers and the Representation of Popular Politics in Venezuela," *A Contra Corriente* 6, no. 2 (2009): 144–72; and Duno-Gottberg, "The Color of Mobs."

12. Noam Lupu, "Who Votes for Chavismo? Class Voting in Hugo Chávez's Venezuela," *Latin American Research Review* 45, no. 1 (2010): 7–32.

13. A similar discourse of respectability is described in Stuart Hall et al., *Policing the Crisis: Mugging, the State, and Law and Order*, 2nd ed. (London: Palgrave Macmillan, 2013).

14. Coronil and Skurski, "Dismembering and Remembering the Nation."

15. In "The Color of Mobs," Luis Duno-Gottberg describes this as "ethno-populism."

16. Francisco Toro, "Venezuela's Elusive Voters," *Latitude* (blog), *New York Times*, 08.02.12. http://latitude.blogs.nytimes.com/2012/08/02/a-broad-swath-of-the-venezuelan-electorate-refuses-to-pick-a-side/.

17. RS 07.01.09.

18. Eurídice Ledezma, "Jorge Tortoza, otra bala perdida," *Exceso*, no. 162 (April 2003): 38–45.

19. Ledezma, "Jorge Tortoza, otra bala perdida."

20. RS 03.11.09.

21. RS 08.31.10.

22. RS 03.11.09.

23. RS 03.01.09.

24. B. Nelson, *The Silence and the Scorpion*, 46–47.

25. In Caracas, the only exceptions were state-owned television channel VTV and newspaper *Últimas Noticias*.

26. "Libertad de expresión bajo fuego cruzado," *El Nacional*, 10.30.01.

27. E.g., "Chávez, como los dictadores," *El Nacional*, 10.29.01; and "Alfredo Peña responde a Chávez," *El Nacional*, 10.06.01.

28. E.g., Britto García, *Venezuela: Investigación de unos medios*.

29. Alejandro Botía, *Auge y crisis del Cuatro Poder: La prensa en democracia* (Caracas: Debate, 2007), 263–70.

30. La Fuente and Meza, *El acertijo de abril*.

31. "La battala final será en Miraflores," *El Nacional*, 04.11.01.

32. Ernesto Villegas Poljak, *Abril, golpe adentro* (Caracas: Editorial Galac, 2010).

33. B. Nelson, *The Silence and the Scorpion*, 216–17.

34. "Jorge Tortoza recibirá homenaje póstumo," *El Nacional*, 06.27.02; "Otorgan Premio Nacional de Periodismo póstumo a Jorge Tortoza," *El Universal*, 07.04.10.

35. "Inauguran Sala de Prensa," *Diario 2001*, 07.24.02.

36. "En Caracas marcha revolucionaria rinde homenaje a Jorge Tortoza," *Venpres*, 04.11.04.

37. "Nombre de Jorge Tortoza sera incluido en el Newseum de Washington," *Diario 2001*, 06.11.02.

38. "Estamos sumidos a una agónica lucha," *Diario 2001*, 06.29.02.

39. In Venezuela, the term *revolution* was associated almost exclusively with President Chávez and his supporters. The opposition discourse favored terms borrowed from liberal democracy.

40. RS 08.01.10.

41. Sigmund Freud, *Totem and Taboo*, 5th ed. (New York: W. W. Norton, 1990); James Frazer, *The Golden Bough: A Study in Magic and Religion* (Oxford: Oxford University Press, 2009); William Roberson Smith, *Religion of the Semites* (New Brunswick, NJ: Transaction Publishers, 2002); René Girard, *Violence and the Sacred* (Baltimore: Johns Hopkins University Press, 1979); Maurice Bloch, *Prey into Hunter: The Politics of Religious Experience* (New York: Cambridge University Press, 1991).

42. Freud, *Totem and Taboo*.

43. Girard, *Violence and the Sacred*.

44. Bloch, *Prey into Hunter*.

45. The difficulty with adapting these theories of sacrifice to populist movements is that they tend to read collective identities as the *outcome* of ritual violence. However, in the case of April 11, political identity predated the outbreak of political violence. Thus, interpreting Tortoza's death through the lens of religious sacrifice tends to obscure the real historical practices through which the violence was appropriated for specific ends. If Tortoza was not a sacrifice in the traditional sense, it is nonetheless clear that a sacrificial *idiom* framed the narrative of his murder. In this case, the sacrificial idiom is related to populism as an element of Christian political theology that links victimhood to popular sovereignty.

46. RS 07.30.10.

47. "Chávez, como los dictadores," *El Nacional*, 10.29.01.

48. A great deal of controversy surrounds this footage because it pinned blame for the death of Chávez's supporters and helped legitimate the president's ouster. The controversy begins in the editing of the footage, as summed up by two dueling documentaries, *The Revolution Will Not Be Televised* (Kim Bartley and Donnacha Briain) and *Radiografía de una mentira*, or *X-ray of a Lie* (Wolfgang Schalk).

49. "Photo del asesino del Jorge Tortoza," *Diario 2001*, 11.26.02.

50. "Identificado presunto asesino," *El Universal*, 01.07.03.

51. "A dos meses de la masacre," *El Nacional*, 06.11.02.

52. Villegas Poljak, *Abril, golpe adentro*.

53. In March 2010, Israel Márquez was murdered outside his home in what the police described as a failed carjacking. He was shot seven times while trying to defend himself and his wife.

54. RS 08.20.10; RS 08.21.10.

55. One year later, *El Nacional* published a list of people presumed responsible for more than twenty crimes on April 11 ("Abril dejó 113 víctimas," 04.11.02). In this article, Nelson Márquez is the person connected to the murder of Jorge Tortoza.

56. "Fiscalía imputará a PM por ocultar datos sobre muerte de Tortoza," *El Mundo*, 09.12.06. Although many observers have expressed skepticism about the case set in motion by public prosecutor Danilo Anderson, it is important to note that the hypothesis of the Márquez brothers was more than a fringe conspiracy theory. Four years earlier, the highly regarded opposition newspaper *Tal Cual* leveled similar charges about a cover-up. *Tal Cual* claimed that the documents were changed, bullets were hidden, and the guns of the Márquez brothers were, in fact, fired ("Caso Tortoza," 06.11.02). This accusation was reprinted the following year in *El Nacional*,

"Policía judicial no pudo identificar en 365 días el asesino de Tortoza," 04.12.03. As late as 2007, reputable journalists such as Vladimir Villegas continued to link Tortoza's murder to the Márquez family ("El crimen de Tortoza o la solidaridad mediática," *El Nacional*, 07.31.07).

57. RS 03.01.09; RS 03.11.09; RS 03.12.09; RS 08.30.10.

58. Carlos Ortiz, ed., *Siete días que estremecieron a Venezuela* (Caracas: Libros de El Nacional, 2002).

59. Thomas Blom Hansen and Finn Stepputat, "Sovereignty Revisited," *Annual Review of Anthropology* 35, no. 1 (2006): 295–315; Thomas Blom Hansen and Finn Stepputat, *Sovereign Bodies: Citizens, Migrants, and States in the Postcolonial World* (Princeton, NJ: Princeton University Press, 2005).

60. RS 08.31.10.

61. Stuart Hall, "Popular-Democratic vs. Authoritarian Populism: Two Ways of Taking Democracy Seriously," in *Marxism and Democracy*, ed. Alan Hunt (London: Lawrence and Wishart, 1980), 157–85.

CHAPTER SIX

1. The critique of objectivity was a common refrain among Venezuelan journalists. They frequently contrasted the illusion of objectivity with a professional commitment to honesty or truthfulness. Although Anglo-American journalists tend to conflate these two ideals, objectivity is qualitatively different than truth telling. I conducted more than eighty interviews with journalists of various political stripes in Venezuela. Only one—who was in a very unusual situation—reproduced the discourse of objectivity common in North America and parts of Western Europe. For an important intervention on truth and journalism that is relevant to this discussion, see Natalia Roudakova, *Losing Pravda: Ethics and the Press in Post-Truth Russia* (New York: Cambridge University Press, 2017).

2. This is not the first time someone has suggested that the press in Latin America is distinctive. It has been established that the region's journalistic tradition is the outcome of a specific social, political, and economic history with its own particular cultural configuration. However, few scholars attempt to understand these differences through the eyes of practitioners or set out a theoretical apparatus for studying the practices of media producers in Latin America. Daniel Hallin and Paolo Mancini have gone furthest in probing how the media work in political systems that are democratic but not explicitly liberal. Their description of polarized pluralist systems is a good starting point for understanding the press in Venezuela. See Daniel Hallin and Paolo Mancini, *Comparing Media Systems: Three Models of Media and Politics* (New York: Cambridge University Press, 2004); Daniel Hallin and Stylianos Papathanassopoulos, "Political Clientelism and the Media: Southern Europe and Latin America in Comparative Perspective," *Media, Culture and Society* 24, no. 2 (2002): 175–95. For an anthropological approach, see Naomi Schiller, "Reckoning with Press Freedom."

3. This is standard security protocol in morgues throughout North America, and unauthorized access of this kind would likely result in criminal charges. This information comes from my communication with the Offices of the Medical Examiners for Massachusetts and New York. RS 08.19.16.

4. The so-called LOPNA, or Ley Orgánica para la Protección del Niño y Adolescente (Organic Law for the Protection of Children and Adolescents), was passed by the Venezuelan National Assembly in April 2000. It was revised in December 2007 and then again in June 2015. It contained a number of provisions that ostensibly

protected children from inappropriate content and unsanctioned representation. In practice, it functioned to check the power of the press.

5. "La sentencia," *Últimas Noticias*, 08.18.10.

6. RS 08.18.10.

7. "Prohibido informar," *El Nacional*, 08.18.10.

8. RS 08.18.10.

9. The rise of denunciation was closely tied to human rights activism in Latin America during this period. Scholars have paid close attention to the compilation and circulation of denuncias as part of a strategy of democratic resistance. On the use of denuncias by human rights activists, see Guest, *Behind the Disappearances*; Tate, *Counting the Dead*.

10. On this quantitative jump in mass mediated scandals, see Aníbal Pérez-Liñán, *Presidential Impeachment and the New Political Instability in Latin America* (New York: Cambridge University Press, 2010).

11. The best and most comprehensive book on this shift is Waisbord's *Watchdog Journalism in South America*. See also Rosental Calmon Alves, "From Lapdog to Watchdog: The Role of the Press in Latin America's Democratization," in *Making Journalists: Diverse Models, Global Issues*, ed. Hugo de Burgh (London: Routledge, 2005), 181–202; and Pérez-Liñán, *Presidential Impeachment*.

12. See Waisbord, *Watchdog Journalism in South America*; and Alves, "From Lapdog to Watchdog."

13. This new style of journalism has been referred to as "the vanguard press," "watchdog journalism," "civic journalism," and "mass-mediated scandal." In Venezuela it was referred to as "the journalism of denunciation" throughout the 1990s. See Waisbord, *Watchdog Journalism in South America*; Sallie Hughes, *Newsrooms in Conflict: Journalism and the Democratization of Mexico* (Pittsburgh, PA: University of Pittsburgh Press, 2006); and Pérez-Liñán, *Presidential Impeachment*.

14. See Angel Rama, "Rodolfo Walsh: La narrativa en el conflicto de las culturas," in *Ficciones Argentinas: Antología de lecturas críticas* (Buenos Aires: Grupo Editorial Norma, 2004).

15. As a journalistic ideal, objectivity emerged in the wake of World War I when doubts about the perfectibility of democracy and the possibility of unvarnished facts crept into the consciousness of North American journalists. See Michael Schudson, *Discovering the News: A Social History of American Newspapers* (New York: Basic Books, 1981).

16. See François-Xavier Guerra, "The Spanish-American Tradition of Representation and its European Roots," *Journal of Latin American Studies* 26, no. 1 (1994): 1–35; and Martín-Barbero, *Communication, Culture and Hegemony*.

17. One of the disservices done to testimonio was the refusal by some North American critics to recognize it as a unique representational practice despite the fact that its authors were explicit on this point. On this authorial voice, see Mary Louis Pratt, "I, Rigoberta Menchú and the 'Culture Wars,'" in *The Rigoberta Menchú Controversy*, ed. Arturo Arias (Minneapolis: University of Minnesota Press, 2001), 29–57.

18. See Miguel Barnet, "La novela-testimonio: Socioliteratura," *Union* 6 (1969): 99–122; John Beverley, "The Margin at the Center: On Testimonio," *Modern Fiction Studies* 35, no. 1 (1989): 11–28; and George Yúdice, "Testimonio and Postmodernism," *Latin American Perspectives* 18, no. 3 (1991): 15–31.

19. Yúdice, "Testimonio and Postmodernism," 17.

20. Beverley, "Margin at the Center."

21. Beverley, "Margin at the Center."

22. The line between literature and journalism is particularly difficult to distinguish in Latin America given the tradition of the *letrado* (man of letters or learned person). Men and later women of letters wrote across many genres, so that literary and journalistic careers overlapped. On the confluence of journalism and literature, see Angel Rama, *The Lettered City* (Durham, NC: Duke University Press, 1996). On the relevance of journalism to testimonio, see Michael Moody, "Isabel Allende and the Testimonial Novel," *Confluencia* 2, no. 1 (1986): 39–43; and Margaret Randall, "Reclaiming Voices: Notes on a New Female Practice in Journalism," *Latin American Perspectives* 18, no. 3 (1991): 103–13.

23. In *War Stories*, Mark Pedelty makes a similar observation about the rejection of "objectivity" and the embrace of truthfulness among Salvadoran reporters.

24. Michel Foucault, *Power/Knowledge: Selected Interviews and Other Writings 1972–1977*, ed. Colin Gordon (New York: Vintage, 1980). For a slightly different application of this concept to media production in Venezuela, see Naomi Schiller, "Liberal and Bolivarian Regimes of Truth: Toward a Critically Engaged Anthropology in Caracas, Venezuela," *Transforming Anthropology* 19, no. 1 (2011): 35–42.

25. With the rise of Donald Trump, professional news organizations in the United States began to explicitly denounce the "lies" of a political figure. The suddenness of this shift is summed up in an August 2015 *New York Times* article on the retirement of the comedian Jon Stewart. In that article, the noted journalist Jeff Greenfield remarks, "There are a lot of journalists who watch Stewart and envy the freedom he has. You can't go on television when you're a journalist and say, 'Senator X is a bald-faced liar.'" What Greenfield described as a taken-for-granted norm of US journalism in 2015 has become decidedly less clear-cut. See Jeff Greenfield, "Jon Stewart, Sarcastic Critic of Politics and Media, Is Signing Off," *New York Times*, 08.06.15.

26. Jürgen Habermas, *The Structural Transformation of the Public Sphere: An Inquiry into a Category of Bourgeois Society* (Cambridge, MA: MIT Press, 1991); Nancy Fraser, "Rethinking the Public Sphere: A Contribution to the Critique of Actually Existing Democracy," *Social Text*, no. 25/26 (1990): 56–80; and Oskar Negt and Alexander Kluge, *Public Sphere and Experience: Toward an Analysis of the Bourgeois and Proletarian Public Sphere* (Minneapolis: University of Minnesota Press, 1993).

27. There is good reason to believe that in the United States a shift is under way.

28. See Fernando Coronil, *The Magical State: Nature, Money, and Modernity in Venezuela* (Chicago: University of Chicago Press, 1997), 357; and Terry Lynn Karl, *The Paradox of Plenty: Oil Booms and Petro-States* (Berkeley: University of California Press, 1997), 156.

29. Andrew Templeton, "The Evolution of Popular Opinion," in *Lessons of the Venezuelan Experience*, ed. Moisés Naím (Washington, DC: Woodrow Wilson Center Press, 1995), 79–114; Pérez-Liñán, *Presidential Impeachment*.

30. See Rogelio Pérez Perdomo, "Corruption and Political Crisis," in Naím, *Lessons of the Venezuelan Experience*, 311–33; and Coronil, *Magical State*.

31. See Kurt Weyland, "The Politics of Corruption in Latin America," *Journal of Democracy* 9, no. 2 (1998): 108–21.

32. See Coronil, *Magical State*; and Karl, *Paradox of Plenty*.

33. See Michael Coppedge, *Strong Parties and Lame Ducks: Presidential Partyarchy and Factionalism in Venezuela* (Stanford, CA: Stanford University Press, 1997); Brian Crisp and Dan Levine, "Democratizing the Democracy? Crisis and Reform in Venezuela," *Journal of Interamerican Studies and World Affairs* 40, no. 2 (1998): 27–61; Miriam Kornblith, *Venezuela en los 90: La crisis de la democracia* (Caracas: Ediciones IESA, 1998); and Buxton, *Failure of Political Reform in Venezuela*.

34. Kirk Hawkins argues that the denunciation of corruption is a hallmark of populism. More important for my argument, he shows that this was a shared feature in the presidential campaigns of both Rafael Caldera (1993) and Hugo Chávez (1998). According to Hawkins, populism was the common denominator of nearly every political project following the fall of Venezuela's pacted democracy (Hawkins, *Venezuela's Chavismo*).

35. Ruth Capriles Méndez, ed., *Diccionario de la corrupción en Venezuela: 1984–1992* (Caracas: Consorcio de Ediciones Capriles, 1989), 3:10.

36. See Rogelio Pérez Perdomo, "Corruption and Business in Present Day Venezuela," *Journal of Business Ethics* 9, no. 7 (1990): 555–66.

37. Templeton in "The Evolution of Popular Opinion" argues that Venezuelans were very tolerant of behavior usually classified as corruption. For example, a 1991 survey that asked respondents to rate certain behaviors found that the majority of Venezuelans did not consider government officials exchanging favors with businessmen bidding on a contract to be especially bad behavior.

38. See Lugo-Ocando and Romero, "From Friends to Foes."

39. C. Pedroza, "La denuncia, genero periodística de la crisis" (thesis, Universidad Central de Venezuela, 1994), 151.

40. Elyina Gallardo and Mildred Hernandez, "El periodismo de denuncia: Destabilizador del sistema democrático?" (thesis, Universidad Central de Venezuela, 1993).

41. Robert Samet, "The Denouncers: Populism and the Press in Venezuela," *Journal of Latin American Studies* 49 (2016): 1–27. As of September 2018, Rangel was 90 years old and still working.

42. See especially Di Tella, "Populism and Reform in Latin America"; Weffort, "State and Mass in Brazil"; and Germani, *Authoritarianism, Fascism, and National Populism*.

43. Laclau, *On Populist Reason*, 73.

44. See Louis Althusser and Etienne Balibar, *Reading Capital* (London: Verso, 1997); Louis Althusser, *Lenin and Philosophy and Other Essays* (New York: Monthly Review Press, 2001); Laclau, *Politics and Ideology in Marxist Theory*; and Laclau and Mouffe, *Hegemony and Socialist Strategy*.

45. Stuart Hall and Lawrence Grossberg, "On Postmodernism and Articulation: An Interview with Stuart Hall," *Journal of Communication Inquiry* 10, no. 2 (1986): 45–60.

46. Laclau and Mouffe, *Hegemony and Socialist Strategy*.

47. Templeton, "The Evolution of Popular Opinion."

48. Marcel Granier, *La generación de relevo vs. el estado omnipotente* (Caracas: Seleven, 1984).

49. The strangeness of this coalition deserves emphasis. It is often forgotten that popular demands for the deepening of democracy were entangled with neoliberal visions of privatization and decentralized control. These two projects overlapped, bringing together revolutionaries and technocrats, ex-guerrillas and the owners of capital. Whereas the former imagined reinventing the state, the latter planned to dismantle it.

50. Tulio Hernández, "Medios y conflicto político," in *Medios de comunicación y democracia* (Caracas: UCAB, 1995), 107–33.

51. J. L. Austin, *How to Do Things with Words* (Cambridge, MA: Harvard University Press, 1975).

52. CNN Wire Staff, "Venezuelan newspaper owner defends photograph that spurred investigation," 08.17.10.

53. This focus on victims and protests was explicit. In my interview with the editor of the crime desk, I was told that she was following orders from above. RS 08.28.08.

54. RS 08.28.08.
55. RS 08.28.08.
56. Andrés Izarra and Félix Lopez, *Los guardianes del periodismo pornográfico* (Caracas: Agencia Bolivariana de Noticias, 2010), 122–23.
57. Izarra and Lopez, *Los guardianes del periodismo pornográfico*, 122–23.
58. Hugo Chávez's final *Memoría y cuenta* was delivered on January 13, 2012.

CHAPTER SEVEN

1. RS 03.26.10.
2. Austin, *How to Do Things with Words*.
3. To maintain anonymity, I have left out dates and modified identifying elements of this profile.
4. The overestimation of homicide statistics is something that I described in Robert Samet, "Getting a Handle on Homicide Rates in Caracas." Dorothy Kronick's research has confirmed these observations. In one of her blog posts, Kronick shows that the homicide statistics that were circulated by the Venezuelan Violence Observatory and widely reported in the international press were inflated by at least 20 percent. Dorothy Kronick, "How to Count Our Dead," *Caracas Chronicles* (blog), 07.01.16, https://www.caracaschronicles.com/2016/07/01/our-dead/.
5. See Peter Sloterdijk, *Critique of Cynical Reason* (Minneapolis: University of Minnesota Press, 1987). For an overview of anthropology's engagement with cynicism, see Hans Steinmüller. "A Minimal Definition of Cynicism: Everyday Social Criticism and Some Meanings of 'Life' in Contemporary China," *Anthropology of This Century* (blog), October 2014, http://aotcpress.com/articles/minimal -definition-cynicism-everyday-social-criticism-meanings-life/.
6. Globovisión was Venezuela's most visible opposition television station and critic of Chávez.
7. "Performativity" is most closely associated with ordinary language philosophy, specifically the work of J. L. Austin. In gender studies and queer studies, performativity has been fruitfully taken up alongside theories of "performance." See Shoshana Felman, *The Scandal of the Speaking Body: Don Juan with J. L. Austin, or Seduction in Two Languages* (Stanford, CA: Stanford University Press, 2002); Judith Butler, *Bodies That Matter: On the Discursive Limits of "Sex"* (London: Routledge, 1993); Eve Kosofsky Sedgwick, *Touching Feeling: Affect, Pedagogy, Performativity* (Durham, NC: Duke University Press, 2003); and Paulla Ebron, "Constituting Subjects through Performative Acts," in *Africa after Gender?*, ed. Catherine M. Cole, Takyiwaa Manuh, and Stephan F. Miescher (Bloomington: Indiana University Press, 2007), 171–90.
8. Although this is often mistaken as a strong "constructivist" argument, no serious theory of performativity suggests that social facts are somehow unreal. Discourse, like any other doing, has effects. A more apt description might be "antiessentialist." See, Sedgwick, *Touching Feeling*, 5.
9. Austin, *How to Do Things with Words*, 6.
10. Austin's typology of speech acts differentiated illocutionary acts and perlocutionary effects. Illocution does something more or less directly (e.g., "commands," "judges," "baptizes") whereas perlocution is an effect that may be provoked in the future (e.g., to persuade or to incite). Although Austin concentrates on the former, it is clear that the illocutionary and perlocutionary are not easily unlinked.
11. Jacques Derrida, "Signature Event Context," in *Limited Inc* (Evanston, IL: Northwestern University Press, 1988).

12. Jacques Derrida famously highlighted the iterative quality of performatives. See Derrida, "Signature Event Context." Although the critical scholarship on performativity usually references Derrida's work, it is worth noting that variations of the theme of iteration (for example, "différance") as the play of repetition and difference have been central to theories of mediation dating back to the ancient Greek concept of mimesis. The novelty (and difficulty) of Derrida's approach was the extent to which he pushed the imitative principle by unmooring it from a point of origin. In this respect, his work bears a close resemblance to C. S. Peirce's idea of "infinite semiosis." See C. S. Peirce, "Questions Concerning Certain Faculties Claimed for Man," *Journal of Speculative Philosophy* 2 (1868): 103–14; Albert Atkin, "Peirce's Theory of Signs," *Stanford Encyclopedia of Philosophy*, Summer 2013 ed., http://plato.stanford.edu/archives/sum2013/entries/perice-semiotics.

13. On the ritualistic quality of performatives and communication more generally, see Derrida, *Limited Inc*, 21. For an anthropological take, see Stanley Tambiah, "A Performative Approach to Ritual," *Proceedings of the British Academy* 65 (1979): 113–69.

14. Butler, *Bodies That Matter*; and Judith Butler, *Excitable Speech: A Politics of the Performative* (New York: Routledge, 1997).

15. Michael Warner, *Publics and Counterpublics* (New York: Zone Books, 2005).

16. The quotation is not from Pascal himself but from Louis Althusser's essay "Ideology and Ideological State Apparatuses," in *Lenin and Philosophy*, 114.

17. In this regard, the "movement" so crucial to the formation of populist identities might better be described as a process of accretion or aggregation that functions via repetition. Jeffrey Juris develops a similar theory of aggregation and the relationship between media, democracy, and political mobilization in "Reflections on #Occupy Everywhere: Social Media, Public Space, and Emerging Logics of Aggregation," *American Ethnologist* 39, no. 2 (2012): 259–79.

18. Benjamin, "Theses on the Philosophy of History."

19. By *ontopolitical*, I am referring to the secular deification of human agency, which is central to both the Enlightenment project and immanent critiques thereof. What some have called the "ontological turn" often papers over the extent to which critiques of secular humanism are parasitically (in Derrida's sense) dependent on it.

20. Wendy Brown, "Wounded Attachments," *Political Theory* 21, no. 3 (1993): 390–410.

21. This distinction was made in Velasco's commentary on a paper delivered at the Watson Institute for International Studies. See Alejandro Velasco, "Where Are the Barrios? Street Protest and Popular Politics in Venezuela, Then and Now" (paper presented at Center for Latin American and Caribbean Studies conference "Venezuela after Chavez," Watson Institute for International Studies, Brown University, Providence, RI, April 30, 2014), https://watson.brown.edu/clacs/files/clacs/imce/publications/Venzuela%20After%20Chavez.pdf.

22. RS 02.12.08.

23. RS 03.08.10.

24. RS 02.12.08.

25. RS 12.19.07.

26. Eleazar Díaz Rangel, "Urge frenar la inseguridad," *Últimas Noticias*, 09.17.08.

27. Wilmer Poleo, "Código Policial: La voz del pueblo," *Últimas Noticias*, 09.29.08.

28. RS 09.26.08.

29. Coronil and Skurski, "Dismembering and Remembering the Nation," 83.

30. Theodore Glasser and James Ettema make a similar observation about populism and the press: "The pitting of the press against power, particularly the power of the state,

reflects a fundamentally populist conception of the press in contemporary society." James Ettema and Theodore Glasser, *Custodians of Conscience* (New York: Columbia University Press, 1998), 3.

31. RS 01.11.08.
32. RS 03.10.08.
33. RS 03.15.08.
34. See Althusser, *Lenin and Philosophy*. Danilyn Rutherford makes a similar observation about the policeman in George Orwell's story "Shooting an Elephant." See Danilyn Rutherford, *Laughing at Leviathan: Sovereignty and Audience in West Papua* (Chicago: University of Chicago Press, 2012).

CHAPTER EIGHT

1. RS 10.02.08.
2. "El Aissami: 20% de los delitos son cometidos por funcionarios policiales." *El Universal*, 06.02.09.
3. Charles Tilly, *Popular Contention in Great Britain, 1758–1834* (Boulder, CO: Paradigm, 2005); Jason Frank, *Constituent Moments: Enacting the People in Postrevolutionary America* (Durham, NC: Duke University Press, 2010). What I am describing is similar to Tania Ahmad's "Socialities of Indignation: Denouncing Party Politics in Karachi," *Cultural Anthropology* 29, no. 2 (2014): 411–32.
4. The term "citizen security" can be traced to the United Nations Development Programme's 1994 Human Development Report, which proposed the concept of "human security."
5. E.g., Daniel Goldstein, "Human Rights as Culprit, Human Rights as Victim," in *The Practice of Human Rights*, ed. Mark Goodale and Sally Engle Merry (New York: Cambridge University Press. 2007), 49–77.
6. Within anthropology, this impasse is best described by Teresa Caldeira and James Holston's writings on "disjunctive democracy." See Teresa Caldeira and James Holston, "Democracy and Violence in Brazil," *Comparative Studies in Society and History* 41, no. 4 (1999): 691–729.
7. In *Philosophy of Right*, Hegel describes abstract right as the by-product of concrete wrong; see Georg Wilhelm Friedrich Hegel, *Hegel's Philosophy of Right*, trans. T. M. Knox (New York: Oxford University Press, 1967), 64–74. Jacques Rancière outlines a similar approach to wrongs in *Disagreement*, as does Elias Canetti in *Crowds and Power* ("the sting" of command); see Jacques Rancière, *Disagreement: Politics and Philosophy*, trans. Julie Rose (Minneapolis: University of Minnesota Press, 2004); and Elias Canetti, *Crowds and Power* (New York: Farrar, Straus and Giroux, 1984). My own formulation is most directly indebted to Wendy Brown's essay "Wounded Attachments."
8. In J. L. Austin's terms, we might say that rights are parasitic on wrongs. Thanks to Frederic Schaffer for this observation. See Frederic Schaffer, *Elucidating Social Science Concepts: An Interpretivist Guide* (New York: Routledge, 2015).
9. Émile Durkheim, *The Elementary Forms of Religious Life*, trans. Karen E. Fields (New York: Free Press, 1995).
10. Ministerio del Poder Popular para la Comunicación y la Información, "Semana 40, La Dolorita en Petare: 3800 funcionarios participan en Plan Caracas Segura," accessed 01.17.14, http://radiomundial.com.ve/node/147141 (content no longer available).
11. Between 1999 and 2012, the Chávez government launched more than twenty security initiatives. See PROVEA, "Derecho a la seguridad ciudadana," *Situación de los derechos humanos en Venezuela: Informe Anual Enero–Diciembre 2012* (Caracas: PROVEA, 2012).

12. RS 01.10.08.
13. RS 01.11.08.
14. Refers to news about celebrities and show business.
15. President Chávez repeatedly stated that the main problem was the perception of insecurity, which Plan Secure Caracas aimed to address.
16. Elizabeth Povinelli, "Defining Security in Late Liberalism: A Comment on Pedersen and Holbraad," in *Times of Security: Ethnographies of Fear, Protest and the Future*, ed. Martin Holbraad and Morten Axel Pedersen (London: Routledge, 2013), 28–32; Michel Foucault, *Security, Territory, Population: Lectures at the Collège de France 1977–1978* (New York: Macmillan, 2009).
17. Popular sovereignty is democracy's constituent power. See Frank, *Constituent Moments*; Schmitt, *Crisis of Parliamentary Democracy*; Sheldon S. Wolin, "'Fugitive Democracy,'" *Constellations* 1, no. 1 (1994): 11–25. The concept of constituent power—as elaborated in political and legal theory—allows that self-government is not limited to national-popular projects. For example, claims made in the name of "the community" draw on constituent power albeit at a different scale. It is important to recognize that shifting scale does not allow us to sidestep the paradox of popular sovereignty.
18. Charlie Devereux and Robert Samet, "Crime Runs Amok in Caracas Slums," *San Francisco Chronicle*, 11.16.08.
19. For an explanation of the historical and political significance of the Caracazo, see Coronil and Skurski, "Dismembering and Remembering the Nation"; Margarita López Maya, "Venezuelan *Caracazo* of 1989."
20. Quoted in Aleida Guevara and Hugo Chávez, *Chávez, Venezuela, and the New Latin America* (London: Ocean Press, 2005), 10.
21. E. Thompson, *Customs in Common*, 185.
22. Thanks to Sonia Alvarez, Angélica Bernal, Barbara Cruikshank, and the "On Protest" working group who pushed my thinking on the relationship between "moments" and "movements."
23. Less frequently it was a kidnapping or a sexual assault.
24. On the relationship between melodrama, the popular, and Latin American politics, see Martín-Barbero, *Communication, Culture and Hegemony*.
25. Alexis Rosas, *El asesinato del los hermanos Faddoul* (Caracas: Editorial Alfa, 2008), 17.
26. Rosas, *El asesinato del los hermanos Faddoul*, 108.
27. PROVEA, "Derecho a la seguridad ciudadana," *Situación de los derechos humanos en Venezuela: Informe Anual Octubre 2005–Septiembre 2006* (Caracas: PROVEA, 2006), 334.
28. Max Weber, *Economy and Society*, vol. 1 (Berkeley: University of California Press, 1978).
29. Tove Tybjerg, "Reflections on 'Charisma,'" *Nordic Journal of Religion and Society* 20, no. 2 (2007): 167–78.
30. Martin Riesebrodt, "Charisma in Max Weber's Sociology of Religion," *Religion* 29, no. 1 (1999): 1–14.
31. Lévi-Strauss, *Introduction to the Work of Marcel Mauss*.
32. Laclau, *On Populist Reason*; Laclau, *Politics and Ideology in Marxist Theory*.
33. See Wolin, "Fugitive Democracy," for a similar description.
34. See James Holston, *Insurgent Citizenship: Disjunctions of Democracy and Modernity in Brazil* (Princeton, NJ: Princeton University Press, 2009); Engin Isin and Patricia Wood, *Citizenship and Identity* (Thousand Oaks, CA: SAGE, 1999); and Bryan S. Turner, "Outline of a Theory of Citizenship," *Sociology* 24, no. 2 (1990): 189–217.

35. See *Inside Out: The People's Art Project* at http://www.insideoutproject.net/en, where Projecto Esperanza's work is featured along with seventy other projects (accessed 12.13.16; 08.29.18).
36. María Fernanda Pérez Rincones, "Projecto Esperanza," *Tribuna del investigador* 12, no. 1–2 (2012): 31–35, at 32.
37. Hobbes, *Leviathan*.
38. "The state is not the reality which stands behind the mask of political practice. It is itself the mask which prevents our seeing political practice as it is." Philip Abrams, "Notes on the Difficulty of Studying the State," *Journal of Historical Sociology* 1, no. 1 (1988): 58–59, at 58.
39. Thinking alongside Wendy Brown or Jacques Lacan, we might refer to this as a "wound." Elias Canetti describes it as a "sting"; Canetti, *Crowds and Power*.
40. See Brown, "Wounded Attachments," for a discussion of how projects for political emancipation form wounded attachments to the state.
41. Karl Marx, *A Contribution to the Critique of Political Economy*, ed. Maurice Dobb (New York: International Publishers, 1979); Raymond Williams, *Marxism and Literature*.

CONCLUSION

1. John Judis, *The Populist Explosion: How the Great Recession Transformed American and European Politics* (New York: Columbia Global Reports, 2016), 14–15. Judis is one of few scholars to provide a working definition of this distinction.
2. Right-wing populism persecutes certain subaltern groups. It incorporates others. See, e.g., Thomas Blom Hansen, *The Saffron Wave: Democracy and Hindu Nationalism in Modern India* (Princeton, NJ: Princeton University Press, 1999).
3. Loïc Wacquant, "Three Steps to a Historical Anthropology of Actually Existing Neo-liberalism," *Social Anthropology* 20, no. 1 (2012): 66–79, at 67.
4. The term *neoliberalism* has come under scrutiny, not undeservedly; I find it useful for describing the assemblage of ideologies, policies, and institutions associated with the political and socioeconomic sea change of the 1970s and 1980s.
5. David Garland, *The Culture of Control: Crime and Social Order in Contemporary Society* (Chicago: University of Chicago Press, 2002).
6. Scholars have grappled with the onset of punitive policies since the 1970s; however, the full extent of the punitive turn only became apparent at the end of the twentieth century. In his 1995 essay "The Philosophy and Politics of Punishment and Sentencing," Anthony Bottoms observed that tough-on-crime policies were driven by a populist dynamic. See Anthony Bottoms, "The Philosophy and Politics of Punishment and Sentencing," in *The Politics of Sentencing Reform*, ed. C. M. V. Clarkson and Rod Morgan (Oxford: Clarendon Press, 1995). Scholars have built on his thesis of punitive populism. The significance of Bottoms's observation is lost if populism is reduced to a conspiracy between unscrupulous politicians and a pitchfork-waving mob. Although punitive populism in North America was part of a counterrevolutionary backlash, it drew together diverse constituencies, including some of those who became its primary targets. More confounding, if anticrime, prosecurity movements eroded liberal democracy, they were nonetheless an outgrowth of democratic institutions (electoral democracy, press freedom, and civil society groups, to name a few). Similar antinomies are reflected in ethnographies of crime and punishment in Latin America. On the rise of punitive paradigm in Europe and the United States, see Michelle Alexander, *The New Jim Crow* (New York: New Press, 2012); Garland, *Culture of Control*; Stuart Hall et al., *Policing the Crisis*; and Jonathan Simon, *Governing*

through Crime: How the War on Crime Transformed American Democracy and Created a Culture of Fear (New York: Oxford University Press, 2009). One the rise of a similar paradigm in Latin America, see Desmond Arias and Daniel Goldstein, *Violent Democracies in Latin America* (Durham, NC: Duke University Press, 2010); Teresa Caldeira, *City of Walls*; Graham Denyer Willis, *The Killing Consensus: Police, Organized Crime, and the Regulation of Life and Death in Urban Brazil* (Oakland: University of California Press, 2015); Angelina Godoy, *Popular Injustice: Violence, Community, and Law in Latin America* (Stanford, CA: Stanford University Press, 2006); Goldstein, *Outlawed*; and Kevin Lewis O'Neill, *Secure the Soul: Christian Piety and Gang Prevention in Guatemala* (Oakland: University of California Press, 2015).

7. The punitive turn was part of the neoliberal revolution. My reading of this relationship is similar, in certain respects, to the one set out by Loïc Wacquant in "Three Steps to a Historical Anthropology of Actually Existing Neoliberalism."

8. Hall explicitly linked these phenomena. See Stuart Hall, "Authoritarian Populism," *New Left Review*, no. 151 (1985): 115–24.

9. Durkheim, *The Division of Labor in Society* (New York: Free Press, 2014).

10. Jean and John Comaroff, *The Truth about Crime* (Chicago: University of Chicago Press, 2016); Carol Greenhouse, "Durkheim and Law: Divided Readings over Division of Labor," *Annual Review of Law and Social Science* 7, no. 1 (2011): 165–85.

11. Scholars have noted the heterogeneous composition of the Bolivarian Revolution and its internal disjunctures. See, for example, Matt Wilde, "Utopian Disjunctures: Popular Democracy and the Communal State in Urban Venezuela," *Critique of Anthropology* 37, no. 1 (2017): 47–66.

12. The punitive turn was well under way before Maduro came to power. See Andrés Antillano, "Crimen y castigo en la revolución bolivariana," *Cuestiones de sociología*, no. 10 (2014), https://www.cuestionessociologia.fahce.unlp.edu.ar/article/view /CSn10a19/6070. The thing that set Maduro apart from Chávez was his adoption of the language of *mano dura*. See Andrés Antillano, Verónica Zubillaga, and Keymer Ávila, "Revolution and Counter-Reformation: The Paradoxes of Drug Policy in Bolivarian Venezuela," SSRN Scholarly Paper, Social Science Research Network, Rochester, NY, September 2016.

13. Marcia Ochoa, *Queen for a Day: Transformistas, Beauty Queens, and the Performance of Femininity in Venezuela* (Durham, NC: Duke University Press, 2014).

14. "Beauty Queen's Killers Nabbed, Venezuela Says," CNN, 01.10.14, https://www.cnn .com/2014/01/09/world/americas/monica-spear-venezuela-beauty-queen-killed /index.html.

15. Antillano, "Seguridad y política."

16. Antillano, "Seguridad y política"; Antillano, "Crimen y castigo"; Antillano, "Re-politizar la inseguridad." *Espacio abierto* 22, no. 3 (2013): 581–91.

17. At least he never embraced it in reference to street crime. Instead, Chávez focused his tough talk on national security. A study of the Chávez administration's security discourse would begin with its attempts to protect the Bolivarian Revolution from an assortment of coup d'états, assassination plots, and covert operations.

18. The official name was Operación de Liberación y Protección del Pueblo, but it's usually referred to as Operación de Liberación del Pueblo, or OLP.

19. Human Rights Watch and PROVEA, *Unchecked Power: Police and Military Raids in Low-Income and Immigrant Communities in Venezuela*, Human Rights Watch, April 2016, https://www.hrw.org/sites/default/files/report_pdf/venezuela0416web.pdf.

20. Andrés Antillano and Keymer Ávila, "¿La mano dura y la violencia policial disminuyen los homicidios?" SSRN Scholarly Paper, Social Science Research Network, Rochester, NY, September 2017.

21. Death masks worn by security agents participating in OLP provide visual evidence. "La aterradora nueva máscara de las OLP," *El Nacional*, 03.11.17, http://www.el-nacional.com/noticias/sucesos/aterradora-nueva-mascara-las-olp_84856.

22. Hanson and Smilde, "Who Is Responsible and What Should Be Done?"

23. Gramsci, *Selections from the Prison Notebooks*.

24. This account is based on interviews that I conducted in July 2014 with former employees of *Últimas Noticias*. Their claims were substantiated by an investigative series conducted by the Instituto Prensa y Sociedad (IPYS). See IPYS, "Despidos y renuncias se produjeron en cadena," accessed 06.15.18, https://ipysvenezuela.org/propietariosdelacensura/cadena-capriles.html.

25. The phrase "left art of security" is borrowed from James Ferguson, "Toward a Left Art of Government: From 'Foucauldian Critique' to Foucauldian Politics," *History of the Human Sciences* 24, no. 4 (2011): 61–68; and inspired by a reading of Austin Zeiderman, *Endangered City: The Politics of Security and Risk in Bogotá* (Durham, NC: Duke University Press, 2016); Austin Zeiderman, "Living Dangerously: Biopolitics and Urban Citizenship in Bogotá, Colombia," *American Ethnologist* 40, no. 1 (2013): 71–87.

26. The rejection of sovereign power that was perhaps appropriate to a previous historical conjuncture is dangerously out of sync with our current predicament. E. P. Thompson put it best. It is good and fine to envision a working-class utopia that "will require no inhibitions and can dispense with the negative restrictions of bourgeois legalism." However, one would be wise to "watch this new power for a century or two before you cut your hedges down." E. P. Thompson, *Whigs and Hunters* (London: Breviary Stuff Publications, 2013), 266–69.

27. Legitimacy is never a fait accompli. As Max Weber was careful to point out, the exercise of force hinges on claims to legitimacy that are always being tested and contested. See Weber, "Politics as a Vocation," in *From Max Weber: Essays in Sociology* (Oxford: Oxford University Press, 1946), 77–128.

28. Benjamin, "Theses on the Philosophy of History."

29. Benjamin, "Theses on the Philosophy of History," 255.

WORKS CITED

Abrams, Philip. "Notes on the Difficulty of Studying the State." *Journal of Historical Sociology* 1, no. 1 (1988): 58–89.

Ahmad, Tania. "Socialities of Indignation: Denouncing Party Politics in Karachi." *Cultural Anthropology* 29, no. 2 (2014): 411–32.

Alcaldía de Chacao. "Plan 180: Propuesta para la justicia y la seguridad en Venezuela." Caracas: Editorial BC Veneuniverso C.A., 2007.

Alexander, Michelle. *The New Jim Crow*. New York: New Press, 2012.

Althusser, Louis. *Lenin and Philosophy and Other Essays*. New York: Monthly Review Press, 2001.

Althusser, Louis, and Etienne Balibar. *Reading Capital*. London: Verso, 1997.

Alvarez, Sonia, Evelyn Dagnino, and Arturo Escobar, eds. *Cultures of Politics, Politics of Cultures: Re-Visioning Latin American Social Movements*. Boulder, CO: Westview Press, 1998.

Alves, Rosental Calmon. "From Lapdog to Watchdog: The Role of the Press in Latin America's Democratization." In *Making Journalists: Diverse Models, Global Issues*, edited by Hugo de Burgh, 181–202. London: Routledge, 2005.

Anderson, Jon Lee. "Slumlord." *New Yorker*, January 28, 2013.

Antillano, Andrés. "Crimen y castigo en la revolución bolivariana." *Cuestiones de sociología*, no. 10 (2014). https://www.cuestionessociologia.fahce.unlp.edu.ar/article/view/CSn10a19/6070.

———. "Repolitizar la inseguridad." *Espacio abierto* 22, no. 3 (2013): 581–91.

———. "Seguridad y política en la Venezuela bolivariana: La seguridad en el debate político venezolano entre 1998–2009." *Espacio abierto* 21, no. 4 (2012): 708.

Antillano, Andrés, and Keymer Ávila. "¿La mano dura y la violencia policial disminuyen los homicidios?" SSRN Scholarly Paper, Social Science Research Network, Rochester, NY, September 2017.

Antillano, Andrés, Verónica Zubillaga, and Keymer Ávila. "Revolution and Counter-Reformation: The Paradoxes of Drug Policy in Bolivarian Venezuela." SSRN Scholarly Paper, Social Science Research Network, Rochester, NY, September 2016.

Arias, Enrique Desmond, and Daniel M. Goldstein, eds. *Violent Democracies in Latin America*. Durham, NC: Duke University Press, 2010.

Atkin, Albert. "Peirce's Theory of Signs." *Stanford Encyclopedia of Philosophy*. Summer 2013 ed. http://plato.stanford.edu/archives/sum2013/entries/perice-semiotics.

Austin, J. L. *How to Do Things with Words*. Cambridge, MA: Harvard University Press, 1975.

Ayala, Felipe Guaman Poma de. *The First New Chronicle and Good Government: On the History of the World and the Incas up to 1615*. Austin: University of Texas Press, 2010.

Babül, Elif. "The Paradox of Protection: Human Rights, the Masculinist State, and the Moral Economy of Gratitude in Turkey." *American Ethnologist* 42, no. 1 (2015): 116–30.

Barnet, Miguel. "La novela-testimonio: Socioliteratura." *Union* 6 (1969): 99–122.

Bartley, Kim, and Donnacha O'Briain. *The Revolution Will Not Be Televised*. Directed by Kim Bartley and Donnacha O'Briain. Documentary film, 2003, 74 min.

Bello Lozano, Humberto. *Historia de las fuentes e instituciones jurídicas venezolanas*. Caracas: Librería La Lógica, 1985.

Benjamin, Walter. *Illuminations*. New York: Schocken Books, 1969.

———. "Theses on the Philosophy of History." In *Illuminations*.

———. "The Work of Art in the Age of Mechanical Reproduction." In *Illuminations*.

Beverley, John. "The Margin at the Center: On Testimonio." *Modern Fiction Studies* 35, no. 1 (1989): 11–28.

Bisbal, Marcelino, ed. *Hegemonía y control comunicacional*. Caracas: Editorial Alfa, 2009.

Blackmore, Lisa. "El Helicoide and La Torre de David as Phantom Pavilions." *Bulletin of Latin American Research* 36, no. 2 (2016): 206–22.

Bloch, Maurice. *Prey into Hunter: The Politics of Religious Experience*. New York: Cambridge University Press, 1991.

Boltanski, Luc. *Love and Justice as Competences: Three Essays on the Sociology of Action*. Translated by Catherine Porter. Cambridge: Polity Press, 2012.

Botía, Alejandro. *Auge y crisis del Cuarto Poder: La prensa en democracia*. Caracas: Debate, 2007.

Bottoms, Anthony. "The Philosophy and Politics of Punishment and Sentencing." In *The Politics of Sentencing Reform*, edited by C. M. V. Clarkson and Rod Morgan. Oxford: Clarendon Press, 1995.

Bourdieu, Pierre. *Outline of a Theory of Practice*. New York: Cambridge University Press, 1977.

———. "The Political Field, the Social Science Field, and the Journalistic Field." In *Bourdieu and the Journalistic Field*, edited by Rodney Benson and Erik Neveu. Cambridge: Polity Press, 2005.

Briceño-León, Roberto. "Violence in Venezuela: Oil Rent and Political Crisis." *Ciência y saúde coletiva* 11, no. 2 (2006): 315–25.

Briggs, Charles. "Mediating Infanticide: Theorizing Relations between Narrative and Violence." *Cultural Anthropology* 22, no. 3 (2007): 315–56.

Brillembourg, Alfred, Kristin Feireiss, and Hubert Klumpner, eds. *Informal City: Caracas Case*. New York: Prestel Publishing, 2005.

Brillembourg, Alfredo, and Hubert Klumpner, eds. *Torre David: Informal Vertical Communities*. Zurich: Lars Muller Publishers, 2012.

Britto García, Luis. *Venezuela: Investigación de unos medios por encima de toda sospecha*. Caracas: Colección Análisis, 2004.

Brown, Wendy. "Wounded Attachments." *Political Theory* 21, no. 3 (1993): 390–410.

Buck-Morss, Susan. "Aesthetics and Anaesthetics: Walter Benjamin's Artwork Essay Reconsidered." *October* 62 (1992): 3–41.

Buitrago Segura, Luis. *Caracas la horrible*. Caracas: Editorial Ateneo de Caracas, 1980.

Butler, Judith. *Bodies That Matter: On the Discursive Limits of "Sex."* London: Routledge, 1993.

———. *Excitable Speech: A Politics of the Performative*. New York: Routledge, 1997.

Buxton, Julia. *The Failure of Political Reform in Venezuela*. Farnham, UK: Ashgate, 2001.

Caldeira, Teresa. *City of Walls: Crime, Segregation, and Citizenship in São Paulo.* Berkeley: University of California Press, 2000.

Caldeira, Teresa, and James Holston. "Democracy and Violence in Brazil." *Comparative Studies in Society and History* 41, no. 4 (1999): 691–729.

Canetti, Elias. *Crowds and Power.* New York: Farrar, Straus and Giroux, 1984.

Cañizález, Andrés. *Los medios de comunicación social.* Curso de formación sociopolitica 26. Caracas: Centro Gumilla, 1991.

———. "Medios y pluralismo en Venezuela." *Chasqui* 98 (2007): 4–9.

Cañizález, Andrés, and Jairo Lugo-Ocando. "The Media in Venezuela." In *The Media in Latin America,* edited by Jairo Lugo-Ocando. New York: Open University Press, 2008.

Capriles Méndez, Ruth, ed. *Diccionario de la corrupción en Venezuela: 1984–1992.* 3 vols. Caracas: Consorcio de Ediciones Capriles, 1989.

Cariola, Cecilia, Miguel Lacabana, and F. J. Velasco. *Impacto socio-ambiental del ajuste estructural: Mercado de trabajo, pobreza y medio ambiente urbano.* Caracas: Cendes, 1999.

Ciccariello-Maher, George. "Collective Panic in Venezuela," *Jacobin,* June 18, 2014. https://www.jacobinmag.com/2014/06/collective-panic-in-venezuela/.

———. *We Created Chávez: A People's History of the Venezuelan Revolution.* Durham, NC: Duke University Press, 2013.

Coing, Helmut. "English Equity and the 'Denunciatio Evangelica' of the Canon Law." *Law Quarterly Review* 71 (1955): 223–41.

Comaroff, Jean, and John L. Comaroff. *The Truth about Crime.* Chicago: University of Chicago Press, 2016.

Cooper, Amy. "The Doctor's Political Body: Doctor–Patient Interactions and Sociopolitical Belonging in Venezuelan State Clinics." *American Ethnologist* 42, no. 3 (August 1, 2015): 459–74.

Cooper, Amy, Robert Samet, and Naomi Schiller. "Protests and Polarization in Venezuela after Chávez." *Cultural Anthropology* (blog), February 5, 2015. https://culanth.org/fieldsights/630-protests-and-polarization-in-venezuela-after-chavez.

Coppedge, Michael. *Strong Parties and Lame Ducks: Presidential Partyarchy and Factionalism in Venezuela.* Stanford, CA: Stanford University Press, 1997.

Coronil, Fernando. *The Magical State: Nature, Money, and Modernity in Venezuela.* Chicago: University of Chicago Press, 1997.

Coronil, Fernando, and Julie Skurski. "Dismembering and Remembering the Nation: The Semantics of Political Violence in Venezuela." *Comparative Studies in Society and History* 33, no. 2 (1991): 288–337.

Corrales, Javier. "In Search of a Theory of Polarization: Lessons from Venezuela, 1999–2005." *ERLACS: European Review of Latin American and Caribbean Studies,* no. 79 (October 15, 2005): 105–18.

Crisp, Brian F., and Daniel H. Levine. "Democratizing the Democracy? Crisis and Reform in Venezuela." *Journal of Interamerican Studies and World Affairs* 40, no. 2 (1998): 27–61.

Crouse, Timothy. *The Boys on the Bus.* New York: Random House Trade Paperbacks, 2003.

Dagnino, Evelina. "Citizenship: A Perverse Confluence." *Development in Practice* 17, no. 4/5 (2007): 549–56.

Daniel, E. Valentine. *Charred Lullabies.* Princeton, NJ: Princeton University Press, 1996.

Denyer Willis, Graham. *The Killing Consensus: Police, Organized Crime, and the Regulation of Life and Death in Urban Brazil.* Oakland: University of California Press, 2015.

Derrida, Jacques. *Limited Inc.* Evanston, IL: Northwestern University Press, 1988.

Di Tella, Torcuato. "Populism and Reform in Latin America." In *Obstacles to Change in Latin America,* edited by Claudio Veliz, 47–72. London: Oxford University Press, 1965.

Ditton, Jason, and Stephen Farrall, eds. *The Fear of Crime.* Burlington, VT: Routledge, 2000.

Douglas, Mary. *Purity and Danger.* New York: Routledge Classics, 2002.

Duno Gottberg, Luis. "The Color of Mobs: Racial Politics, Ethnopopulism and Representation in Venezuela in the Chávez Era." In Smilde and Hellinger, *Venezuela's Bolivarian Democracy,* 271–97.

———. "Social Images of Anti-Apocalypse: Bikers and the Representation of Popular Politics in Venezuela." *A Contra Corriente* 6, no. 2 (2009): 144–72.

Duque, José Roberto. *Guerra nuestra: Crónicas de desamparo.* Caracas: Editorial Memorias de Altagracia, 1999.

Durkheim, Émile. *The Division of Labor in Society.* New York: Free Press, 2014.

———. *The Elementary Forms of Religious Life.* Translated by Karen E. Fields. New York: Free Press, 1995.

Dussel, Enrique. *Twenty Theses on Politics.* Translated by George Ciccariello-Maher. Durham, NC: Duke University Press, 2008.

Ebron, Paulla. "Constituting Subjects through Performative Acts." In *Africa after Gender?,* edited by Catherine M. Cole, Takyiwaa Manuh, and Stephan F. Miescher, 171–90. Bloomington: Indiana University Press, 2007.

Eiss, Paul. *In the Name of El Pueblo: Place, Community, and the Politics of History in Yucatán.* Durham, NC: Duke University Press, 2010.

Ellner, Steve. "Recent Venezuelan Political Studies: A Return to Third World Realities." *Latin American Research Review* 32, no. 2 (1997): 201–18.

Ellner, Steve, and Daniel Hellinger, eds. *Venezuelan Politics in the Chávez Era: Class, Polarization, and Conflict.* Boulder, CO: Lynne Rienner, 2003.

Ellner, Steve, and Miguel Tinker Salas, eds. *Venezuela: Hugo Chávez and the Decline of an "Exceptional Democracy."* Lanham, MD: Rowman and Littlefield, 2007.

Ericson, Richard, Patricia Baranek, and Janet Chan. *Representing Order: Crime, Law, and Justice in the News Media.* Toronto: University of Toronto Press, 1991.

Ettema, James, and Theodore Glasser. *Custodians of Conscience.* New York: Columbia University Press, 1998.

Feldman, Allen. *Formations of Violence: The Narrative of the Body and Political Terror in Northern Ireland.* Chicago: University of Chicago Press, 1991.

Felman, Shoshana. *The Scandal of the Speaking Body: Don Juan with J. L. Austin, or Seduction in Two Languages.* Stanford, CA: Stanford University Press, 2002.

Ferguson, James. "Toward a Left Art of Government: From 'Foucauldian Critique' to Foucauldian Politics." *History of the Human Sciences* 24, no. 4 (2011): 61–68.

Fernandes, Sujatha. *Who Can Stop the Drums? Urban Social Movements in Chávez's Venezuela.* Durham, NC: Duke University Press, 2010.

Ferrándiz, Francisco. "The Body as Wound: Possession, Malandros, and Everyday Violence in Venezuela." *Critique of Anthropology* 24, no. 2 (2004): 107–33.

Fisher, Jo. *Mothers of the Disappeared.* Boston: South End Press, 1999.

Fishman, Mark. *Manufacturing the News.* Austin: University of Texas Press, 1988.

Fitzpatrick, Sheila, and Robert Gellately, eds. *Accusatory Practices: Denunciation in Modern European History, 1789–1989.* Chicago: University of Chicago Press, 1997.

Forcione, Alban K. *Majesty and Humanity: Kings and Their Doubles in the Political Drama of the Spanish Golden Age.* New Haven, CT: Yale University Press, 2009.

Foucault, Michel. *Power/Knowledge: Selected Interviews and Other Writings, 1972–1977.* Edited by Colin Gordon. New York: Vintage, 1980.

———. *Security, Territory, Population: Lectures at the Collège de France 1977–1978.* New York: Macmillan, 2009.

Fournier, Paul. *Les officialités au moyen âge*. Paris: E. Plon et cie, 1880.

Frank, Jason. *Constituent Moments: Enacting the People in Postrevolutionary America*. Durham, NC: Duke University Press, 2010.

Fraser, Nancy. "Rethinking the Public Sphere: A Contribution to the Critique of Actually Existing Democracy." *Social Text*, no. 25/26 (1990): 56–80.

Frazer, James. *The Golden Bough: A Study in Magic and Religion*. Oxford: Oxford University Press, 2009.

Freud, Sigmund. *Beyond the Pleasure Principle*. Edited by James Strachey. New York: W. W. Norton, 1990.

———. *Totem and Taboo*. 5th ed. New York: W. W. Norton, 1990.

Gabaldón, Luis, and Andrés Antillano, eds. *La policía venezolana: Desarrollo institucional y perspectivas de reforma al inicio del tercer milenio*. Vols. 1–3. Caracas: Conarepol, 2007.

Gallardo, Elyina, and Mildred Hernandez. "El periodismo de denuncia: Destabilizador del sistema democrático?" Thesis, Universidad Central de Venezuela, 1993.

García Guadilla, María-Pilar. "Crisis, actores sociales y geografía urbana: Segregación urbana y castas socio-ecologicas." Working paper. Universidad Simon Bolívar, 1993. http://observatoriogeograficoamericalatina.org.mx/egal4/Geografiasocioeconomica/Geografiaurbana/13.pdf.

Garland, David. *The Culture of Control: Crime and Social Order in Contemporary Society*. Chicago: University of Chicago Press, 2002.

Germani, Gino. *Authoritarianism, Fascism, and National Populism*. New Brunswick, NJ: Transaction Publishers, 1978.

Girard, René. *Violence and the Sacred*. Baltimore: Johns Hopkins University Press, 1979.

Godoy, Angelina Snodgrass. *Popular Injustice: Violence, Community, and Law in Latin America*. Stanford, CA: Stanford University Press, 2006.

Goldstein, Daniel. "Human Rights as Culprit, Human Rights as Victim." In *The Practice of Human Rights*, edited by Mark Goodale and Sally Engle Merry, 49–77. New York: Cambridge University Press. 2007.

———. *Outlawed: Between Security and Rights in a Bolivian City*. Durham, NC: Duke University Press, 2012.

Gómez Grillo, Elio. *La historia fea de Caracas y otras historias criminológicas*. Caracas: Academia Nacional de la Historia, 1982.

González, David. "La urbe de los sucesos." *Comunicación* 142 (2008): 20–23.

González Mejías, Josbelk, and Dorothy Kronick. "Measuring Lethal Violence in Venezuela." Working paper, Center for Inter-American Policy and Research, Tulane University, New Orleans, last modified April 13, 2008. Microsoft Word file.

Gramsci, Antonio. *Selections from the Prison Notebooks*. New York: International Publishers, 1971.

Granier, Marcel. *La generación de relevo vs. el estado omnipotente*. Caracas: Seleven, 1984.

Grattan, Laura. *Populism's Power: Radical Grassroots Democracy in America*. New York: Oxford University Press, 2016.

Greenhouse, Carol J. "Durkheim and Law: Divided Readings over Division of Labor." *Annual Review of Law and Social Science* 7, no. 1 (2011): 165–85.

Guerra, François-Xavier. "The Implosion of the Spanish Empire." In *The Collective and the Public in Latin America*, edited by Luis Roniger and Tamar Herzog. Eastbourne, UK: Sussex Academic Press, 2000.

———. "The Spanish-American Tradition of Representation and Its European Roots." *Journal of Latin American Studies* 26, no. 1 (1994): 1–35.

Guest, Iain. *Behind the Disappearances: Argentina's Dirty War against Human Rights and the United Nations*. Philadelphia: University of Pennsylvania Press, 1990.

Guevara, Aleida, and Hugo Chávez. *Chávez, Venezuela, and the New Latin America*. London: Ocean Press, 2005.

Guilhaumou, Jacques. "Fragments of a Discourse of Denunciation (1789–1794)." In *The French Revolution and the Creation of Modern Political Culture*, vol. 4, *The Terror*, edited by Keith Michael Baker, 139–56. Oxford: Pergamon, 1994.

Gürsel, Zeynep. "U.S. Newsworld: The Rule of Text and Everyday Practices of Editing the World." In *The Anthropology of News and Journalism*, edited by Elizabeth Bird, 35–53. Bloomington: Indiana University Press, 2009.

Guss, David M. *The Festive State: Race, Ethnicity, and Nationalism as Cultural Performance*. Berkeley: University of California Press, 2000.

Habermas, Jürgen. *The Structural Transformation of the Public Sphere: An Inquiry into a Category of Bourgeois Society*. Cambridge, MA: MIT Press, 1991.

Hale, Chris. "Fear of Crime: A Review of the Literature." *International Review of Victimology* 4, no. 2 (1996): 79–150.

Hall, Stuart. "Authoritarian Populism: A Reply to Jessop et al." *New Left Review*, no. 151 (1985): 115–24.

———. "Notes on Deconstructing 'the Popular.'" In *People's History and Socialist Theory*, edited by Raphael Samuel. London: Routledge and Kegan Paul, 1981.

———. "Popular-Democratic vs. Authoritarian Populism: Two Ways of Taking Democracy Seriously." In *Marxism and Democracy*, edited by Alan Hunt, 157–85. London: Lawrence and Wishart, 1980.

Hall, Stuart, Chas Critcher, Tony Jefferson, John Clarke, and Brian Roberts. *Policing the Crisis: Mugging, the State, and Law and Order*. 2nd edition. London: Palgrave Macmillan, 2013.

Hall, Stuart, and Lawrence Grossberg. "On Postmodernism and Articulation: An Interview with Stuart Hall." *Journal of Communication Inquiry* 10, no. 2 (1986): 45–60.

Hallin, Daniel, and Charles Briggs. "Biocommunicability: The Neoliberal Subject and Its Contradictions in News Coverage of Health Issues." *Social Text* 25 (2007): 43–66.

Hallin, Daniel, and Paolo Mancini. *Comparing Media Systems: Three Models of Media and Politics*. New York: Cambridge University Press, 2004.

Hallin, Daniel, and Stylianos Papathanassopoulos. "Political Clientelism and the Media: Southern Europe and Latin America in Comparative Perspective." *Media, Culture and Society* 24, no. 2 (2002): 175–95.

Hansen, Thomas Blom. *The Saffron Wave: Democracy and Hindu Nationalism in Modern India*. Princeton, NJ: Princeton University Press, 1999.

Hansen, Thomas Blom, and Finn Stepputat. *Sovereign Bodies: Citizens, Migrants, and States in the Postcolonial World*. Princeton, NJ: Princeton University Press, 2005.

———. "Sovereignty Revisited." *Annual Review of Anthropology* 35, no. 1 (2006): 295–315.

Hanson, Rebecca. "Civilian Policing, Socialist Revolution, and Violent Pluralism in Venezuela." PhD diss., University of Georgia, 2017.

Hanson, Rebecca, and David Smilde. "Who Is Responsible and What Should Be Done? Public Opinion on Crime and Citizen Security Reform in Venezuela." Paper presented at conference "The Paradox of Violence in Venezuela," Tulane University, New Orleans, October 29–31, 2015.

Haraway, Donna. "Situated Knowledges: The Science Question in Feminism and the Privilege of Partial Perspective." *Feminist Studies* 14, no. 3 (1988): 575–99.

Hawkins, Kirk A. *Venezuela's Chavismo and Populism in Comparative Perspective*. New York: Cambridge University Press, 2010.

Hegel, Georg Wilhelm Friedrich. *Hegel's Philosophy of Right*. Translated by T. M. Knox. New York: Oxford University Press, 1967.

Hellinger, Daniel. "Chávez and the Intellectuals." *NACLA Report on the Americas* 45, no. 4 (2012): 51–52.

Herman, Edward S., and Noam Chomsky. *Manufacturing Consent: The Political Economy of the Mass Media*. New York: Pantheon, 2002.

Hernández, Tosca. *La ideologización del delito y de la pena*. Caracas: Universidad Central de Venezuela, 1977.

Hernández, Tulio. "Medios y conflicto político." In *Medios de comunicación y democracia*, 107–33. Caracas: Universidad Católica Andrés Bello, 1995.

Hobbes, Thomas. *Leviathan*. London: Penguin Books, 1982.

Holston, James. *Insurgent Citizenship: Disjunctions of Democracy and Modernity in Brazil*. Princeton, NJ: Princeton University Press, 2009.

Hughes, Sallie. *Newsrooms in Conflict: Journalism and the Democratization of Mexico*. Pittsburgh, PA: University of Pittsburgh Press, 2006.

Human Rights Watch and PROVEA. *Unchecked Power: Police and Military Raids in Low-Income and Immigrant Communities in Venezuela*. Human Rights Watch, April 2016. https://www.hrw.org/sites/default/files/report_pdf/venezuela0416web.pdf.

Illuminati, Giulio. "The Frustrated Turn to Adversarial Procedure in Italy." *Washington University Global Studies Law Review* 4, no. 3 (2005): 567–81.

Informativovenez. "Mario Silva: Asesinato de Javier Garcia no es por inseguridad." YouTube, posted June 17, 2008. Video, 7:13. https://www.youtube.com/watch?v=XtPxuVxrMW4.

Instituto Prensa y Sociedad. "Despidos y renuncias se produjeron en cadena." Accessed June 15, 2018. https://ipysvenezuela.org/propietariosdelacensura/cadena-capriles.html.

Isin, Engin, and Patricia Wood. *Citizenship and Identity*. Thousand Oaks, CA: SAGE, 1999.

Ivancheva, Mariya. "The Bolivarian University of Venezuela." *Learning and Teaching* 6, no. 1 (2013): 3–25.

Izarra, Andrés, and Félix López. *Los guardianes del periodismo pornográfico*. Caracas: Agencia Bolivariana de Noticias, 2010.

James, William. *Pragmatism and Other Writings*. Edited by Giles Gunn. New York: Penguin Classics, 2000.

Jameson, Fredric. "Cognitive Mapping." In *Marxism and the Interpretation of Culture*, edited by Cary Nelson and Lawrence Grossberg, 347–57. Chicago: University of Illinois Press, 1988.

Jarman, Rebecca. "Representing the Barrios: Culture and Politics in the Venezuelan City 1958–2008." PhD diss., Cambridge University, 2016.

Joseph, Gilbert, and Daniel Nugent, eds. *Everyday Forms of State Formation: Revolution and the Negotiation of Rule in Modern Mexico*. Durham, NC: Duke University Press, 1994.

Judis, John. *The Populist Explosion: How the Great Recession Transformed American and European Politics*. New York: Columbia Global Reports, 2016.

Juris, Jeffrey S. "Reflections on #Occupy Everywhere: Social Media, Public Space, and Emerging Logics of Aggregation." *American Ethnologist* 39, no. 2 (2012): 259–79.

Jusionyte, Ieva. *Savage Frontier: Making News and Security on the Argentine Border*. Oakland: University of California Press, 2015.

Kantorowicz, Ernst. *The King's Two Bodies*. Princeton, NJ: Princeton University Press, 1957.

Kappeler, Aaron. "From Reactionary Modernization to Endogenous Development: The Revolution in Hydroelectricity in Venezuela." *Dialectical Anthropology* 41 (2017): 241–62.

Karl, Terry Lynn. *The Paradox of Plenty: Oil Booms and Petro-States.* Berkeley: University of California Press, 1997.

Kazin, Michael. *The Populist Persuasion: An American History.* Ithaca, NY: Cornell University Press, 2017.

Kornblith, Miriam. *Venezuela en los 90: La crisis de la democracia.* Caracas: Ediciones IESA, 1998.

Kronick, Dorothy. "How to Count Our Dead." *Caracas Chronicles* (blog), July 1, 2016. https://www.caracaschronicles.com/2016/07/01/our-dead/.

Laclau, Ernesto. *On Populist Reason.* New York: Verso, 2005.

———. *Politics and Ideology in Marxist Theory: Capitalism, Fascism, Populism.* New York: Verso, 1979.

———. "Populism: What's in a Name?" In Panizza, *Populism and the Mirror of Democracy,* 32–49.

Laclau, Ernesto, and Chantal Mouffe. *Hegemony and Socialist Strategy: Towards a Radical Democratic Politics.* New York: Verso, 1985.

La Fuente, Sandra, and Carlos Meza. *El acertijo de abril: Relato periodístico de la breve caída de Hugo Chávez.* Caracas: Ediciones Cyngular, 2004.

Las Casas, Bartolomé de. *Brevísima relación de la destrucción de las Indias.* Edited by José Miguel Martínez Torrejón. Barcelona: Galaxia Gutenberg : Círculo de Lectores, 2009.

Latour, Bruno. *Science in Action: How to Follow Scientists and Engineers through Society.* Cambridge, MA: Harvard University Press, 1987.

Ledezma, Eurídice. "Jorge Tortoza, otra bala perdida." *Exceso,* no. 162 (April 2003): 38–45.

Lee, Murray. *Inventing Fear of Crime.* London: Routledge, 2013.

Lefebvre, Henri. *The Production of Space.* Cambridge, MA: Wiley-Blackwell, 1992.

Lefort, Claude. "Permanence of the Theologico-Political." In *Democracy and Political Theory.* Cambridge: Polity Press, 1991.

Lévi-Strauss, Claude. *Introduction to the Work of Marcel Mauss.* Translated by Felicity Baker. London: Routledge, 1987.

———. *Totemism.* Translated by Rodney Needham. Boston: Beacon Press, 1971.

López Maya, Margarita. "The Venezuelan *Caracazo* of 1989: Popular Protest and Institutional Weakness." *Journal of Latin American Studies* 35, no. 1 (2003): 117–37.

Lucas, Colin. "The Theory and Practice of Denunciation in the French Revolution." *Journal of Modern History* 68, no. 4 (1996): 768–85.

Lugo-Ocando, Jairo, and Juan Romero. "From Friends to Foes." *Sincronía* 4 (Spring 2003). http://sincronia.cucsh.udg.mx/lugoromero.htm.

Lupu, Noam. "Who Votes for Chavismo? Class Voting in Hugo Chávez's Venezuela." *Latin American Research Review* 45, no. 1 (2010): 7–32.

Lynch, Kevin. *The Image of the City.* Cambridge, MA: MIT Press, 1960.

Márquez Balza, Damarys. *El reportero de sucesos.* Caracas: Ediciones Joel, 1983.

Martín-Barbero, Jesús. *Communication, Culture and Hegemony: From the Media to Mediations.* London: SAGE, 1993.

Marx, Karl. *A Contribution to the Critique of Political Economy.* Edited by Maurice Dobb. New York: International Publishers, 1979.

Matza, Tomas, and Kevin Lewis O'Neill. "Introduction: Politically Unwilling." *Social Text* 32, no. 3 (2014): 1–10.

Mauss, Marcel. "Techniques of the Body." *Economy and Society* 2, no. 1 (1973): 70–88.

Mazzarella, William. "Affect: What Is It Good For?" In *Enchantments of Modernity*, edited by Saurabh Dube, 291–309. New York: Routledge, 2009.

———. "'Very Bombay': Contending with the Global in an Indian Advertising Agency." *Cultural Anthropology* 18, no. 1 (2003): 33–71.

McEvoy, Claire, and Gergely Hideg. *Global Violent Deaths, 2017*. Geneva: Small Arms Survey, 2018.

McLuhan, Marshall. *Understanding Media: The Extensions of Man*. New York: MIT Press, 1984.

Ministerio del Poder Popular para la Comunicación y la Información. "Semana 40, La Dolorita en Petare: 3800 funcionarios participan en Plan Caracas Segura." Accessed January 17, 2014. http://radiomundial.com.ve/node/147141 (content no longer available).

Ministerio Público. *Informe anual de gestión 2016*. Caracas: Ministerio Público, 2017. https://observatoriodeviolencia.org.ve/wp-content/uploads/2017/08/MP_InformeAnual Gesti%C3%B3n_2016-1.pdf.

Moody, Michael. "Isabel Allende and the Testimonial Novel." *Confluencia* 2, no. 1 (1986): 39–43.

Morgan, Edmund S. *Inventing the People: The Rise of Popular Sovereignty in England and America*. New York: W. W. Norton, 1989.

Muñoz, Agustín Blanco. *Habla el comandante*. Caracas: Catedra Pio Tamayo, 1998.

Naím, Moisés, ed. *Lessons of the Venezuelan Experience*. Washington, DC: Woodrow Wilson Center Press, 1995.

Negt, Oskar, and Alexander Kluge. *Public Sphere and Experience: Toward an Analysis of the Bourgeois and Proletarian Public Sphere*. Minneapolis: University of Minnesota Press, 1993.

Nelson, Anne. "No Gloom Here: In Latin America, Newspapers Boom." Media Shift, May 11, 2011. http://mediashift.org/2011/05/no-gloom-here-in-latin-america-newspapers -boom131/.

Nelson, Brian A. *The Silence and the Scorpion: The Coup against Chávez and the Making of Modern Venezuela*. New York: Nation Books, 2009.

New York City Police Department. "Historical New York City Crime Data." Accessed June 15, 2018. https://www1.nyc.gov/site/nypd/stats/crime-statistics/historical.page.

Nugent, David. "Democracy Otherwise: Struggles over Popular Rule in the Northern Peruvian Andes." In *Democracy: Anthropological Approaches*, edited by Julia Paley, 21–62. Santa Fe, NM: School for Advanced Research Press, 2008.

Ochoa, Marcia. *Queen for a Day: Transformistas, Beauty Queens, and the Performance of Femininity in Venezuela*. Durham, NC: Duke University Press, 2014.

O'Neill, Kevin Lewis. *Secure the Soul: Christian Piety and Gang Prevention in Guatemala*. Oakland: University of California Press, 2015.

Ortiz, Carlos, ed. *Siete días que estremecieron a Venezuela*. Caracas: Libros de El Nacional, 2002.

Panizza, Francisco. *Populism and the Mirror of Democracy*. New York: Verso, 2005.

Pasquali, Antonio. *Comunicación y cultura de masas*. Caracas: Monte Ávila Editores, 1960.

Pedelty, Mark. *War Stories: The Culture of Foreign Correspondents*. New York: Routledge, 1995.

Pedrazzini, Yves, and Magaly Sánchez. *Malandros, bandas, y niños de la calle*. Valencia, Venezuela: Vadell Hermanos Editores, 1992.

Pedroza, C. "La denuncia, genero periodística de la crisis." Thesis, Universidad Central de Venezuela, 1994.

Peirce, Charles S. "Questions Concerning Certain Faculties Claimed for Man." *Journal of Speculative Philosophy* 2 (1868): 103–14.

Pérez-Liñán, Aníbal. *Presidential Impeachment and the New Political Instability in Latin America*. New York: Cambridge University Press, 2010.

Pérez Perdomo, Rogelio. "Corruption and Business in Present Day Venezuela," *Journal of Business Ethics* 9, no. 7 (1990): 555–66.

———. "Corruption and Political Crisis." In Naím, *Lessons of the Venezuelan Experience*, 311–33.

Pérez Rincones, María Fernanda. "Projecto Esperanza." *Tribuna del investigador* 12, no. 1–2 (2012): 31–35.

Perlman, Janice. *The Myth of Marginality: Urban Poverty and Politics in Rio de Janeiro*. Berkeley: University of California Press, 1980.

Portes, Alejandro, and Bryan Roberts. "The Free-Market City: Latin American Urbanization in the Years of the Neoliberal Experiment." *Studies in Comparative International Development* 40, no. 1 (2005): 43–82.

Povinelli, Elizabeth. "Defining Security in Late Liberalism: A Comment on Pedersen and Holbraad." In *Times of Security: Ethnographies of Fear, Protest and the Future*, edited by Martin Holbraad and Morten Axel Pedersen, 28–32. London: Routledge, 2013.

Pratt, Mary L. "I, Rigoberta Menchú and the 'Culture Wars.'" In *The Rigoberta Menchú Controversy*, edited by Arturo Arias, 29–57. Minneapolis: University of Minnesota Press, 2001.

PROVEA. "Derecho a la seguridad ciudadana." *Situación de los derechos humanos en Venezuela: Informe Anual Octubre 2005–Septiembre 2006*. Caracas: PROVEA, 2006.

———. "Derecho a la seguridad ciudadana." *Situación de los derechos humanos en Venezuela: Informe Anual Octubre 2006–Septiembre 2007*. Caracas: PROVEA, 2007.

———. "Derecho a la seguridad ciudadana." *Situación de los derechos humanos en Venezuela: Informe Anual Octubre 2008–Septiembre 2009*. Caracas: PROVEA, 2009.

———. "Derecho a la seguridad ciudadana." *Situación de los derechos humanos en Venezuela: Informe Anual Octubre 2009–Septiembre 2010*. Caracas: PROVEA, 2010. https://www.derechos.org.ve/web/wp-content/uploads/20_seguridadciudadana.pdf.

———. "Derecho a la seguridad ciudadana." *Situación de los derechos humanos en Venezuela: Informe Anual Octubre 2010–Septiembre 2011*. Caracas: PROVEA, 2011.

———. "Derecho a la seguridad ciudadana." *Situación de los derechos humanos en Venezuela: Informe Anual Enero–Diciembre 2012*. Caracas: PROVEA, 2012.

Rama, Angel. *The Lettered City*. Durham, NC: Duke University Press, 1996.

———. "Rodolfo Walsh: La narrativa en el conflicto de las culturas." In *Ficciones Argentinas: Antología de lecturas críticas*. Buenos Aires: Grupo Editorial Norma, 2004.

Rancière, Jacques. *Disagreement: Politics and Philosophy*. Translated by Julie Rose. Minneapolis: University of Minnesota Press, 2004.

Randall, Margaret. "Reclaiming Voices: Notes on a New Female Practice in Journalism." *Latin American Perspectives* 18, no. 3 (1991): 103–13.

Rentschler, Carrie. *Second Wounds: Victims' Rights and the Media in the U.S.* Durham, NC: Duke University Press, 2011.

Rey, Germán. *El cuerpo del delito: Representación y narrativas mediáticas de la (in)seguridad ciudadana*. Bogotá: Centro de Competencia en Comunicación para América Latina, 2005.

Riesebrodt, Martin. "Charisma in Max Weber's Sociology of Religion." *Religion* 29, no. 1 (1999): 1–14.

Rosas, Alexis. *El asesinato del los hermanos Faddoul*. Caracas: Editorial Alfa, 2008.

Rotker, Susana, ed. *Citizens of Fear: Urban Violence in Latin America*. New Brunswick, NJ: Rutgers University Press, 2002.

———. "We Are the Others." In *Citizens of Fear*, 224–39.

Roudakova, Natalia. *Losing Pravda: Ethics and the Press in Post-Truth Russia.* New York: Cambridge University Press, 2017.

Rutherford, Danilyn. *Laughing at Leviathan: Sovereignty and Audience in West Papua.* Chicago: University of Chicago Press, 2012.

Sahlins, Marshall, and David Graeber. *On Kings.* Chicago: HAU Books, 2017.

Salas, Yolanda. "Imaginaries and Narratives of Prison Violence." In Rotker, *Citizens of Fear,* 207–23.

Samet, Robert. "The Denouncers: Populism and the Press in Venezuela." *Journal of Latin American Studies* 49 (2016): 1–27.

———. "Getting a Handle on Homicide Rates in Caracas." *Venezuelan Politics and Human Rights* (blog), August 17, 2012. http://venezuelablog.tumblr.com/search/samet?og=1.

Sánchez, Rafael. *Dancing Jacobins: A Venezuelan Genealogy of Latin American Populism.* New York: Fordham University Press, 2016.

Sanjuán, Ana María. "Democracy, Citizenship, and Violence in Venezuela." In Rotker, *Citizens of Fear,* 87–101.

Santner, Eric L. *The Royal Remains: The People's Two Bodies and the Endgames of Sovereignty.* Chicago: University of Chicago Press, 2012.

Savage, Ritchie. *Populist Discourse in Venezuela and the United States.* Cham, Switzerland: Springer, 2018.

Schaffer, Frederic Charles. *Elucidating Social Science Concepts: An Interpretivist Guide.* New York: Routledge, 2015.

Schalk, Wolfgang, dir. *Radiografía de una mentira.* Anzoátegui, Venezuela: Fog Wolf Productions, 2004. DVD, 80 min.

Scheper-Hughes, Nancy. *Death without Weeping: The Violence of Everyday Life in Brazil.* Berkeley: University of California Press, 1993.

Schiller, Naomi. *Channeling the State: Community Media and Popular Politics in Venezuela.* Durham, NC: Duke University Press, 2018.

———. "Liberal and Bolivarian Regimes of Truth: Toward a Critically Engaged Anthropology in Caracas, Venezuela." *Transforming Anthropology* 19, no. 1 (2011): 35–42.

———. "Reckoning with Press Freedom: Community Media, Liberalism, and the Processual State in Caracas, Venezuela." *American Ethnologist* 40, no. 3 (2013): 540–54.

Schivelbusch, Wolfgang. *The Railway Journey: The Industrialization of Time and Space in the Nineteenth Century.* Berkeley: University of California Press, 2014.

Schmitt, Carl. *The Crisis of Parliamentary Democracy.* Cambridge, MA: MIT Press, 1988.

———. *Political Theology.* Chicago: University of Chicago Press, 1985.

Schudson, Michael. *Discovering the News: A Social History of American Newspapers.* New York: Basic Books, 1981.

Sedgwick, Eve Kosofsky. *Epistemology of the Closet.* Berkeley: University of California Press, 1990.

———. *Touching Feeling: Affect, Pedagogy, Performativity.* Durham, NC: Duke University Press, 2003.

Sewell, William. "Space in Contentious Politics." In *Spaces of Contention: Spatialities and Social Movements,* edited by Walter Nicholls, Byron Miller, and Justin Beaumont. London: Ashgate, 2013.

Shils, Edward. *The Torment of Secrecy: The Background and Consequences of American Security Policy.* Glencoe, IL: Free Press, 1956.

Silver, Allan. "The Demand for Order in Civil Society." In *The Police: Six Sociological Essays,* edited by David J. Bordua, 1–24. New York: Wiley, 1967.

Simon, Jonathan. *Governing through Crime: How the War on Crime Transformed American Democracy and Created a Culture of Fear*. New York: Oxford University Press, 2009.

Skurski, Julie. "The Leader and the 'People': Representing the Nation in Postcolonial Venezuela." PhD diss., University of Chicago, 1993.

Sloterdijk, Peter. *Critique of Cynical Reason*. Minneapolis: University of Minnesota Press, 1987.

Smilde, David. "Crime and Revolution in Venezuela." *NACLA Report on the Americas* 49, no. 3 (2017): 303–8.

Smilde, David, and Daniel Hellinger, eds. *Venezuela's Bolivarian Democracy: Participation, Politics, and Culture under Chávez*. Durham, NC: Duke University Press, 2011.

Smith, William Robertson. *Religion of the Semites*. New Brunswick, NJ: Transaction Publishers, 2002.

Spivak, Gayatri Chakravorty. "Subaltern Studies: Deconstructing Historiography." In *Selected Subaltern Studies*, edited by Ranajit Guha and Gayatri Chakravorty Spivak. Oxford: Oxford University Press, 1988.

Steinmüller, Hans. "A Minimal Definition of Cynicism: Everyday Social Criticism and Some Meanings of 'Life' in Contemporary China." *Anthropology of This Century* (blog), October 2014. http://aotcpress.com/articles/minimal-definition-cynicism-everyday -social-criticism-meanings-life/.

Stephen, Lynn. "Women's Rights Are Human Rights: The Merging of Feminine and Feminist Interests among El Salvador's Mothers of the Disappeared (CO-MADRES)." *American Ethnologist* 22, no. 4 (1995): 807–27.

Tambiah, Stanley. "A Performative Approach to Ritual." *Proceedings of the British Academy* 65 (1979): 113–69.

Tate, Winifred. *Counting the Dead: The Culture and Politics of Human Rights Activism in Colombia*. Berkeley: University of California Press, 2007.

Taussig, Michael. *Shamanism, Colonialism, and the Wild Man: A Study in Terror and Healing*. Chicago: University of Chicago Press, 1991.

Templeton, Andrew. "The Evolution of Popular Opinion." In Naím, *Lessons of the Venezuelan Experience*, 79–114.

Thompson, E. P. *Customs in Common: Studies in Traditional Popular Culture*. New York: New Press, 1993.

———. *Whigs and Hunters*. London: Breviary Stuff Publications, 2013.

Thompson, Hunter S. *Fear and Loathing on the Campaign Trail '72*. New York: Simon and Schuster, 2012.

Tilly, Charles. *Popular Contention in Great Britain, 1758–1834*. Boulder, CO: Paradigm, 2005.

———. "Spaces of Contention." *Mobilization: An International Quarterly* 5, no. 2 (2000): 135–59.

Toro, Francisco. "Venezuela's Elusive Voters." *Latitude* (blog), *New York Times*, August 2, 2012. http://latitude.blogs.nytimes.com/2012/08/02/a-broad-swath-of-the-venezuelan -electorate-refuses-to-pick-a-side/.

Turner, Bryan S. "Outline of a Theory of Citizenship." *Sociology* 24, no. 2 (1990): 189–217.

Tybjerg, Tove. "Reflections on 'Charisma.' " *Nordic Journal of Religion and Society* 20, no. 2 (2007): 167–78.

United Nations Department of Economic and Social Affairs. "2018 Revision of World Urbanization Prospects." May 16, 2018. https://www.un.org/development/desa /publications/2018-revision-of-world-urbanization-prospects.html.

United Nations Office on Drugs and Crime (UNODC), Jean-Luc Lemahieu, and Angela Me. *Global Study on Homicide*. Vienna: UNODC, 2013.

Urribarrí, Raisa. "De comunitarios a gobunitarios: Los medios alternativos en tiempos de revolución." In *Hegemonía y control comunicacional*, edited by Marcelino Bisbal, 155–90. Caracas: Editorial Alfa, 2009.

Velasco, Alejandro. *Barrio Rising: Urban Popular Politics and the Making of Modern Venezuela*. Oakland: University of California Press, 2015.

———. "Where Are the Barrios? Street Protest and Popular Politics in Venezuela, Then and Now." Paper presented at Center for Latin American and Caribbean Studies conference "Venezuela after Chavez," Watson Institute for International Studies, Brown University, Providence, RI, April 30, 2014. https://watson.brown.edu/clacs/files/clacs/imce/publications/Venezuela%20After%20Chavez.pdf.

Vera-Rojas, María. "En nombre del amor: Políticas de la sexualidad en el proyecto socialista bolivariano." *Cuadernos de literatura* 18, no. 36 (2014): 58–85.

Villegas Poljak, Ernesto. *Abril, golpe adentro*. Caracas: Editorial Galac, 2010.

Wacquant, Loïc. "Three Steps to a Historical Anthropology of Actually Existing Neoliberalism." *Social Anthropology* 20, no. 1 (2012): 66–79.

Waisbord, Silvio. *Watchdog Journalism in South America*. New York: Columbia University Press, 2000.

Warner, Michael. *Publics and Counterpublics*. New York: Zone Books, 2005.

Weber, Max. *Economy and Society*. Vol. 1. Berkeley: University of California Press, 1978.

———. "Politics as a Vocation." In *From Max Weber: Essays in Sociology*, 77–128. Oxford: Oxford University Press, 1946.

Weffort, Francisco. "State and Mass in Brazil." *Studies in Comparative International Development* 2, no. 12 (1966): 187–96.

Weiner, Norbert. *The Human Use of Human Beings*. Boston: Da Capo Press, 1988.

Weisbrot, Mark, and Tara Ruttenberg. "Television in Venezuela: Who Dominates the Media?" *MR Online*, December 13, 2010. http://mrzine.monthlyreview.org/2010/wr131210.html.

Weyland, Kurt. "Clarifying a Contested Concept: Populism in the Study of Latin American Politics." *Comparative Politics* 34, no. 1 (2001): 1–22.

———. "The Politics of Corruption in Latin America." *Journal of Democracy* 9, no. 2 (1998): 108–21.

Wilde, Matt. "Utopian Disjunctures: Popular Democracy and the Communal State in Urban Venezuela." *Critique of Anthropology* 37, no. 1 (2017): 47–66.

Williams, Raymond. *Marxism and Literature*. Oxford: Oxford University Press, 1977.

Wilpert, Gregory. "The 47-Hour Coup That Changed Everything." *Venezuelanalysis* (blog), April 13, 2007. https://venezuelanalysis.com/analysis/2336.

Wolin, Sheldon. "'Fugitive Democracy.'" *Constellations* 1, no. 1 (1994): 11–25.

———. "The People's Two Bodies." *Democracy* 1, no. 1 (1981): 9–24.

World Bank. "Individuals Using the Internet (% of Population)." Accessed September 23, 2018. https://data.worldbank.org/indicator/IT.NET.USER.ZS?locations=VE&year=2011.

———. "Mobile Cellular Subscriptions (per 100 People)." Accessed September 23, 2018. https://data.worldbank.org/indicator/IT.CEL.SETS.P2?locations=VE&view=map&year=2011.

Worsley, Peter. "The Concept of Populism." In *Populism: Its Meaning and National Characteristics*, edited by Ghita Ionescu and Ernest Gellner. London: Macmillan, 1969.

Wright, Winthrop R. *Café con leche: Race, Class, and National Image in Venezuela*. Austin: University of Texas Press, 1993.

Yanagisako, Sylvia Junko. *Producing Culture and Capital: Family Firms in Italy*. Princeton, NJ: Princeton University Press, 2002.

Yúdice, George. "Testimonio and Postmodernism." *Latin American Perspectives* 18, no. 3 (1991): 15–31.

Zeiderman, Austin. *Endangered City: The Politics of Security and Risk in Bogotá*. Durham, NC: Duke University Press, 2016.

———. "Living Dangerously: Biopolitics and Urban Citizenship in Bogotá, Colombia." *American Ethnologist* 40, no. 1 (February 1, 2013): 71–87.

Zubillaga, Verónica. "The February Protests and the Unequal Experience of Violence." *Cultural Anthropology* (blog), February 5, 2015. https://culanth.org/fieldsights/637-the -february-protests-and-the-unequal-experience-of-violence.

———. "Menos desigualdad, más violencia: La paradoja de Caracas." *Nueva sociedad* 243 (2013): 104–18.

INDEX

Italic page numbers refer to figures.